Around the World in Sandals

*Enjoy!
Russell &
Penny*

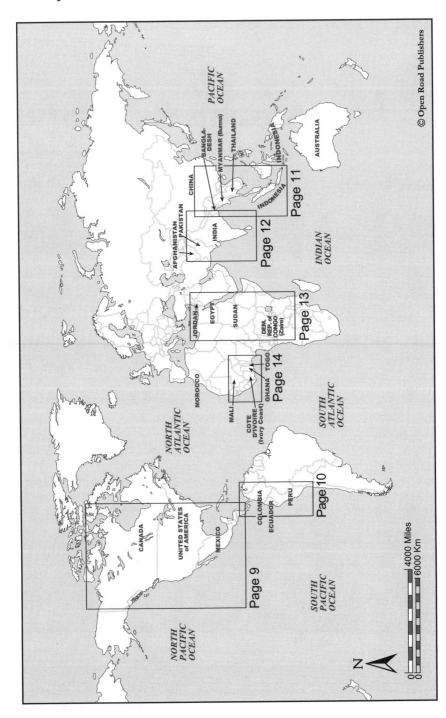

Around the World in Sandals

Russell and Penny Jennings

OPEN ROAD PUBLISHERS
Vancouver, BC, Canada

ISBN 0-9691363-4-X

First Edition, 2005

Library and Archives Canada Cataloguing in Publication

Jennings, Russell, 1943-
Around the world in sandals: tales of discovery and discomfort / by Russell and Penny Jennings.

ISBN 0-9691363-4-X

1. Voyages and travels. 2. Jennings, Russell, 1943- – Travel.
I. Jennings, Penny, 1941- II. Title.

G440.J45A3 2005   910.4'092   C2004-905673-5

Acknowledgements
To Julie Lees for story editing and critiquing the manuscript.
To Galina Korobova for cover and map preparation.
To Mark Hoffmann (Babblefish Design) for page layout and prepress preparation (mhoffmann@babblefishdesign.com).

Publisher
Open Road Publishers
3316 West 8th Avenue
Vancouver, BC, V6R 1Y4, Canada

Fax: +1 604 734 1586
Email: jennings@worldweatherguide.com
Web site: www. worldweatherguide.com

Cover photo: Kuta Beach, Bali, Indonesia (Jennings)
Printed in Canada

5

CONTENTS

Maps of authors' routes

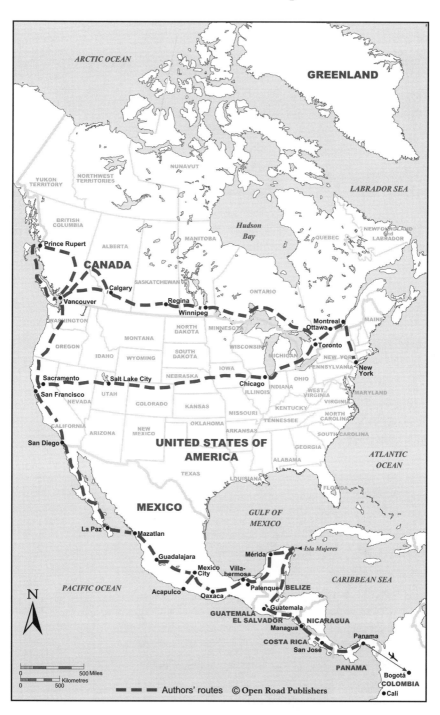

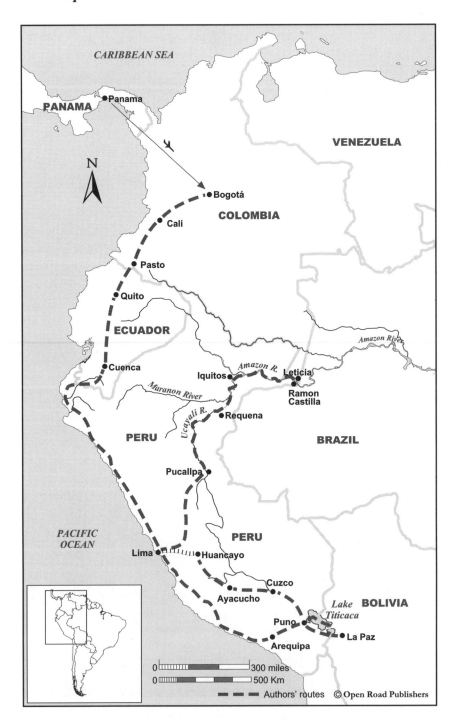

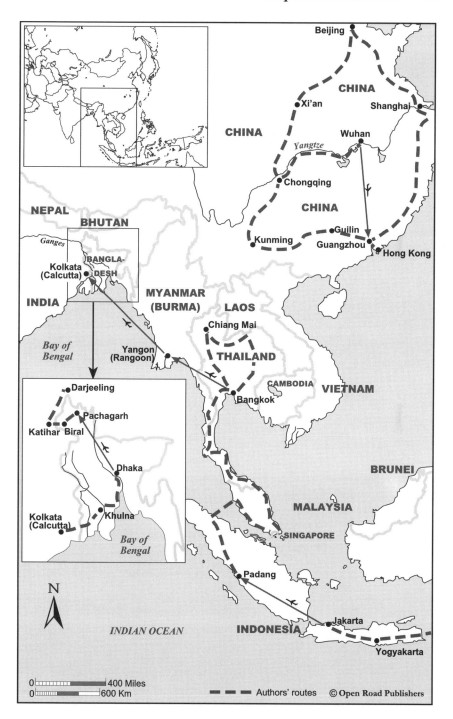

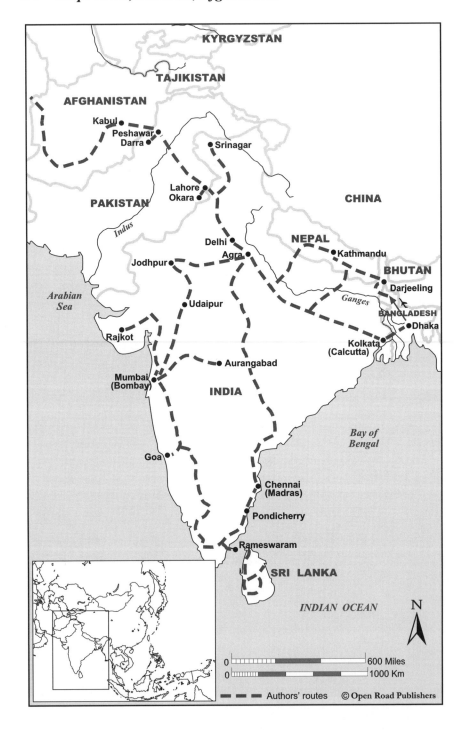

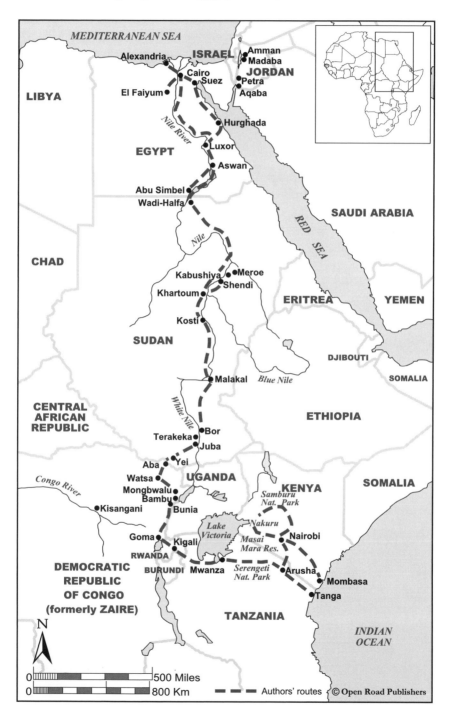

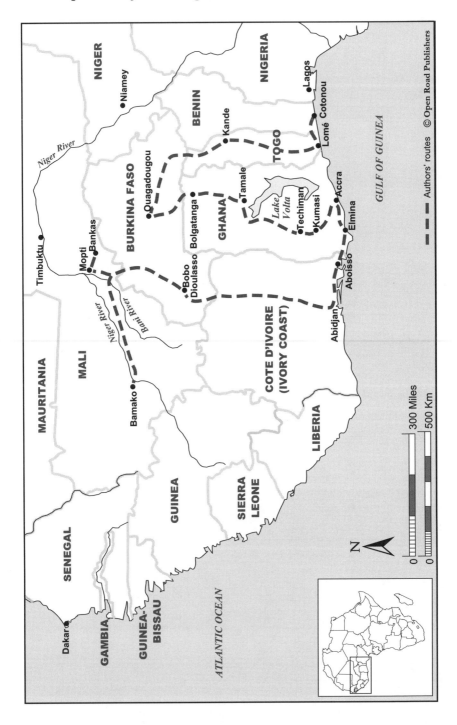

Introduction

What the reader needs to know

Hi! We are Russell and Penny Jennings.

Often the highlight of travel is not the destination but the journey to get there and the people met along the way.

In our anecdotes, any resemblance to actual persons, living or dead, is *not* coincidental. The characters and their names are *real* except in special instances when we changed the names to protect the guilty.

We wrote detailed journals when we travelled which enabled us to recount our experiences accurately. Even the dialogue is a fair representation of what was said.

Our travel adventures are in the first person singular with the *I* always referring to Russell. If the *I* referred to Penny in some stories, and to Russell in others, we would all be confused.

Now for some trivia about us.

A few words from Russell

I'm from Melbourne, Australia.

My first recollection of wanting to travel dates to when I was about nine years old. I took a world atlas, a notebook and a pen and started writing. When my mother asked me what I was doing, I replied: "I'm writing down all the countries and cities I want to visit one day."

But it takes money to travel. I earned diplomas in Sales and Marketing, and Accountancy, the latter of which enabled me to work as an accountant in Johannesburg, London, Melbourne and Papua New Guinea.

I also worked at a variety of jobs: insurance salesman, seaman on a freighter, radio show producer and host, truck driver, travel agent, newspaper columnist, tour escort, oil rigs roustabout, and presenter of night school courses on archaeology, religions and world cultures.

When I travelled I carried a backpack, hitchhiked and used public transportation, stayed in hostels, no-star hotels and under the stars.

I had been content travelling solo, leaving my footprints across Africa, Asia, North America, Europe and Australia.

I was in my tenth year of *work and travel, travel and work* when I met Penny on a blind date in Vancouver and asked her to put on a backpack and join me. It was something completely out of character for me to do. But my gut instinct told me I was doing the right thing; it had never failed me in my encounters with people in the past.

I was captivated by Penny's winning smile, her directness and her care and consideration of others. And she was easy to look at.

It took almost two months of cajoling before she agreed to travel south with me, initially to Mexico, then to South America.

A few words from Penny

The small town of Cloverdale in Surrey, British Columbia is where I was born and raised.

In my high school yearbook I wrote that my ambition was to go to Australia.

In my twenties I visited Hawaii and Trinidad and Tobago but visiting Australia became a forgotten dream.

The thought of travelling was on my mind when I bought a forty-volume collection of *The World and Its People* which described the people and cultures of all countries. But going to those places remained another dream.

My life centred around my family, the church where I taught Sunday school and sang in the choir, and the bank where I worked for seventeen years – in the same office. My life was predictable from one day to the next, or one week or one month to the next. I was content but something, unknown to me, was saying it was time for a change. But what sort of change, I could not envision.

My settled life suddenly turned upside down in July 1975 when I reluctantly agreed to go on a blind date with an Australian whom, my girlfriend assured me, was "just passing through Vancouver on his way to South America and I wouldn't have to see him again."

She was wrong. And this book proves how much.

The blind date story by Russell

The year 1970 saw me in Johannesburg, working to fund future travels.

From my apartment doorway I saw a backpacker knocking on my friend's door down the hall.

"He's out of town for a few days," I said. "If you want a place to sleep you can use my floor."

"Thanks. My name's Mike."

Before he left after a few days, this easy-going guy handed me a piece of paper. "My address," he said. "Look me up if you're ever in Vancouver." His tone was sincere.

Five years later I surprised Mike by knocking on his door.

Mike's lady-friend, Lamont, had a friend named Penny. Mike suggested we all go out for dinner.

Penny's response was negative. Her previous blind date had been a disaster. He had spoken two words all night, neither of them to her. But Lamont and Mike persisted and got Penny to change her mind. They told her I was just passing through Vancouver and she wouldn't see me again.

Later at the restaurant, the four of us loosened up on the dance floor. Penny and I danced comfortably together; I felt as if we had been dancing together for years. We all returned to our table and sipped our drinks. Conversation was difficult over the band but Lamont managed to ask, "Where are you going next, Russell?"

"Penny and I are going to South America," I responded, raising my voice over the din.

Lamont, stunned, looked at Penny. "You're going to South America?"

Penny was taken by surprise.

"Sure, why not?" she answered with a tongue in cheek grin. She glanced at me sideways as if to say "I'll go along with your little joke."

Then Penny asked, "What do I take?"

I could hardly believe my ears. This was fantastic. I grabbed a paper napkin and jotted down a list: backpack, clothing, passport, sandals, towel, bathing suit. . .

"Wait!" said Penny. "What's a backpack?"

Mike leaned forward and yelled. "It's a bag you carry on your back to hold your clothes and toothbrush. You can borrow mine."

"Just a moment," said Penny. "Let's not get serious about South America. I'm joking about going there. I've got a job I like – I've been working for a bank for seventeen years. I have a car and am renting an apartment."

My euphoria nose-dived, but I wouldn't let go.

"What you should do," I suggested, "is leave your job, sell your car, quit your apartment and come."

Penny looked astonished but thoughtful. She needed time to recover. We all sat in silence for a few moments. I happened to glance at my watch. Eight o'clock. I have known Penny for two hours. Have I been too fast?

"Let's dance," I suggested. As we stood up Penny picked up the napkin with the list and slipped it in her purse.

Would Penny accept my impromptu offer? Why should she? She has just met me. These thoughts raced through my head as we danced. I seriously felt we would be a great travelling team. The whole of me felt the good chemistry between us.

My intended short stay stretched to four weeks while I tried to convince Penny to join me in discovering the wonder and magic of foreign lands.

I met her family. Her brother and four sisters acknowledged that Penny had travelled to Hawaii to the security of a hotel and to Trinidad and Tobago to the security of friends, but to travel into unfamiliar or even familiar territory with a stranger was beyond their comprehension.

I respected the concern her family had for each other and felt the odds stacking against me.

Nevertheless Penny and I had grown fond of each other in a very short time. She expressed interest in travelling to South America but it was out of character for her to just switch off the light, close the door and go travelling.

There had to come a day when a decision had to be made. Penny brought up the topic. "I can't think properly while you're around," she said. "You're confusing my life and my family is concerned. I think you should continue your travels without me. You've been here for a month now and I'm delaying you."

I was devastated but I understood the disruption I was causing the Robinson family.

I decided to hitchhike around the United States for about a month. Before leaving I went to Penny's apartment and gave her a piece of paper. "Here are two addresses in the States where you can write to me if you like." Then I added hopefully, "The invitation is still open if you change your mind."

We embraced and bade each other a fond farewell. I hoped it was not forever.

My travelling days ticked by. New adventures, new acquaintances, new sights and then in Nashville, a letter from Penny.

"Four weeks holiday are due to me," she wrote. "I'll travel with you as far as Mexico on one condition, that if I don't like backpacking you take me to the nearest airport and I fly home."

I was excited. I read the letter again and again to make sure I wasn't mistaken.

I replied immediately, accepting her condition. But, I wrote, if you can manage four weeks, why don't you ask for an additional two weeks so we can see Mexico in depth?

I hurried back to Vancouver. Unknown to Penny, I had left some belongings at Mike's. I wanted to have an excuse to return in case I had to ask her again to come travelling.

After we embraced she told me the good news, that she had been given the extra two weeks. Then she added: "But I'm only going as far as Mexico. Right?"

"Right," I answered, hoping she would change her mind.

As Penny had to work for a few more days we agreed to meet

in southern California, in San Diego. I was to leave immediately to hitchhike and she would fly later.

Penny took to backpacking with amazing ease. We travelled well together and had similar interests.

The six-week holiday stretched to four months after Penny asked for and was granted a two-and-a-half-month leave of absence from the bank. Our travels continued through Central America into South America and beyond.

The years between our later backpacking adventures were spent managing a travel agency in Vancouver and escorting tour groups to destinations to which we had travelled independently.

Are you ready to join us?
Slip into your sandals and let's go.

Mexico

The sun worshipper

Oaxaca to Villahermosa and Palenque, October 1975
See map, page 9

The bus from Oaxaca to Villahermosa pulled away in the middle of the night.

In a driving rain storm.

I slept reasonably well, even though my seat wouldn't recline.

Beside me sat Penny who snoozed off and on, also in a non-reclining seat. She was new to backpacking and sleeping on buses. It was tolerable but not fun to be buffeted by rough roads, jolted upright when the wheels hit a pothole or having our lolling heads jerk us awake when the bus swerved or stopped.

I awoke with a start when the bus lurched. I looked at Penny. She was wide awake, staring out the window into the blackness.

"Don't worry about me," she said with a smile, "I'm enjoying the scenery."

I liked her cheerful attitude. I squeezed her arm.

When dawn broke we saw the rain had stopped. The lush, green vegetation glittered in the early morning sunlight.

We struck up a conversation with another passenger, Gerard, an accountant from Paris on a three-week holiday. He was short, of slim build, with a narrow face and aquiline nose. I assumed he was a sun worshipper because his face was tanned nut-brown, as was his chest, exposed under an open bolero jacket. Gerard must have enjoyed attracting attention because he wore six silver chains around his neck, four copper bracelets on each wrist, a bright red head scarf with matching red earrings and tight blue jeans that were rolled up to just below the knee to reveal his high-heeled alligator boots. He was a likeable extrovert.

In Villahermosa we booked rooms in the same hotel and agreed to sightsee together. Penny and I had come to see some unusual stone sculptures.

Almost 100 kilometres west of Villahermosa lies La Venta where, in 1925, an expedition discovered stone sculptures of human heads and animals, alongside altars and urns in an almost impenetrable forest. The heads, some weighing as much as twenty tonnes, were particularly puzzling because the faces were distinctly negroid. They were sculpted from basalt – a dense, dark volcanic rock – during the Olmec period of 3,000 years ago.

Because the stone carvings were threatened with destruction by oil exploration nearby, many stone figures were hauled to a wooded area, now the Parque la Venta, near Villahermosa.

In the park the three of us followed a winding dirt path enveloped by thick, dark, forest growth. The pathway was full of puddles from an earlier rain storm and the vegetation drooped heavily with water droplets. Rotting leaves squished under our sandals, giving off that wonderful smell of decay. Mosquitoes increased the farther we walked into the park. We soon came upon the massive stone heads and stood beside them to gauge their height; they were just over two metres high.

I looked intently at the faces. "They're definitely negroid with their prominent lips and wide flat noses. Although there aren't any historical records of Africans living in Central America, these heads must be sculptures of real people. They are too accurate to be a coincidence."

Carved above the faces were caps which looked like helmets worn by American footballers. "That *must* be a coincidence," I surmised.

When we tried to photograph the massive heads, we disturbed a swarm of mosquitoes which rose from the dark vegetation and woodland pools. They attacked us, driving their sucking tubes into our arms, neck and hands. It was a feeding frenzy. I smacked at them, squashing their bodies which left smudges of blood on my arms. Penny swatted them with her hat. "They're ferocious," she exclaimed. "I've never seen anything like it. This is awful!"

Gerard jumped around beside me, going berserk, his camera dangling uselessly as he waved his arms. In his sleeveless jacket which would not button at the front, he was offering himself as a filling station for thousands of buzzing insects. After being bitten relentlessly he bade a quick *au 'voir* and dashed along the pathway to the park gate. Five minutes later we sprinted along the same escape route.

The next day Penny and I decided to visit Palenque. In the lobby we bumped into Gerard who told us he would take a later bus.

The Mayan ruins at Palenque lie three hours by road southeast of Villahermosa. They were inhabited as early as 600 BC but did not become known to the Western world until the middle of the eighteenth century.

On the way there our bus drove into a downpour that lasted just fifteen minutes and then the sun came out, bringing heat and humidity. The area is one of the wettest in the world.

Upon arrival in Palenque we saw that the buildings were built on a plateau overlooking a plain, and that the site was surrounded by dense forest. The tallest structure was a pyramid capped by a temple containing inscriptions carved in stucco, many of which had not been deciphered. To reach this *Temple of the Inscriptions*, a modern-day name, we climbed the stone stairs on the outside of the pyramid that would have been used centuries ago by the Mayan priests and courtiers.

Once inside the temple at the top we saw the entrance to the internal stairway that descended into the heart of the pyramid. This entrance had been rediscovered in the early 1950s and had taken three years of sifting through rubble to completely clear the steps of the passage.

To make the descent easier for visitors, electric light bulbs had been installed. We probably would have felt more like explorers if we had to crawl down the passage holding lighted tapers or flaming torches, but we appreciated the modern lighting. The ceiling of the tunnel was high enough for us to stand upright as we descended the steep stairway.

At the bottom, which was at ground level, the stairway opened into a small stone-walled room. A low-wattage bulb dangled from the ceiling, casting a subdued, yellowish light. As we started exploring we both confessed to an eerie feeling.

We peeked into an alcove that contained a stone sarcophagus about four metres long and one metre wide.

My heart jumped.

"This is what we've come to see," I said in a hushed, excited tone. "It's been my ambition to see this for years. Look at the lid of the sarcophagus."

We peered at a five-tonne slab with a carving of a half-sitting, half-crouching figure. Some say it is Pakal, a 7th-century AD Mayan ruler; others say it represents the position of falling into the underworld at time of death, while others say it depicts a spaceman at the controls of a spaceship. Proponents of this assumption believe that extraterrestrials landed on earth. They point to the "clearly discernible" helmet, hand-throttle, pedal and oxygen apparatus. It may have been Pakal but we agreed he looked like a spaceman.

Not being an archaeologist I could only regard the carved man as weird and unique. I couldn't imagine the number of hours required by artisans to carve the features and the accompanying symbols and word pictures.

When originally discovered, the sarcophagus contained the skeleton of a man in his forties. He wore a mask of jade with jade plugs in his earlobes. His decayed body was adorned with jade necklaces, rings on his fingers and hundreds of jade disks which at one time had been sewn onto a shroud. The adornments had been transferred to the National Museum of Anthropology in Mexico City. I felt like an intruder in a man's private chamber as we explored the sanctuary where he had rested undisturbed for 1,300 years.

We retraced our steps to daylight. From the top of the pyramid we gazed down to a small temple on our left and spotted a body spread-eagled on its steps. As we approached we saw it was none other than the sun-worshipping Gerard, still wearing his alligator boots, rolled-up jeans and sleeveless, open-fronted jacket. But he had changed from his red scarf to blue, with matching blue earrings. We were pleased to see a familiar face and he, likewise. We shook hands enthusiastically and waited together for the bus to take us back to Villahermosa.

Upon arriving at dinner time we asked Gerard to join us at a nearby restaurant. As we strolled towards the eatery, local men on the sidewalk wolf-whistled. Penny was quite sure they were not wolf-whistling her when she saw Gerard preening himself, obviously enjoying the attention.

In the restaurant Gerard excused himself and disappeared into the washroom. Within moments he returned wearing not his blue scarf, but a green one with matching green earrings. He had changed for dinner! Gerard was just as unique as the man carved on the lid of the sarcophagus.

The next day we went our separate ways.

From the seats of our outbound bus as it rumbled down the main street we spotted a pair of alligator boots tiptoeing around puddles on the sidewalk. We waved to their owner but he didn't see us. On his head he wore a purple scarf with matching earrings.

There could only be one Gerard!

Mexico

Island of adventure

Mystery boat trip at Isla Mujeres, October 1975
See map, page 9

The twin-decked ferry pitched and rolled as it chugged across the strait from Puerto Juarez on the Mexican mainland to Isla Mujeres, a small island off the northeast coast of Yucatan Peninsula. Penny and I were itching for a few days of sun and sand.

About thirty locals were on the ferry, returning to their homes on the island. The only other passengers were us – the lone gringos – and three trussed up pigs which squealed constantly during the forty-five minute ride.

In the distance, Isla Mujeres looked like a big sand dune capped with palm trees. We docked in the early afternoon when the Mexican sun was bathing the island in white heat.

We strolled along unpaved streets covered with drifts of sand blown in from the beach. The streets were lined with two- and three-storey hotels and seafood restaurants, all painted in bright reds, greens, yellows and blues. The atmosphere boosted our holiday spirit. We passed a restaurant with its fish menu displayed in the window. Our mouths watered. We put a fresh seafood dinner on the top of our list for an evening meal.

Wedged between the colourful buildings, small shops displayed tourist knickknacks. I smiled at a little shop selling postcards and magazines. A sign proudly announced "Broken English Spoken Perfectly."

The village had a casual atmosphere and not many visitors. Perfect for a few days' break from our travels.

The next morning, as we shuffled through the ankle deep sand of the main street to explore our surroundings, a young local man approached us. He asked if we'd like to join a group on an all-day boat trip to a beach and that lunch would be included. The trip sounded good but I was wary.

Over the past few weeks there was no shortage of people wanting to sell something or offer a service. The challenge was to figure out the good offers from the bad. Although the price seemed reasonable, the young fellow wasn't able to tell us much about the trip because of his limited English.

This was our first morning on the island. We decided against committing a full day to an unknown venture. We thanked him and watched as he disappeared around a corner.

Had we made the right decision? The thought nagged me. Penny spoke for both of us. "We'll never know what we missed if we don't go on the trip. It doesn't matter where it's going."

"You're right," I said, and we both took off in pursuit. We soon found him and signed up. The thought of a mystery trip smacked of adventure.

We backtracked through the sand to our hotel then, armed with lip salve, suntan lotion, bathing suits and towels, hurried to the dock.

The white hulled motor launch was bobbing against the pier. We spotted a few people under a canopy that shaded the rear half of the vessel. A crewman waved us onto the boat to meet our fellow passengers: three Mexican couples and four American girls. The skipper spoke in halting English. His two affable crew members spoke no English but smiled a lot.

The inboard motor sputtered alive, a crewman untied the hawser and we headed out to sea, straight towards the horizon. Penny checked our map to see which little island was out there but the map showed nothing. No one looked anxious. I guessed everyone had blind faith in the skipper.

The waves in the turquoise sea became choppier. Looking back I saw Isla Mujeres fade into a blurry, hazy speck. Almost an hour went by before the skipper cut the engine and the two crewmen grabbed dive masks and snorkels.

What now?

They lowered themselves over the side carrying string bags, and disappeared. Intrigued, and beckoned by the crystal clear water, I jumped in and watched them below me as they breast-stroked down to the sea bed. I held my breath and dived, trying to catch up to them. I watched them gather large conch shells and drop them into the bags but I couldn't swim any deeper. My ears throbbed; it was time to surface.

One of the American girls leaned over the side. "What's happening down there?"

"They're collecting conch shells," I said as I dogpaddled to keep my head above water. "I don't know why. The only thing I know about them is that you can drill a hole and blow it like a trumpet."

"How big are they?"

"About the size of a football."

"I'm coming in."

With that said she flung her leg over the side.

Suddenly the skipper yelled, "No, no, no."

I looked up and saw the skipper was agitated. I supposed it was because he was ultimately responsible for his passengers and didn't want to be put at risk. Maybe he'd had a bad experience with a previous group who, like me, had recklessly leapt over the side. I'm sure he would have stopped me had he been fast enough.

The crewmen continued diving until they had gathered a dozen glistening pink conch shells between them.

Conversation between our fellow day trippers had been impossible because of the noisy engine. This quiet conch-collecting interlude gave us a chance to get to know each other. Of the Mexican couples, Meix and Marie-Carmen, from Mexico City, were on their honeymoon, and the four American girls were nurses from San Francisco.

Satisfied with the collection of conch shells, the skipper revved the engine and turned back towards Isla Mujeres. While we motored along, a crewman hooked lumps of blubbery white meat out of the shells. He diced the meat and marinated it in lime juice. I assumed this snail delicacy would be served at lunch.

On the way we stopped while the crewmen tossed soda crackers overboard. Hundreds of fish surfaced to take the bait. Quickly the crewmen leaned over the side with nets and hauled aboard a dozen or more large ones before they got away.

The fish flipped and flopped on the floor of the boat, causing a slight panic among the passengers. We yanked up our feet to escape their gnashing teeth. They were supposed to be our lunch, not us theirs.

The skipper steered towards the southern end of the island and after another hour arrived at the edge of a mangrove swamp. A crewman stood on the bow and pointed left then right, directing the skipper who maneuvered the boat around stands of mangroves. Soon the boat shuddered as it slid onto a bank draped with rotting mangrove roots. Our interest piqued when the two crewmen jumped off the bow with machetes and hacked at the dead branches that were above the waterline. They piled these onto the forward deck. Fuel for a cooking fire?

Next, we headed along the coast and arrived at a white-sand beach. Under a dome of blue sky, friendly palm fronds waved a greeting and created shady patches on the sand.

We sloshed through shallow water between the boat and the beach. A spirit of well-being rippled through the group. I heard enthusiastic comments about the sunny weather, our picturesque surroundings and how our mystery trip was full of surprises like the unexpected stops for conch, fish and firewood.

Above the high tide mark where the coconut palms grew, I was surprised to see an open-air beach bar. The building's three walls were constructed of adobe bricks, the roof with grass thatch and the floor, cement. The bar was well-stocked with spirits and Corona beer. Apart from the coconut palms it provided the only shelter from the sun's midday rays.

About fifty feet offshore stood a fenced enclosure, the size of a volleyball court. Stakes had been driven into the sandy sea bed and wire mesh stretched along the fence. What was penned inside?

While the two crewmen started a fire to barbecue the fish, the skipper invited us to follow him. Intrigued, everyone trailed him, wading into waist deep water towards the pen.

"Two Caribbean sea turtles are inside," he said as, one by one, we hoisted ourselves onto some cross spars that held the stakes together, and jumped into the pen.

Did anyone feel nervous about the unknown? Maybe because everyone was going into the pen, not one of us asked about potential danger.

As we huddled in a corner the skipper clapped his hands. Within moments two large brown shells, each about one metre in diameter, broke the surface. This was incredible. I had never imagined in the morning when we boarded the boat, that by noon we would be in a pen with turtles. Why were they here?

From what the skipper said, we deduced that the turtles were part of a conservation programme. But we couldn't be sure. The skipper was a real-life example of "Broken English Spoken Perfectly."

The skipper swam slowly to the nearest turtle, approaching it from the rear. With outstretched arms he grabbed the edges of the shell and dragged himself onto its back. This must have agitated the turtle because it dived, forcing the skipper to release his grip. It then resurfaced next to its mate.

With a sweep of his hand from us towards the turtles, the skipper indicated that each of us could take a turn in riding one. Penny took a deep breath to boost her confidence then bravely paddled to one, hoisted herself up and hung on while it carried her for about thirty seconds before starting to dive. She anticipated the dive and sucked air into her lungs. The turtle descended at a forty-five-degree angle in a bid to shake off its freeloader. She held on until her air gave out, then let go and surfaced.

"That was fabulous," she blurted between gulps of air. "Never thought I'd ever ride a turtle. A bit scary, not knowing if it would turn around and nip me!"

Shouts and gasps rose behind us. We swung around to see the skipper holding up by the tail, a shark about one-and-a-half metres long. It wasn't a dangerous shark, he assured us. It was a non-biting nurse shark that frequented the waters of Isla Mujeres.

After our turtleback riding we all left the pen and splashed our way back to the sandy beach. It was an experience not to be missed but I was disappointed. I hadn't taken my movie camera to capture the action. Could I encourage Penny to go back into the pen?

"Are you kidding?" Her voice rose in surprise. "What about the shark?" There was a hint of fear in her tone.

"The skipper said it wasn't dangerous," I said.

Having been easily convinced it was safe, or being more courageous than I thought, she bravely heaved herself up onto a spar, swung her leg over and dropped into the pen, then clapped her hands.

She turned to me. "Are you coming in?"

"No," I said. "I'll film from outside the pen. It's safer."

She laughed.

As if they sensed her presence, two big brown shells broke the surface. I started the camera rolling to record the event.

She selected one and dragged herself onto its back. Just as she sensed it was going to dive she turned and yelled, "Watch for the shark!" Then her body slid below the surface. For a moment just the white soles of her feet were visible, then they disappeared. Thankfully the shark didn't show itself even though it was supposed to be harmless.

After a few long moments her blonde head popped up, a smile of achievement on her face. I was enthused with the variety of shots I got for my film. She climbed out of the pen, swung her lithe body over the top spar and plopped into the water beside me. I slipped my arm around her waist and drew her towards me.

"That was fantastic," I said, admiring her fearlessness as I gave her a peck on the cheek.

"I did it only for you," she said, then added jokingly: "Just don't ask for an encore."

Meanwhile, the crew had prepared our lunch and arranged for us to use the tables and chairs in the open-air bar on the beach. Our eyes popped when they brought each of us a freshly barbecued fish whose head and tail draped over the sides of the dinner plates. We squeezed lemon juice over them, separated delicate flakes of fish with our fingers, savoured the tasty morsels, and smacked our lips.

The crew added peas and chopped onions to the snails they had marinated in lime juice on the boat. With our forks we spiked the conch. The idea of eating raw conch from the shells had not appealed to me but they proved to be digestible and tasted tangy with the lime juice. I couldn't imagine a seafood dinner in a town restaurant beating this experience.

Meix and Marie-Carmen generously bought brandy and tequila for the table. We raised our glasses in a toast to the skipper and crew for the great day. The barman slipped an audio cassette into the tape player, then the amplifier exploded with guitars, trumpets and violins of *mariachi* musicians playing Mexico's famous *La Bamba*. We pushed back our chairs and scrambled onto the sandy dance floor, kicking up the sand as we tangoed, mamboed and rock'n'rolled.

Colombia

Suspicious passenger

Cali to Pasto, November 1975
See map, page 10

"My money pouch is missing from my bag," Penny whispered frantically.

"Are you sure?" I asked.

"Yes."

"How much was in it?"

"Fifteen hundred dollars in travellers cheques."

"Wow! Look again."

Penny leaned down and felt under the bus seat to check inside her bag again. "It's definitely missing," she insisted anxiously.

Penny and I were travelling on buses through Colombia. To get here we had bused from Mexico, through Central America to Panama City, then flown into Bogota, Colombia's capital.

Having reached Cali, in southwestern Colombia, we bought tickets for an evening bus to our next city, Pasto. Our backpacks were stashed in the baggage compartment in the side of the bus. When we boarded in the evening we placed our two day-packs under our seats.

After the bus pulled out of the terminal, we immediately fell into an exhausted sleep. I awoke when the man sitting behind us turned the volume up on his radio. I glanced at Penny who was wide awake.

"That guy is really inconsiderate of other passengers," I whispered. "I wish he'd turn his radio down." Although he couldn't have heard my comment he unexpectedly turned it down and started rustling paper instead.

Then all went quiet. We dozed but I was jolted awake when he cranked it up again. These noisy disturbances continued sporadically. He was getting on my nerves. I thought of complaining to the man but because we were the only foreigners I didn't want to cause a fuss. The other passengers lolled in their seats snoozing; they showed no signs of being perturbed. I guessed we would just have to endure the noise.

The bus stopped several times during the night, allowing passengers to disembark and others to board.

I woke up again when Penny shifted about in her seat. It was pitch black outside. My watch showed three-thirty. Penny said she felt cold and reached under the seat for her jacket which she had wrapped around her bag. The jacket lay crumpled on the floor. Grabbing for her bag, she found it open. Frantically she rummaged inside to make sure everything was still there.

That's when she told me her money pouch was missing.

Penny's belt had two pouches, one for money, the other for her passport.

"How come it was in your bag?" I asked incredulously. We usually wore our money belts all the time.

"I thought I would be able to sleep better," she said in a hushed tone. She checked the remaining pouch.

"At least my passport wasn't taken," she said thankfully.

"I wonder who it could be?" I said.

"It must be the man behind us. He was there most of the night with his noisy radio," Penny whispered. "Who else could it be?"

We decided to make it obvious to him we were aware Penny's bag had been tampered with, hoping he would miraculously find the cheques and hand them over. I looked over the seat directly at him. He wore a brown woollen cap and a black scarf drawn across his mouth. He had a radio glued to his ear. His dark eyes looked up at me, but they were half closed.

Penny started moving her bag around under the seat in another attempt to make him come clean. It didn't work.

Several times over the next two hours I looked at him again to let him know we were awake, aware and suspicious. But each time he looked up at me his eyes lacked any expression. He looked secure in his own cosmos.

"He has to be the guy," I told Penny. "Any normal person would be curious or annoyed."

I checked the luminous dial of my watch. Six a.m. In half an hour we would be arriving in Pasto. We quickly devised a plan to put into effect upon arrival. Although we were seated in the middle of the bus Penny needed to be one of the first off. From outside the bus she would watch for my upturned thumb through the window, which meant I had caught the thief. Then she would run to find a police-man to detain the culprit. My downturned thumb would indicate that we were out of luck.

As soon as the bus turned into the terminal she leapt out of her seat and nimbly forged over boxes, bags and bundles piled in the aisle and waited outside for my signal.

I turned and watched our suspect as he gathered his two bags and his radio and stood up in the aisle. I rose immediately and blocked his way. I had never done anything like this before. I pointed to one of his bags then reached for it and unzipped it. Fortunately, he just stood there staring with his dark expressionless eyes. I rifled through the bag; my fingers sifted furiously through clothes and plastic bottles. Nothing!

I took his second bag. Fortunately, he did not protest. I felt isolat-ed and vulnerable. By this time passengers had jammed up behind him in the aisle. I was surprised no one objected. They watched curiously.

What's wrong with the guy? He's so passive. Maybe he's on some type of drug. I became nervous as I rifled through his second bag. Again, nothing. He must have the cheques. They must be on him. My hands flew into the pockets of his jacket and trousers. Still nothing! I was totally out of my element. The crowd of passengers became more curious but, more than that, they were getting agitated. What am I doing here? My heart pumped furiously. I stopped and took a breath.

"He perdido mi catera," I said loudly, hoping I was pronouncing my Spanish correctly for "I have lost my wallet."

Now that they understood they poked around under the seats but found nothing. Meanwhile my suspect just stood there.

I wasn't cut out for this. What did I just do? I stepped aside to let everyone pass, and flopped into my seat. Phew! What if he had become obnoxious and wanted to argue and fight? Did he have a weapon? What if the other passengers had disapproved of what I, the gringo, was doing? How would they have reacted? There was much I didn't know about Latin temperament.

I looked out the window and gave the "thumbs down" signal to Penny. But she didn't react. I then realized, because of the tinted windows, she couldn't see inside the bus. So, our plan was rendered useless.

I reached under the seat for my bag and discovered it had been slashed.

So, the thief carried a knife!

I shuddered to think of the outcome had the situation become ugly. I checked inside my bag; fortunately, everything was still there.

I joined Penny outside. She looked despondent about her loss.

"At least the thief was kind enough to leave my passport," she said, trying to look on the bright side.

Upon reaching our next major city, Quito in Ecuador, Penny reported the theft to American Express and listed the numbers of the stolen travellers cheques on the claim form. Later she was reimbursed.

The confrontation haunted me.

Had I frisked the wrong person? I'm sure he was guilty but I hadn't found the cheques on him. Had he passed them to an accomplice? If that was so I would have to concede that he had outsmarted us.

However, the thief couldn't cash the cheques now that American

Express had the numbers, and they would notify all agents through their head office.

So, in the end, we outsmarted him. Or hoped we did.

Ecuador

Bowler hats and blankets

Customs checkpoint, November 1975
See map, page 10

Gravel flew out from under the tires of the taxi. Clouds of dust floated behind us as the driver tried to get Penny and me to the Colombia-Ecuador border post before it closed for siesta at noon. We arrived five minutes before closing and were quickly rubber-stamped out of Colombia and, in a nearby office, into Ecuador.

The taxi driver directed us to a minibus taking on passengers for Quito, Ecuador's capital. When all thirteen seats were occupied, the bus driver jumped aboard and started up the engine.

Next to me in the back seat sat a wide-beamed, elderly Indian woman with a pile of bowler hats on her head. I counted seven and wondered why she wore so many. On her lap was stacked a pile of red and green blankets. Next to her was a young man who wore four bowler hats. Their feet rested on cardboard boxes bound with tape.

Next to Penny sat a young woman in her twenties. As she gazed at the mountain scenery, the large elderly woman placed a bowler hat on her head and put one on the head of a passenger in front. I was surprised when neither of them voiced an objection.

As we watched, bemused by these antics, the young woman accepted two pairs of shoes which she put into a paper bag and placed next to her feet. It seemed that the passengers were comfort-able with the elderly woman's behaviour, because no words were exchanged.

The driver forged his way to the Pan-American Highway and we settled into our seats for the five-hour drive to Quito. We were only about five kilometres into the journey when we saw a truck beside the road and a uniformed official signalling us to stop. The young woman looked at us and muttered *Aduana* (Customs) and the elderly woman quickly dumped a blanket onto the young man's lap. Our driver geared down and stopped a few metres beyond the truck.

The customs officer demanded the driver open the rear door of the minibus where most of the baggage was stored. While the officer opened a bag for inspection, another customs officer spoke through the window of the minibus to the young man who had the folded blanket on his lap. The officer asked to see the contents of the box beneath his feet but the young man refused.

The officer raised his voice and drew his gun. He held it by the barrel in a menacing gesture, as if it were a club. The other officer quickly appeared, leaned through the door of the minibus, seized the cardboard box and ripped open one side. Bottles of pink liquid that looked like hand lotion fell onto the ground. I thought this was a heavy-handed action and felt sorry for the young fellow who was then ordered out of the minibus. He climbed out clutching the elderly woman's blanket. I was stunned when the two officers confiscated the blanket as well as the box of lotion and put them in their truck.

The elderly woman and the other passengers feigned innocence with deadpan faces when they were questioned about the goods they carried. No one appeared intimidated by the officers; inspections had likely happened to them many times before.

The officers showed no interest in Penny and me or what we carried in our backpacks. I guessed that some of the passengers were smuggling goods from Colombia, where they were cheaper, to Ecuador where they can be sold at a profit in the local weekly markets, and that they had not paid customs duty at the Ecuador border post.

The officers appeared satisfied with their morning's cache of a blanket and lotion which they could sell, and the passengers seemed content because that was all they lost. It was a small price to pay for the profits they would make.

As we drove away the other passengers glanced at each other – with satisfied looks on their faces and bowler hats on their heads.

Ecuador

Intriguing discoveries

With Padre Crespi in Cuenca, November 1975
See map, page 10

I thought we had stepped back into another century as we gazed at the man who came through the doorway. Padre Crespi wore an ankle-length black habit, shiny with wear, yet it fitted comfortably. Cuffs on both long sleeves were frayed. The partially-stooped priest extended his bony hand as he greeted us in Spanish. The top of his head was bald, fringed by long wisps of grey hair. His unruly grey beard brushed his chest. Deep creases lined his face, a face that had seen more than 80 years. His eyes, bright as raindrops, sparkled agelessly in their ancient setting.

The previous day, while gathering general information in the Quito tourist office, Penny and I came across a rather interesting pamphlet about a priest-archaeologist, Padre Carlo Crespi, who lived in Cuenca, a town south of Ecuador's capital, Quito.

Born in Italy in 1891, he became a priest as well as a scholar of science, archaeology, music and education. In 1923, he sailed to Ecuador to do missionary work and was now a priest at the Church of Maria Auxiliadora.

Through his friendship with the Indians over several decades, they had brought him gifts of ancient objects discovered in caves throughout the countryside. The profusion of artifacts had prompted him to catalogue them. The Vatican gave him permission to open a museum which, by 1960, had grown into one of the largest in Ecuador. Many of the artifacts, he maintained, belonged to Middle Eastern and Mediterranean cultures. He had deduced that Phoenicians (from the region of present-day Lebanon) had crossed the Atlantic Ocean around 1200 BC and sailed up the Amazon, making contact with the people of present-day Ecuador by navigating some of the tributaries that fed the great river.

In July 1962 tragedy struck the museum when an arsonist burned it down. Padre Crespi was able to salvage a few of the artifacts which he continued to display.

The man intrigued us. We had to meet him. The next morning we hopped a bus for Cuenca.

The Santa bus line carried us for ten bone-rattling hours in a rickety, squeaky bus over some of the roughest mountain roads imaginable from Quito to Cuenca. The pamphlet from the Quito tourist office gave Padre Crespi's address as the Colegio Salesiano. We found the building and were admitted into an ante-room by a young priest in a black suit who asked us to wait there.

Padre Crespi entered and greeted us with a friendly *buenos dias* in a rasping authoritative voice. Cloaked in his black robe with a cobweb trailing from his sleeve he looked as if he had just crept out of the crypt.

After shaking hands he told us in Spanish, with an intermittent sprinkling of English, of the two large rooms containing artifacts he had rescued from the fire. He led us to the first room where I was overwhelmed by the floor to ceiling shelves cluttered with skulls, vases, stone carvings and sheets of engraved metal. A subtle odour of decay permeated the still air. Cobwebs of delicate lace hung from the high ceiling.

"Everything is pre-Inca," he told us in Spanish. "Some pieces are more than 5,000 years old."

On a shelf lay a stone sculpture, about twenty centimetres long, of a mermaid. Mermaids, I knew, belonged to the mythology of lands bordering the Mediterranean. Padre Crespi held up a stone carving of a winged bull, a guardian idol in early Middle Eastern culture when Babylon was at the height of its civilization.

Next, he showed us a large metal sheet with an engraving of a minotaur, a "half-man, half-bull" of Cretan mythology. "These objects arrived here on Phoenician trading ships about 3,000 years ago," he said. I was enthused and puzzled but kept an open mind as he reached for another artifact from a shelf.

Penny nodded towards a small stack of *Archaeology* magazines dated 1960, gathering dust on a shelf. Interesting, I thought, considering they were American publications in English, a language he didn't speak except for a few hackneyed phrases.

Next off the shelf was a metal sheet engraved with real and imagined animals: a camel, a six-legged bird, dinosaurs and multi-headed snakes. I wondered what they meant and waited for an explanation. But he didn't offer one.

In the second room I pointed to more metal sheets – like rolls of linoleum – some of which had the lustre of gold and others, silver. We unrolled a silver sheet about 1.3 metres wide and ten metres long. It contained several engravings of animals we didn't recognize. Maybe extinct or mythological? We weren't sure.

There were also engravings of hooded cobras and elephants, busts of people and curious symbols that resembled letters of an alphabet. The snake, we knew, was significant in many cultures as a wise, spiritual being, but seeing engravings of elephants was a mystery since they have been extinct in South America for at least 12,000 years. Elephant bones had been discovered and dated to that period.

Were the engravings thousands of years old, made when elephants roamed South America, or were they crafted by local artisans? If engraved recently, who today would spend countless hours hammering seemingly unfamiliar and unrelated motifs out of gold and silver sheets? And how were these sheets made? And what was their purpose? And for whom were the sheets intended? My mind spun with questions when the priest opened a book of gold-coloured metal sheets about thirty centimetres wide and one metre long which he described as an ancient medical dictionary.

He flipped over the sheets like the pages of a book, thanks to wire rings that had been inserted in two holes punched along the side of each sheet. Whether the wire binding was old or new we couldn't tell.

Human skeletons were engraved onto the sheets, and symbols appeared next to the various parts of the human anatomy as if to name them, or explain their function. I was fascinated as I studied the engravings more closely. The individual metal sheets definitely did appear to be part of a dictionary. At least to my unpractised eye.

While carefully handling the gold- and silver-coloured sheets I imagined those early metal smiths blending another base metal to add strength. Possibly zinc. But, like everything else we were seeing, I couldn't be sure about anything.

From a cluttered shelf Padre Crespi produced another startling gold sheet engraved with a pyramid. The apex was pointed, unlike a Meso-American Mayan pyramid which is crowned with a temple. The engraver had etched rectangular blocks into the side of his pyramid, presumably to indicate it was constructed with cut stones. To us it looked decidedly Egyptian.

The priest explained that the local Indians had been bringing these items to him over the years. Some objects, he told us, were found in caves but others came from their homes where they made them to give as gifts to him. Penny pointed to a clay sculpture on a shelf which looked rudimentary. It had gold-coloured beer bottle caps pressed into it. She whispered to me: "Beer bottle caps."

Padre Crespi overheard and understood what she said. He responded with a gravelly laugh and quickly set us straight: *"Oro, oro, no cerveza."* (Gold, gold, not beer.) To him, if the item was yellow, it was gold. He then pointed to lumps of clay with clear broken glass embedded into them. "Pre-Inca. With diamonds," he insisted. Another lump of clay had green broken glass poked into it. "Emeralds," he said.

We glanced at each other, realizing because of his advancing age his cognitive abilities were waning. We concluded that a few home-made gifts had landed in his museum collection and he now couldn't tell the difference between old and new.

After almost two hours with this erudite man, listening to explanations in a mix of Spanish, English and his native Italian, it was time to leave. We thanked him in the three languages and slipped him the expected donation to his favourite charity.

Under a flawless blue sky we sat on a park bench to collect our thoughts and reflect.

"What do you make of all this?" Penny said.

"I think the word bizarre sums it up. I'm keeping an open mind. Some of the things don't have a logical explanation, like the long rolls of sheet metal."

"I wish we'd asked Padre Crespi for his opinion about the rolls," Penny said.

We were so overwhelmed by the artifacts we forgot to ask obvious questions. I mulled over the engravings of elephants. "I bet they're African because elephants roamed North Africa's Mediterranean coastline during Phoenician times."

I pondered some of the objects – the mermaid, winged bull, minotaur, and elephant and pyramid engravings – and likened them to pieces of a jigsaw puzzle. I shuffled them around in my mind, trying to complete the picture. But I couldn't do so. A piece was missing, rendering the puzzle incomplete.

What was the missing piece?

I realized it was my need for proof that these artifacts really were transported across the Atlantic Ocean and along the Amazon more than 3,000 years ago. At that time Phoenicia was a maritime power with trading outposts in present-day Morocco from where expeditions may have crossed the Atlantic.

Padre Crespi, a man of letters, and a renowned archaeologist, definitely believed in the voyages.

Peru

Soccer pervades the airwaves

The missing bag in Lima, November 1975
See map, page 10

A shadowy figure in a long brown coat ambled along the aisle of the bus in the semi-darkness. He was a short, quick-eyed man whose head darted left and right while deft fingers riffled through his roll of Peruvian bank notes as he sought customers.

Penny and I had arrived by bus at Huaguillas, a town in Ecuador near the Peruvian border, at two-thirty in the morning. Because of the early hour, the driver let passengers sleep in their seats until sunrise when the border would open.

At first light he allowed the shadowy figure – an early-rising money-changer – to board the bus. His offer was 52 soles for each American dollar, much better than the bank's exchange rate of 43.50 soles. The offer of 20 percent more of Peruvian currency was a compelling reason for us to change US$200.

I carried a leather shoulder bag in which I kept used movie and slide films. To anyone else, the films were worthless. To me they were priceless. It was definitely a bag to be guarded diligently. Unbeknownst to Penny, I buried our newly acquired currency in the same bag. I did this in case we had to open our money belts to show our cash and travellers cheques at the Peruvian immigration and customs control office. The border officials had been instructed by the government to restrict people from bringing an excessive amount of Peruvian currency into the country, and 10,400 soles was regarded as excessive. On the travellers grapevine we heard of others who had their "unofficially acquired" soles confiscated.

The Peruvian sole, a weak currency, could be bought cheaply outside Peru as we had done. The government preferred that visitors change their money at a bank rather than have the profit from the transaction go to the likes of "a shadowy figure in a long brown coat."

My philosophy was to help the man in the street – as long as the price was right.

The bus took us through the Ecuador border control to the Peruvian side. We got off and approached the border office. Behind the desk sat a man with a square jaw that hinted at a streak of belligerence and impatience. He was listening intently to a soccer broadcast. I felt like an intruder. He flipped open our passports, thumped them with his stamp and waved us away. I almost apologized for interrupting his soccer game.

In Lima on the following Saturday morning we went to the railway station to buy train tickets to Huancayo. Reputed to have the best Sunday market in Peru, it was reached by the highest standard gauge railway in the world. I set off to buy the tickets while Penny watched over our bags. The station was a mass of chaotic humanity. In the main hall people scampered in all directions. Some carried luggage; others were empty handed. Vendors sold soccer cards, candy and gum, yelling to attract prospective buyers.

With tickets in hand I weaved through the throng, caught Penny's eye and gave the thumbs-up signal to indicate we had seats on the train.

As we picked up our bags I said, "The brown leather bag. Do you have it?"

Penny looked around and became alarmed. "Don't you have it?"

"No," I said.

We quickly checked again. It had disappeared! I thought of the movie and slide films of Panama and Ecuador. And the US$200 worth of Peruvian currency.

"It must have been snatched when I was returning with the tickets," I said. "Wait here, I'll check the men's toilet."

I dashed into the toilet, quickly scanned the men standing at the urinals and, not seeing a brown leather bag, dashed to the toilet stalls and ran in a hunched position, peering beneath the doors at legs with trousers around the ankles. I hoped no one took me for a pervert! Everything appeared normal. I dashed out and yelled to Penny, "I'll check the street!"

The chance of finding the thief wandering in the street outside the station was slight but it seemed my only option. I looked at scores of people, scoured the ground, scanned a couple of overflowing garbage cans but discovered nothing. I returned discouraged.

The train whistle blew. We ran to the train and found our seats.

As the train pulled away, vendors snaked their way along the aisle selling oranges, limes, tamales, soft drinks, flowers and pictures of local soccer players. Young men flipped through the cards, and chose their favourites. Soccer certainly was a popular sport.

We swayed from side to side in a carriage with about fifty Indians. Most men wore brown ponchos and colourful, knitted woollen caps with earflaps while many women wore black skirts, red shawls and lampshade-hats with fringes of red or black tassels.

Opposite us sat an elderly Indian lady with a plump, agreeable face. Her head was crowned with an eye-catching white wide-brimmed hat with a large black bow. A red shawl covered her ample bosom. When we acknowledged her with *buenos dias* she smiled, revealing brown, crooked teeth that would make a dentist despair.

I told her in broken Spanish the saga of the missing bag. She discussed it with the young man beside her, then announced our misfortune to the passengers in the seats behind her. It was common among village people to broadcast everyone's business.

Passengers farther along the aisle called out for details. The Indian lady was quite a talker. She yelled out the details to them and they passed them on. Soon everyone knew the story. The lady pointed to the luggage racks and under the seats, suggesting I should check the train. Maybe the thief is on the train, she said.

I crouched on the floor and peered under the seats then prowled along the aisle, scanning the luggage racks. Fifty pairs of eyes followed me. I felt as if I was invading people's privacy. I dawdled slowly from one carriage to the next, perusing every part of each rack. These were passengers who didn't know what I was looking for. They stared. I heard whispers behind me. I felt uncomfortable and eventually retraced my footsteps.

"It's useless to look further," I told Penny. "The bag has gone."

She looked distraught. "Was there anything else in the bag besides the film?" I told her about the cash.

She sagged lower into her seat. With our combined expenses averaging $12 a day, I figured we had lost sixteen days of funds. I hoped the thief would spend the windfall wisely.

We peered out the window and consoled ourselves with the beauty through which we were travelling. High, rock strewn mountain peaks covered with snow were framed by the window. Below us the Rimac bubbled over rocks. Sometimes it was on our left and sometimes on our right as the train criss-crossed the river.

At this high altitude of 3,000 metres the air was rarefied. As the train crawled forward and upward to higher elevations a lady behind us called for oxygen. An attendant appeared with an inflated rubber oxygen bottle to which a nozzle was attached, and revived her. We suffered slight headaches which we cured with a couple of strong aspirins.

We passed through the village of Galera which boasts the highest standard gauge railway station in the world at 4,781 metres. Eleven hours after leaving Lima the train clattered into Huancayo station.

The Sunday market, mainly occupying one long street, attracted hundreds of Indians to the stalls selling farm produce, plastic basins, pots and pans, hats, coats and a colourful blur of blankets made from alpaca and llama wool.

Normally we would have been enthusiastic about the array of goods but we were uncharacteristically quiet. The loss of the films devastated us. Could we ever find them? Penny must have read my thoughts. "I suggest we return to Lima," she said, "to see if anyone has turned the bag into the police."

I agreed. I didn't expect to get back the money, but hoped that the bag, with the films, had been handed in. We could either return to

Lima immediately or stick to our plan of travelling in the Andes.

The lure of the Andes mountains won.

After exploring Cuzco, Machu Picchu, Lake Titicaca and Bolivia we returned to Lima and started our inquiries. We headed to the railway station. In the crowd we found a policeman who did not understand our Spanish, let alone our English, but who led us along a busy street to a police car. The policeman in the car listened politely as Penny and I strung together Spanish words for our unintelligible discourse about the stolen bag. Then the officer dutifully radioed headquarters. He probably told them about two idiotic foreigners speaking mumbo jumbo.

Within five minutes another police car arrived with three policemen to take us to the precinct headquarters. On the way they wanted to know our problem so we repeated our story. This time we took turns in looking up key words in our English-Spanish dictionary. I think one man got the gist of our story, mainly because he listened while the other two ignored us and discussed something more interesting to them: soccer.

The interested policeman escorted us into headquarters, an old building with a stuccoed facade which, like its neighbouring buildings, needed another coat of yellow paint. Inside, policemen in their blue uniforms milled about chatting and laughing with a dozen or so civilians. A radio blared in the corner with a handful of men listening intently to the broadcaster's every word. It must be a soccer game in progress.

The atmosphere didn't seem conducive to giving a report in a language we could not speak. Nevertheless, our escort introduced us to the duty officer, then disappeared. I asked the officer if there was a room where they stored lost and found bags. He looked at me blankly.

A man in a suit and tie, who was blessed with a smattering of English, relayed our story of theft and hopeful recovery to the officer. He told us the officer would assist us as soon as the game was over. Five minutes later cheers rose from the group gathered around the radio. Obviously the result was favourable. Now the police station could get back to normal. Or was this normal?

The officer led us along a concrete-floored corridor and directed us into a little office which had a window with bars. The stench of stale urine permeated the air. Obviously the room had more than one use. Furnishings consisted of a desk and chairs. This was what I imagined an interrogation room to be like. We sat down. The officer followed and closed the door, imprisoning the stench. He wanted to hear the story and write it down.

I laboured over the details in Spanish as he scribbled. Halfway through my explanation the door swung open and another officer entered, updated his colleague on the *futbol* score and took over the pen. He wanted to hear the story from the beginning. Penny sighed when I started to repeat the story in Spanish. The policeman looked up and said, "Speak English." I started in English, but he looked exasperated and said, "I don't understand."

The situation had become ludicrous. And the dead air and stench of stale urine was impregnating our clothes.

I started to gag. "Do you have a lost property office?" I asked in Spanish between gags.

"No."

Penny and I looked at each other and realized without saying a word that further pursuit was futile. We stood up, shook his hand to end our business, and left the stuffy office.

Outside in the warm sunshine we agreed they'd never get the thief, but they'd always get the soccer score!

Peru

Almost over

The road from Huancayo to Cuzco, November 1975
See map, page 10

The bus was old with a badly maintained interior. The fabric of the seat covers was torn and the metal of the armrests exposed. Some seats wouldn't recline; others refused to stay upright. The floor, covered with large sheets of tin, was blanketed in dust. The only paint we could see was on the ceiling.

Bus fares in Peru were kept low, enabling more locals to travel.

Unfortunately, the low ticket prices didn't allow enough money to maintain the buses properly. This bus was the only one scheduled for today with seats available.

After eyeing the interior, I could only hope the engine and chassis received some semblance of maintenance as the route through the Andes was to be one of narrow, unpaved mountain roads with steep precipices.

In the morning the engine grumbled as the bus pulled away from the Andean market town of Huancayo. Penny and I were starting a forty-hour trip to Cuzco, the ancient Inca capital high in the Andes. The passengers included twenty-five Peruvians, most of whom were Indian women with babies. They each wore a number of skirts, probably their entire wardrobe, as was the common practice. Their babies wore colourful, knitted woollen caps and lay cradled in their arms or swaddled in a blanket slung over their backs. This forced the women to perch on the edges of their seats. They were a solemn group, rarely smiling or talking. Other passengers besides Penny and me included two American girls who were Peace Corps volunteers and two Canadian guys who worked for CUSO, a Canadian aid organisation.

After leaving Huancayo the bus crawled down the side of a mountain and bounced and bucked across a valley floor. We passed the familiar Andean sights of farmers plowing fields with oxen, and herders taking pigs, sheep, horses, cattle and alpacas to newer pastures.

The bus started to ascend, hugging the valley side. The Andes mountains, some draped with forests and others denuded of vegetation at higher elevations, loomed majestically around us as we climbed higher.

A large truck came around a blind curve and squeezed between us and the vertical cliff face. I was startled at how dangerously close our bus veered to the edge of the steep precipice. Rocks worked loose from the shoulder of the road and tumbled into the valley below. A woman sitting ahead of us crossed herself and mumbled quietly as she fingered her rosary beads. It made me a little nervous; I hoped her prayers were being heard. I had read in newspapers back home about buses tumbling off the Andean roads, killing everyone on board. I prayed we would not become such a statistic.

As the bus lurched higher into the mountains, the panoramic views of the Andes grew more impressive. Many peaks showed their grey rock-strewn surfaces; other mountaintops were painted with splashes of red and cream-coloured earth. A blue haze obscured the more distant forested mountains.

The bus strained with its engine howling in protest until it crested a rise. After it panted for a few moments at the top, the bus descended along another curvy road which gripped the steep mountainside. Below us white fluffy clouds hung lazily over the valleys. It is not often one travels by road above the clouds. I stared mesmerized, trying to capture the panorama for my memory bank. Then I lost the scene when the road curved.

On one side of us loomed a high cliff and on the other, a vertical drop. Suddenly an unusual grinding noise from the wheels beneath our feet snapped me back into reality. Penny almost leapt off her seat. "What's that noise?" Moments later there was a screech of tortured metal as the bus's rear end hit the roadway.

We all rocketed out of our seats and fell back with a thud. Penny's head collided with mine and she flopped into her seat winded. Dust from the floor swirled around the interior like a fog. It was difficult to breathe.

The bus slid, careening crazily over the loose gravel as the terrified driver gripped the wheel and feverishly pumped the brakes. The bus finally ground to a halt near mounds of rocks and earth discarded by road workers at the edge of the precipice. Someone cheered the driver.

"I can't breathe!" Penny gasped. She had turned a ghostly white. An arm from behind darted through the dust and jerked open a sliding window. I shoved Penny's head towards the fresh air. She sucked it in with quick shallow breaths. Concerned travellers clustered around.

"I'll be okay," she assured us bravely. "But my back hurts. And my legs feel numb."

Hearing her say that worried me. Then she smiled and said, "I'll be fine. Go have a look to see what's wrong; it's probably just a flat tire."

I joined the other travellers to check the damage. It was definitely more than a flat tire.

Metal parts, including the two sets of spring rods, lay scattered over the roadway. I was horrified to find the rear wheels, still attached to their axle, standing alone behind the bus. The wreck would be going no farther for some time, that was for sure.

Penny leaned out the window. "The feeling has returned to my legs," she said.

What a relief!

I told her about the wheels then reboarded the bus. One of the CUSO aid workers was walking her up and down the sloping aisle. The three other Westerners came aboard to check on her condition. "I can walk but my back hurts," she said. Our mutual concern for

Penny drew us close together.

Within half an hour another bus lumbered around the curve and stopped behind us. I dashed to check it for space. Its rooftop luggage rack was piled high with bundles, boxes and trussed up pigs and goats. The interior was crammed with passengers. Nevertheless about a dozen or more Peruvians from our bus clambered aboard and squeezed in with their babies, bags and bundles. The motor throbbed and the bus lurched forward. Moments later, only a cloud of dust remained. We were stranded. I had no idea when another bus would come along as there was very little traffic on this route.

I returned to our bus to check on Penny. She was calmly writing. To take her mind off the pain in her back she had put her thoughts into verse which she called Almost Over.

> The seats were broken, the windows cracked,
> People kept coming until it was packed.
> The engine started with a loud stutter
> It lurched ahead with a protesting mutter.
> With moans and groans it rounded each curve
> Climbing up and over with many a swerve.
> A grinding of metal was heard 'neath our feet!
> Dust filled our lungs, we were tossed in our seat!
> The driver, whose knuckles had turned white
> Suddenly gripped the wheel with fright.
> The rear wheels had broken away from the bus
> We wondered if this was the end of us.

An hour later another bus rumbled into view. The sign on the front said AYACUCHO, a town enroute to Cuzco. I ran to the bus. It was already full but the passengers crowded together to make space.

I dashed back to get Penny but she was sitting as still as a statue, grimacing. "I'm sure I've just pulled a muscle but my back hurts too much to move," she said. "I'd rather stay on this bus."

"If you want us to stay here, that's okay by me."

I told the other travellers we'd stay behind but they didn't think it was a good idea, not knowing how long we would have to wait.

We watched them disappear into the other vehicle and saw a cloud of black diesel smoke cough out of the exhaust pipe as it prepared to leave.

Suddenly, its door swung open and one of the American girls leapt out and raced towards us.

"We're not leaving you behind," she said. "The bus is full but we're bunching up tighter to make room for you."

Penny admitted it was better to go than endure a long, cold night not knowing if we'd be rescued. We transferred to the bus that looked as run down as our abandoned wreck.

I dared not look underneath to examine the chassis.

Instead, I boarded with a strong, silent prayer.

Peru (Part 1)

Race against time

Boat hunting in Pucallpa, December 1975
See map, page 10

A few minutes before midnight our bus rumbled along the quiet, muddy streets of Pucallpa, a town on Peru's Ucayali River. Penny and I, weary after the thirty-one-hour journey from Lima, checked into the hotel nearest the bus station. The sleepy-eyed clerk showed us the last vacant room. He flicked the light switch. Nothing happened. With a sigh he dragged a chair across the room and stood on it to unscrew the bulb. As he turned it, a flash of light illuminated the room and sparks burst from the fixture. He flew off the chair and thudded on the floor. His eyes almost popped out of their sockets but he recovered sufficiently to give us two candles.

We were into our fourth month of travel in Central and South America and looked forward to a leisurely trip on the Amazon River. But first we had to travel down the Ucayali River to connect with the Amazon. Penny had to return to work by the fifth of January which only gave us about twenty-five days to reach Leticia in Colombia from where she could fly to Vancouver. We hoped we would make it in time.

In the morning we decided on an immediate plan of action. We needed to change money, find a boat going downstream to Iquitos and buy food for the river trip. At the hotel desk sat the clerk who had almost been electrocuted. To find a boat he told us to enquire at the Port Captain's office in a grey building behind the main market.

We entered the office, a room with a cement floor muddied by boatmen coming in and out. On a grey wall hung a blackboard displaying arrivals and departures.

Slouching in chairs sat three seemingly disinterested clerks with deadpan faces. I asked about boats going downstream. My question roused a clerk enough for him to point to the blackboard and mutter "*Campeon*. Today. Puerta La Hoyada." Then he lazily pointed down the road which we assumed was the direction of the port called La Hoyada.

We were buoyed by the news and hurried along the rain-soaked street to the river where we found boats tied to stakes rammed into the muddy embankment. The water level was low, exposing broad expanses of soggy riverbank crisscrossed with deep ruts made by heavy cargo trucks. Our sandals slid and skidded as we picked our way around puddles and a discarded cargo of decaying mangoes and bananas. Fat black pigs grunted as they nuzzled into rotting mangoes while ugly black vultures strutted around pecking at the bananas and decomposing fish.

We spotted a boat with men milling around. It was about ten metres long with a white-painted superstructure with crew's quarters on the main deck, and the wheel house and captain's cabin on the top. The boat rode low in the water with the gunwales just a few centimetres above the waterline.

"It wouldn't take much for a wave to wash over the main deck," I said.

"And look how narrow the gang plank is," Penny said with a shudder as we watched porters carry sacks of grain from the muddy riverbank to the deck.

We followed the porters on board and found the captain, a thin man with deep lines etched into his tanned, leathery face. He said he was leaving in half-an-hour and we could sleep in the crew's quarters. The trip would take nine days for a price of 1,200 soles per person (US$27 each including meals).

Penny and I exchanged glances. In half-an-hour we would have to change money, retrieve our bags from the hotel, buy food and board the boat. It would be a race against time. We decided to try so we bounded across the mud flats, clambered up the riverbank and hailed a cruising taxi. *"Banco de la Nacion,"* I said. We agreed on ten soles and got in. Upon arrival at the bank, Penny gave the driver ten soles and we quickly jumped out, only to see a sign saying CLOSED.

We heard an angry yell and swung around to see the taxi driver shaking his fist and rushing towards us with fire in his eyes. He yelled, *"Diez libres"* (Ten libres). Ten libres was the local slang for 100 soles. He wanted ten times more than we had paid him! Either we misunderstood his initial fare, or he was playing a game to get more money. As the driver shouted angrily I pulled at the bank's door but it was locked. A bank official saw us and opened the door a crack. I explained we wanted to cash travellers cheques. Behind us the taxi driver was breathing fire. I turned to see Penny trying to placate him with another ten soles.

Together we slipped into the bank and changed some travellers cheques. On the sidewalk the taxi driver stood with his arms folded in defiance. The bank clerk confirmed that 100 soles was the correct fare. As we left we topped up the driver's outstretched palm and apologized for the misunderstanding.

Our hotel, a couple of blocks away, occupied the floor above a row of six shops. As we started towards it to collect our luggage I sprinted ahead, yelling over my shoulder to Penny that I would start packing.

I put on a burst of speed, held onto my hat, careened around a corner and got a shock. All the doors of the half-dozen shops and hotel were painted blue, something I hadn't noticed when we left earlier. Which door was ours? My heart pounded. I dashed towards the first one. Pushed it open. I guessed right. Darted upstairs, found our room, swept up clothes like a whirlwind and rammed them into our backpacks.

Precious seconds ticked by but Penny had not arrived. Maybe she had hurtled past the confusion of doors or pushed open the wrong one. Racing against time, I scurried up the stairs to the rooftop where our laundry was drying in the warm sun, scanned the streets below and spotted her. My first two yells caused her to look around bewildered, but at my third call she looked up. I signalled I would meet her at the doorway. We connected, but time was running out; we still had to buy food for the trip.

Forty minutes had passed since we had spoken to the Campeon's master. Had he already sailed? To find out, we left our backpacks in the hotel room, leapt down the stairs two at a time and kept up the momentum as we pounded along the road, swerving to avoid people, potholes and puddles. We arrived at the Campeon, chests heaving with exhaustion, and saw that porters were still shouldering sacks up the gangplank.

The vessel settled deeper into the water. Penny looked concerned. I felt dubious. It didn't look safe.

"A few more sacks of grain," I said, gasping for breath, "will sink this tub. I wouldn't want to spend nine days on it."

Penny agreed. "We should look around for a better boat."

Although disappointed after scrambling to prepare for the trip, I nodded in agreement, still breathless from our race against time.

Peru (Part 2)

Unforeseen challenges

Down the Ucayali River, Pucallpa to Iquitos, December 1975
See map, page 10

I covered my face with my hat to stifle the stench of rotting bananas and fish on Pucallpa's muddy, garbage-strewn riverbank. Penny and I were seeking a boat heading to Iquitos.

Trading activity on the river had slowed for two reasons: the Christmas holiday season was approaching and the annual rains had not yet raised the river level sufficiently for all vessels. Our choices were almost zero.

Farther along the riverbank we spotted a truck being unloaded near a boat; we hurried to investigate. A flat-topped barge, about fifteen metres long, was being loaded with crates of mangoes, beer, Inca Cola, bunches of plantain bananas and plastic bags of household detergent.

The barge was chained to a diesel-powered double-decked tugboat named *Benavente* that was going to push the barge along the river.

We walked up the plank onto the Benavente and located the captain, a short, beefy man wearing a pleasant smile and a dirt-stained skipper's cap. "Five days to Iquitos," he said in Spanish. "We leave tomorrow morning at five. We have a cabin for you; you can move in tonight. The fare is 1,100 soles each, including food." This worked out to an acceptable US$25 each.

He showed us to one of the ten cabins on the main deck, all of which were crew's quarters, including the one he had chosen for us. He spoke to two crew members who were lying on the bunks. Dutifully, they left. "Your cabin," he said. Then his eyes lingered on the Australian bush hat perched on my head. "I like your hat." For a moment I thought he was going to ask for it. I wasn't keen to give it away; it was the only one I had.

Bunk beds stood against one wall, taking up most of the floor space. The thin mattresses were filled with straw that had compacted into a series of rock-hard lumps. They were stained with grease and judging from the accumulation of dust, dirt and dead cockroaches the floor had not seen a broom for years. The window which opened to the passageway along the side of the boat was covered with fine wire mesh to keep out bugs, but it was full of gaping holes.

"Looks great," said Penny enthusiastically. "Lets take it. After cleaning, it will be fine." I admired her go-with-the-flow attitude.

We counted out 2,200 soles into the captain's hand. He invited us to eat with the crew but we declined. We had heard about other travellers becoming ill eating food cooked on the river boats. We left to buy supplies. In the market we bought mosquito coils, canned tuna, fresh carrots and oranges, cans of fruit, cans of juice, strawberry jam and soda crackers.

With our backpacks and supplies we returned to the cabin. We noticed that both a light switch and a light bulb were missing. A quick word to the captain brought a crewman who, within five minutes, had wired in a switch and provided a bulb.

We covered the greasy mattresses with thick brown paper we had bought originally to wrap parcels for mailing home.

Penny glanced at the dirty walls and floor. "Where is the grease coming from?"

"There's the culprit," I said, pointing upwards. In the corner of the cabin above the beds a thick metal chain protruded through a fist-sized hole in the ceiling. It then wound around a pulley and exited at a right angle through a hole in the wall. The chain was taut and smeared with grease. I looked up through the ceiling hole and saw that it was attached to the helm and realized it connected to the rudder. When the helm was turned left or right the chain would move and spatter grease over the bunks and floor.

Penny quickly offered a solution: "Let's wrap newspaper around the pipe. That should stop the grease from spattering."

Satisfied with our housekeeping, we left our cabin to watch the activity on the barge. Although darkness was falling quickly, as it does in the tropics, the workers continued to stack crates and sacks and lash them to the deck. Someone, somewhere, flicked a switch and the entire barge became bathed in light from bulbs strung between poles that lined both sides of the deck. The wheelhouse and all the cabins were brightly lit.

While the workers covered the cargo with tarpaulins (it was the rainy season) we returned to our cabin, closed the door and flopped onto the bunks, tired from hunting down river boats and dashing around town. I reached up and switched off the light.

Almost instantly we heard cries from the crew. We wondered what calamity had occurred. Crewmen in the other cabins began yelling. Someone rapped at our door, but we didn't answer it. I felt apprehensive. Silhouettes passed our window. One of the shadowy figures stopped suddenly, poked a flashlight through the window, pointed it first at Penny and then at me and jabbered at us. He shone the beam onto the light switch, pointed to it, ranted again and vanished.

"I think he's concerned about the switch," Penny whispered. I looked out the window and noticed the barge was in darkness, then there was another rap at the door. I opened it, a hand shot forward, felt for the switch and turned it on.

Cries of "hurrah" exploded from the barge and from the cabins as light was restored to the entire ship! To return our cabin to darkness we avoided the switch. Instead, Penny reached up to the ceiling and unscrewed the light bulb.

The "five in the morning" departure time passed without any signs of activity. It was not until three-thirty p.m. that the captain returned at a half-run, clutching a sheaf of papers and smiling broadly. He rushed up the plank and yelled in Spanish, "Let's go!" The engine started up and after five minutes we were chugging past idle boats and the Campeon, a boat we almost sailed on, which was supposed to have left the day before "in half-an-hour."

The brown river was smooth and about 500 metres wide. Scrub and tall trees lined the riverbanks. Beyond the trees we occasionally glimpsed thatch-roofed huts. Fishermen in dugout canoes angling for their supper had to brace themselves as our wake rocked their flimsy craft.

As dusk approached we pulled ashore at a quiet bend in the river. A crewman jogged down the gangplank with a wire rope, crawled up the embankment and tied it to a tree, thus securing the barge for the overnight stay. The engines stopped, and a generator started humming to provide electric light.

When dusk turned to darkness we were joined by mosquitoes that entered through the rip in the window screen. They carried malaria, a disease we definitely wanted to avoid. We slapped at them and mashed them into a pulp, leaving red blotches of our blood. We also sprayed ourselves and the mesh screen with insect repellent and lit mosquito coils. The pungent smoke curled upwards, clawed at our eyes and stung our nostrils but repelled the pesky insects.

Some skippers of cargo boats made extra money by taking on and dropping off passengers at the small villages along the river. Trailing behind the Benavente was a 'runabout' with an outboard motor. As we approached a village we slowed down and the runabout took passengers ashore. The Benavente then resumed its downstream speed of about twelve knots. An hour or more later the speeding runabout caught up with our barge with a couple of new passengers.

As we approached another village we saw the captain speak to the bosun who immediately came over to us. His belly arrived first, an ample one covered partly by an old yellow T-shirt. With his smattering of English he invited us to go ashore in the runabout as they had to drop off two passengers. Pleased to be asked, we joined a teenager and her mother, a colossal woman with puffed cheeks and stained teeth who clasped a box of baby chicks to her chest.

The crewman piloting the runabout drove it against the riverbank. The other crewman counted fifteen on his fingers to indicate how many minutes they were staying, then walked along the riverside with the mother and daughter.

We clambered up the riverbank and entered the village square around which stood a church, a shop, and homes built with wooden planks and thatch. The place was deserted except for a young girl carrying a bucket of river water to her home. We went to the shop to buy drinks and while there heard hymns coming from the church, reminding us this was Sunday. The music drew us towards the door of the Evangelical Church, but as fifteen minutes had passed we didn't go in.

Back at the riverbank we couldn't see the runabout. Had they forgotten us? The barge by now would be a long way down the river. But where was the runabout? Some village women appeared behind us and started telling us something but we could not interpret their hand movements, and definitely not their language.

Suddenly we heard a holler. Our crewman was standing on high ground, shouting and waving to us.

"Gracias," I yelled, thankful the boat hadn't left. We picked our way along the trail towards him. He pointed to the riverbank where they had moved the runabout. We climbed into the boat and were surprised when the other crewman piled about a dozen turtles around our feet. They were alive but trussed with cord to immobilize them. I imagined turtle soup on the menu – for every meal. I was pleased we had our own provisions.

Back on board I looked for my hat which I had carelessly left behind when we went ashore. I always wore it, rain or shine.

"My hat is missing," I said to Penny as I searched the cabin.

"Surely no one would have come in and taken your hat."

"I remember leaving it on the bunk."

It wasn't valuable but I had a sentimental attachment to it. I had worn it for many months and because it was made of soft cloth, I could stuff it in my pocket.

"Why don't you ask the bosun?" Penny suggested.

I found the bosun. "I think the captain stole it," he said.

At that moment the captain appeared and the bosun said something which prompted the captain to invite me to his cabin to look around. I felt uncomfortable checking his living quarters but it was he who had asked me to do so. I followed him up the iron ladder to his cabin behind the wheelhouse.

The captain's quarters were cramped. On nails around the walls hung trousers, T-shirts, a bunch of bananas, a rain cape, a rain hat but not my hat. On one wall was pinned a map of the Amazon region and nearby, a clock. Bolted to the wall in a corner hung a washbasin, stained brown by river water sediment. In another corner stood a collapsible table propped up by a folding leg. It was cluttered with an empty mug, an ashtray full of cigarette butts and a sheaf of papers that looked like a cargo manifest. I lifted the papers but my hat wasn't under them.

His bed was built against the wall, and beneath the bed were four sliding drawers containing, I assumed, additional clothes. I was tempted to rummage through the contents but I concluded that if he had taken the hat he would have stashed it elsewhere, otherwise he would not have opened his cabin for inspection. I shrugged my shoulders and he shrugged his. I resigned myself to never seeing the hat again.

Dark storm clouds gathered above us and by late afternoon a wild rainstorm lashed the decks and pounded the superstructure. Rain sprayed through our window, dampened the bunk beds and pooled on the floor. Quickly we ripped open some plastic bags and clipped them to the metal window frame with clothes pegs to stop the rain from blowing in.

Just then a stream of water poured through the ceiling. Penny grabbed an empty juice can to catch the flow while I raced topside to find the source. The driving rain sounded like ten thousand drums.

I discovered the wheelhouse door open and rain blowing in. It was puddling on the floor, leaking into our cabin below. I slammed the door behind me and mopped up the water with newspapers and rags. Penny called, saying the water had stopped.

The helmsman glanced at me curiously then quickly turned back to concentrate on steering the ship. The heavy rain had reduced visibility to only a few metres beyond the bow.

The captain entered the wheelhouse, signalled the engineer to reduce speed then ordered the helmsman to pull to the riverbank where a few village huts stood above the high water mark. We lit our mosquito coils and relaxed on our bunks.

When we awoke the next morning, the sun sat low in the sky and the foliage along the river bank glistened from the rainstorm. Water hyacinths with beautiful mauve blooms floated by peacefully. Wondering where we were, we took our map to the bosun. The captain and a crew member arrived and the three of them started jabbing the map with their fingers, arguing among themselves. To this day we still wonder where we were.

As the Ucayali River is narrow we were always in view of the river banks. Children from the villages came to the muddy banks to wave at passing boats. It was a diversion from their rural life. Their only connections with the outside world were the riverboats.

The Benavente chugged on. The crew washed the decks. We watched the cooks expertly remove three turtles from their shells, cut out the liver and eggs and put almost everything else into a big pot of river water. A cooking fire burned slowly in an empty oil drum. The cooks placed the partly cleaned turtle shells over the embers to cook the meat that was still clinging to the undersides. Chickens clucked around the deck, oblivious that their next stop was probably the cooking pot.

Four days had passed. We expected to arrive in Iquitos the next day.

In the late afternoon large buildings came into view. We checked our map and guessed it was Requena. Several ships of about 5,000 tonnes were berthed at the docks. As we approached, a dugout canoe came alongside with two men who climbed aboard and inspected the crates of mangoes while the Benavente nudged its way between smaller vessels; then the engine stopped. The bosun told us the boat was stopping here for the night. As we sat on the deck a crewman walked up and said "Iquitos" and pointed towards the town. We were not due in Iquitos for another twenty-four hours so we ignored him. However, uncertainty gnawed at me.

"Wait here. I'll check," I said to Penny.

I walked down the plank, up a slippery embankment, through a lumber yard, along a path of sawdust and along a muddy track to the main road where I saw a sign that read IQUITOS. To confirm it I stopped a taxi. Yes. We had arrived!

When I returned to the barge I learned that Penny had confirmed our location with the bosun. We took up his offer to stay on board for the night.

At two-forty-five a.m. we were awakened by another steady stream of water coming through the ceiling. Wind howled and thunder growled as rain once more lashed the barge.

Water leaked straight onto and through my straw mattress, through Penny's mattress below and onto the floor. We each curled up at the ends of our bunks – the only dry places – to escape the unscheduled baptism. Maybe we should have gone into Iquitos for the night but it was now three-thirty a.m. and finding a hotel at that hour would have been difficult.

When the sun rose we hoisted our backpacks over our shoulders, said goodbye to the crew and waved to the captain who was standing in the wheelhouse.

I pointed to my bare head, giving him a chance to return my hat, but all he did was shrug with a good humoured grin.

Peru (Part 3)

The shrunken head

Jungle journey at Iquitos, December 1975
See map, page 10

Rita leaned across the dinner table towards Penny and me and whispered, "I've got one."

"A shrunken head?" Penny said.

"Yes."

"Do you have it with you?"

"No, it's at home. I'll tell you about it later."

Earlier in the day in Iquitos, Penny and I had boarded a motor launch which putted along the Nanay River, a tributary of the Amazon in Peru. A thatch-roofed canopy protected us from the tropical sun. This mid-December day was near the start of the wet season. The air hung heavily with moisture, the result of the previous night's rainstorm.

Also on board were two other travellers. Rita was in her sixties, a slender woman, lightly tanned, her greying hair swept back into a bun. She lived in Australia but was visiting her daughter, Jan, who lived and worked in Lima. Jan, a stout, jocular woman laughed easily and heartily. The four of us formed an immediate bond.

In Iquitos we had all booked an excursion to visit tribal groups who lived along tributaries accessible only by boat.

After motoring along the Nanay the boat entered a narrow tributary, the Momon. Long, thin vines draped into the river from over-hanging tree branches. The jungle, thick and lush, looked impenetrable. It resembled a Tarzan movie set. From the top branches of a tall cedar a fluttering flock of green and yellow parakeets took to the air, disturbed by the noise of the motor. In tranquil coves along the river, white fluffy clouds and the riverside vegetation of palms and grasses reflected in the glass-smooth water.

Thirty minutes later we rounded a bend and arrived at the Amazon Safari Camp, a collection of bamboo and palm-thatch buildings perched on stilts in the jungle above the river's high water mark. The Momon can rise by thirty-five feet in the wet season. From the small floating dock a raised walkway snaked uphill. It was two metres high, built of bamboo poles and planks, and wobbled as we filed along it, cautiously gripping the railings.

The lodge at the top of the riverbank housed a reception office and dining room. From this building more raised walkways led to guest rooms, also built on stilts.

"Everything is raised," explained the smiling clerk, "so we are above floodwaters and the animals: the tapirs, peccaries, sloths, anacondas, ants, centipedes and jaguars."

I raised my eyebrows. "Jaguars?"

"Very unlikely," said the man, "but one was seen on a trail some months ago."

The guest rooms, constructed from the plentiful bamboo and palm-thatch, had insect screens over the window openings. Aside from the beds there was a small wooden side-table on which sat a water pitcher, a wash basin and a kerosene lantern. The cleanliness of this spartan accommodation in the depths of the Amazon impressed us.

In the evening, under the light of the lanterns, we were served a buffet meal of chunks of beef, rice, tomatoes and potatoes, followed by a dessert of pineapple and a choice of tea or coffee.

"I'm pleased the four of us are the only guests," Penny said. "I feel like we are on a private expedition."

A man approached our table – a twenty-something, gaunt man of medium height with a shock of black curly hair falling over his coppery brown forehead. His brown eyes sparkled like raindrops.

"My name is Francisco and I will be your guide in the jungle. I'll explain the cultures of the Amazonian tribes." He chattered away with much enthusiasm about the excursion for the following morning – a visit to the Jivaro tribe.

The Jivaro, he explained, were not indigenous to the area but had been relocated here by the Peruvian Government because of tribal disturbances in their homeland near the Peru-Ecuador border. Their forebears were headhunters who used to shrink heads. This had been practised by warriors of opposing tribes. Kill an enemy, shrink his head and absorb his power and strength. The more heads, the greater your respect in the clan.

It was then that Rita leaned over the table and whispered that she had a shrunken head at her home in Australia but would tell us about it later.

The guide continued, mentioning that tourists in the early days paid high prices for shrunken heads, thus pitting tribe against tribe to secure heads for the market. The shrinking of human heads has been banned by the government, he said, but monkey heads are still shrunk occasionally.

With the thought of shrunken heads in our minds Penny and I went to our room.

"I'd like to see Rita's shrunken head one day," I said.

"The whole business sounds gruesome," Penny said pensively, "but I'd like to see it too. What a bizarre souvenir. I bet many innocent people were killed to satisfy the demand."

During the night the sounds of the jungle were like an out-of-tune orchestra. The birds, crickets, frogs and the occasional howl of a distant monkey lulled us to sleep.

After breakfast we set off with Francisco who was dressed in jungle greens and armed with a machete to cut new pathways when necessary. Rain had fallen overnight, making the jungle paths slippery. Francisco slashed at a vine, tore strips from it and explained it was used for making baskets. As we passed beneath a tree with hairy red pods shaped like mussel shells, he picked one and opened it to reveal red seeds.

"It is *achiote*," he said. "It is like paprika. The Indians paint themselves with it."

Farther along the path we halted at a moving line of foliage that crossed in front of us. Closer examination showed the line was actually an army of cutter ants marching in single file, each carrying a piece of leaf many times its body size. The trail of ants continued into the jungle along the ground and over fallen tree branches; they must have numbered in the tens of thousands.

Francisco turned to us. "They are taking the leaves to their underground nests. They use the leaves as compost on which to grow fungi, their food."

Our trail led us to a ravine. We looked down to where a creek bubbled over rocks and decaying vegetation. The only way to cross was by treading carefully over a tree trunk covered with damp moss.

"I don't like the look of this," said Penny with a hint of trepidation.

With the guide's helping hand she gingerly shuffled across. Then we followed a slippery path out of the ravine and into a plot of manioc.

The long narrow stalks of manioc grew to shoulder height. Tending her plants was a plump, young Indian woman with long black hair and copper-toned skin. She pulled up a root to show us what her people subsisted on. The tuber would be scraped, boiled then eaten as a mush or dried into small balls to be stored for later consumption. When we entered the village compound we saw half a dozen open-sided huts. Nursing a baby in front of one of them sat a young chubby woman. Long black hair framed her face.

"She looks young to be a mother," Penny said. "How old is she?"

Francisco rattled off something in the Jivaro dialect.

"She said she's fourteen. It's common for girls to marry young." While he spoke, two chickens pecked and clucked over a discarded banana peel. The chicken is one bird that you can rely on   seeing anywhere in the world.

Nearby, two men sat cross-legged, wrapping the barrel of a

blowgun with a thin flat vine. Blowguns are used to shoot birds, monkeys and other small game, explained our guide. As we approached, both men rose. They were bare-chested and wore knee length skirts of blue cotton. Their pale brown faces were decorated with streaks of red paint – paste from the achiote plant. Francisco spoke to them and they agreed to demonstrate their prowess with their three-metre long blowguns.

From short quivers hanging from their waists they withdrew darts; to each dart was attached a flight made from a small ball of kapok. The darts were needles, about the length of one's hand, obtained from a tree that has needles growing out of its trunk – nature's way of protecting it from animals.

On a tree in their village compound I pinned two bank notes and stood back. From a distance of fifteen paces they raised their long blowpipes, sucked air until their cheeks bulged, then blew with a hissing noise. Both darts pierced the bank notes – which the men kept as their reward.

On the return journey to the lodge, a twenty-metre high kapok tree towered over us along the trail. The white, silky fibres that surrounded the seeds were bursting out of their capsule-shaped brown pods.

Balls of fibre lay scattered on the ground and surrounding bushes, giving the impression of a recent snowfall. Penny bent down and picked up a fluffy ball. "It is so soft, no wonder it's used in pillows."

I picked some up and rolled it between my fingers. "And the Jivaros have a steady supply of kapok for their darts."

At the lodge, around the luncheon table, I turned to Rita. "I'm interested in hearing about the shrunken head. How did you get it?"

"From a friend who got it from someone who got it from the Jivaros in the 1930s."

"Has it turned mouldy with age?" Penny asked.

"No, it's completely dry. All the moisture was removed."

"How do you shrink a head?" I was curious.

"I've been asked many times so I had to find out for myself long ago. Apparently, once you have the severed head, you sew the mouth closed.

"To remove the skull you need a sharp knife. Start at the hairline at the middle of the forehead and slice the skin in a straight line to the back of the neck. Then peel back the skin from the top of the head to the sides and remove the skull.

"The next thing to do is to sew up the scalp then heat the head over a fire to allow fat to drain away. You add a herbal solution to tan the skin then fill the empty head with hot sand and pebbles to puff out the cheeks and to dry out the inside of the head.

"You then hang it over the embers to remove any remaining moisture. After that you remove the sand and pebbles and there you have it, a shrunken head!"

"You say you have it at home? Where in Australia?" I asked.

"I live in Berridale in the Snowy Mountains. Come and see it if you are ever travelling in my part of the country."

Amazed at what I had heard, I now wanted to see it. One year later Penny and I were driving in the Snowy Mountains and made a point of detouring through Berridale. Rita wasn't hard to find; she lived in a small farming community where everyone knew each other.

As we got out of our car at her farm she walked towards us and quickened her pace when she recognized us. She welcomed us into her home.

Over a cup of tea she showed us the shrunken head which had been gathering dust on a shelf. The size of a small grapefruit, it had short hair and eyelashes still attached. The skin was leathery and black, a result of the dehydration process. It gave me a weird feeling to hold the shrunken head of a man in my hands – a head that once laughed and cried.

Peru (Part 4)

Risky undertaking

Down the Amazon, Iquitos to Leticia, December 1975
See map, page 10

The soles of our sandals became caked with sticky mud as Penny and I picked our way along the slippery embankment of the Amazon River at the Peruvian river port of Iquitos. We were looking for a boat to take us downstream to the Peru-Colombia border.

The previous night's torrential downpour had thundered like a shower of ball-bearings on our hotel's tin roof. Water had gushed over the sides of the eaves and puddled on the street, forming a lake.

The early morning sun crawled out from behind the forest and turned up the heat. Perspiration beaded on our skin in the thick, humid air. My shirt felt like a wet rag. We trudged past flat-topped barges, single- and double-decked cargo boats, old hulks on their sides, houseboats floating on balsa logs, and dugout canoes.

From makeshift food stalls constructed of wooden poles and palm-thatch, meals were being served to the labourers who repaired and loaded the boats.

We plodded by customers hunched over dishes of rice, meat and beans and passed through a small flock of black-winged vultures, the unofficial garbage collectors, that pecked at banana peels, rotten mangoes and discarded scraps of meat and fish from the food stalls. The scavengers were doing an admirable job of garbage removal but they were slow, picky eaters. It was now midday, the sun had increased the humidity, and a pungent odour of rotting food permeated the air.

I asked one of the customers who was shovelling beans into his mouth if there was a boat going downstream. He pointed with his spoon to a short, squat, trading boat with a white hull – the *Condesa*.

We boarded the boat and found the captain, a thick log of a man in his forties with an intelligent, aggressive face and a devilish smile. Dressed in grubby shorts and a T-shirt, he was supervising the loading of oil drums. He would leave the next day, December the twenty-fourth, and for the four-day trip he would charge 400 soles (nine dollars) each. He left us so we could think about it.

The Condesa was about twelve metres long with a roofed single deck. The captain's cabin and wheelhouse were located at the forward part of the deck while at amidships there was an open-sided, roofed area where passengers hung hammocks for sleeping. We would be the only gringos. An Indian family – a woman in her fifties, a woman in her twenties and her two young children, a boy and a girl – were the only other passengers.

The engine room and the galley were in the stern.

We checked out the rest of the small vessel. On one side of the deck stood about eight 44-gallon drums roped together. I was alarmed at what I saw. "There's no railing on this side of the boat," I pointed out to Penny. "The barrels have been put here so no one will fall overboard." I tried to sound reassuring.

Although the boat already sat low in the water, we watched labourers load more cargo: sacks of flour and sugar, and crates of beer and soft drinks. The Condesa, a trading boat, would be stopping at riverside villages to deliver cargo.

"A good thing about this boat," Penny said, "is that it's leaving soon. I don't like reminding myself, but I have to be back at work on the fifth of January. That's two weeks from now." She hesitated for a moment, then added: "I'd much rather continue travelling."

"Why don't you?"

"I couldn't just quit without giving the proper one month's notice.

I guess it's called loyalty."

As soon as I had asked the question I realized it wasn't in her character to abandon her workmates.

The captain came and told us he was going all the way to Ramon Castilla. I pulled the map from my shoulder bag. The town was the Amazonian river port in Peru from where we would cross the river to Leticia in Colombia.

We agreed to join the Condesa and dropped 800 soles into the captain's palm. He happily went on his way.

Penny brightened up. "I'm really looking forward to a leisurely trip down the Amazon; it will be a great ending to a fabulous four months."

We linked arms and strolled into Iquitos to shop for the journey.

We bought hammocks and food (canned tuna fish, peaches, pears, strawberry jam, processed cheese, juice and crackers) and Penny added a loaf of raisin bread, protectively wrapped in paper. "A Christmas Day treat," she explained. We also bought Christmas decorations of green, red and silver tinsel.

On board we attached our hammocks to hooks in the ceiling. Penny quietly sang Christmas carols as she hung up tinsel and a paper bell cut from a magazine. "I feel a bit homesick," she said. "I've never been away from home at Christmas time."

The crew loaded more drums of fuel into the hold and onto the deck and placed crates of bottles on top. The captain walked by, perusing his expanding cargo and looked quizzically at the strips of tinsel stuck to the ceiling. *"Navidad,"* (Christmas), Penny said. He shrugged and continued with his work. His mind was not on Christmas; he seemed engrossed in finding space for more cargo that sat on the riverbank.

December the twenty-fourth, the supposed day of departure, came and went.

On Christmas Day, Penny ceremoniously unwrapped our special treat – the loaf of raisin bread. "The bread is alive! Look at all the ants," she exclaimed as she leaped to her feet and quickly shook the loaf and wrapping paper over the railing. Dozens of ants tumbled to a watery grave.

She cut a slice; more ants crawled out and covered her hand. She flicked them off and shook the bread over the side again. "I'm not going to let a few ants spoil our Christmas treat."

Not to be deterred, she continued to shake the bread each time she sliced a piece. With the ants gone we spread the slices with our special purchases of strawberry jam and cheese and celebrated her victory over the ants. It was a Christmas dinner we will always remember.

A few moments later we heard a shout, the engine started and the boat pulled away from the riverbank. I felt good being on the river again after a week in Iquitos.

The Amazon widened downstream from Iquitos. Logs floated by – a hazard to small vessels. Green foliage of hyacinth plants floated on top of the murky water. Trees more than thirty metres high dotted the hinterland while spindly trees and scrub hugged the riverbank. On the first day we approached a village of huts surrounded by plots of pineapples and banana trees. Cows grazed near the huts. Dugout canoes lay above the waterline. The engineer cut the motor and we drifted to the river's edge where a crewman jumped ashore and tied the bow hawser to a tree, and another crewman lowered a gangplank.

While a drum of diesel fuel was offloaded we had the opportunity to look at both sides of the Condesa's hull. On the starboard side – the one with the broken railing – we were disturbed to see that something, probably a log, had previously collided with the boat, cracked the hull and pushed the planks inward, leaving gaps where water could enter. Fortunately, the damage appeared to be only above the waterline. Or so I thought.

As we sailed downstream the water was so smooth it enabled us to detect a slight list of the boat towards the starboard side.

A crewman obviously noticed it too. He opened the hatch cover of the hold, which was directly under our hammocks, and descended a short ladder. He bellowed to another crewman who jumped down after him. The next sound we heard was the throb of the bilge pump.

A crewman leapt out of the hold with a hose and hung it over the side of the boat. Brown water spewed into the river.

Throughout the afternoon the pump was switched on now and again to rid the bilge of excess water. I tried to look on the bright side. "With a cracked hull, a bilge filling with water and a listing boat we're in for an entertaining time."

Penny looked at me sideways. She knew the danger.

As we neared the next village a crewman went down into the hold to ready some drums of diesel fuel for unloading, but rushed back excitedly. I peered into the hold.

"The water is rising and we're listing more," I said, trying to stay calm so as not to upset Penny who was clinging to the railing.

"Are we going to sink?"

"Of course not," I said. "At least, I hope not."

The captain ran towards the commotion and yelled rapid-fire directions to his crew. He appeared to be in control. One crewman leapt into the wheelhouse and cut the engine. Another sprang overboard and landed in water that was armpit-deep then dived to inspect the hull. Another crewman jumped over the side to help him.

Although the bilge pump continued to suck up water, there was an endless pool in the hold. The boat began to list more.

The captain peeled off his clothes to his bleached white briefs and leapt over the side to join the two crewmen already in the brown water. Soon the three men were diving to find the hole, then the captain surfaced and yelled something. Another crewman tossed pieces of burlap sack to him, then went into the hold, apparently to assist with the repairs from inside the hull.

We gripped the railing of the troubled boat. I feared we would sink, and hoped the crew knew what they were doing. I felt it best to stay out of their way. We were inexperienced with shipwrecks.

The only other passengers, the Indian family, stood huddled together by the railing holding cloth bags containing their possessions. They were ready to abandon ship.

For more than an hour the boat drifted aimlessly near the river's edge. Village men sat on the bank, watching patiently. I heaved a sigh of relief when the pump finished emptying the bilge and the boat righted itself. Then two crewmen rolled two fuel drums over the side to the villagers on the riverbank who had ordered them.

Had the water problem been solved? I doubted it. I would be surprised if there was anywhere along the river, except Iquitos, where the boat could be dry docked for repair. I tried to be optimistic and hoped the rest of the trip would be clear sailing.

As darkness engulfed us we listened to the jungle noises of crickets and the calls of distant birds. Then the engine was restarted and we headed downstream into the blackness while a spotlight shone from the wheelhouse to pick out any floating logs. Tired from all the excitement, we lay sleepily in our hammocks and swung gently to and fro as a soft breeze blew across the deck. The four hammocks of the Indian family hung, like ours, above the hatch cover of the hold.

Out of the darkness, black flying cockroaches the size of one's thumb emerged, attracted by the electric light bulb that illuminated our space. They flew into the bulkheads, hit them with a noisy thud, then dropped writhing onto the deck.

Penny pulled her cotton hammock around her into a protective cocoon. A persistent cockroach found the opening in the end of Penny's hammock and both she and it went berserk. She leapt out and left the cockroach to buzz crazily inside. We heard it thrash around against the insides of the hammock in a panic, until it finally found its way out.

The Condesa rounded a bend and pulled over to the riverbank for the night. The electric light was turned off and the cockroach attacks ceased. I heard Penny heave a sigh of relief.

The next morning, while the rising sun flickered through the trees, we continued downstream. A light rain fell. On our port side it was a thrill to see porpoises leaping beside the boat. We stopped twice more to offload drums.

Every hour the bilge pump rhythmically sucked up excess water and discharged it over the side through the hose. Just before four in the afternoon the captain ordered the helmsman to steer the boat into a side channel. I looked inquiringly at the captain who explained with sign language that it was a short cut.

I discovered after speaking in laboured Spanish with a crewman that the captain had been a school teacher of Peruvian history. He changed his occupation when he saw the economic gains to be made by being a skipper of a trading boat. Extra money was made by smuggling goods and carrying passengers. His method was simple. He under-declared the quantity of cargo to avoid wharf charges and applicable taxes. At the various river stops he delivered the goods that had been ordered, then sold his undeclared cargo at inflated prices to villagers along the backwater channels.

The bow cut a swath through a mass of water hyacinths that almost covered the entire channel. About fifteen minutes later the boat shuddered as it hit something. The engineer revved the engine in reverse but we listed to starboard. The captain dashed into the wheelhouse and grabbed the helm. He spun it left and right but the rudder didn't respond. As the boat listed more we gripped the railing to keep our balance.

"We're stuck in the mud!" Penny exclaimed.

The captain ordered two crewmen to jump over the side into the chest deep water. He threw a four-metre pole after them which they grabbed and rammed under the hull to lever the boat off the mud.

The boat remained steadfast on the mud bar. The captain, eager to help his men, stripped again to his briefs, now the brown colour of the muddy Amazon. They pushed upwards on the lever, their muscles bulging. They strained to their limits, but the hull refused to budge.

Two Indians in a canoe appeared unexpectedly. Dressed in shorts and coloured T-shirts, they sat and watched impassively. Seeing them gave the captain an idea because he immediately reboarded the Condesa and dashed to the bow where there was a winch drum and thick wire cable. He called to the Indians, passed them the cable and pointed to a tree by the river. They took the cable, paddled to the riverbank and wrapped it around the tree. The captain and a crewman strained to turn the winch handle but the boat stayed put. All this time the Condesa's engine laboured and the propellers continued to churn the mud.

I felt helpless as we watched the men working frantically. I could only hope we would not keel over. We clung to the railing.

The captain became visibly agitated when the boat listed more. He shouted at two crewmen and ordered them to move two fuel drums to the port side of the deck to counter the starboard list, and to start the bilge pump. Nothing helped; the boat stayed stuck. Two crewmen tried to turn the winch handle again but the cable just hung limply between the boat and the tree. More canoes arrived. Word of a disabled boat must have spread quickly to the nearby village.

The captain walked cautiously around the sloping deck and counted the drums. He hollered abruptly at the crew to jettison some of the cargo to allow the boat to float free.

"There goes our safety barrier," I said as oil drums, which had replaced the missing railing, were dumped over the side. Another dozen or so drums were hauled from the hold.

They hit the water with a splash, disappeared for a moment then bobbed up and floated like corks. We counted seventeen drums. Because the current was sluggish in this backwater channel they floated around aimlessly. All this time the engine ran nonstop.

Then, without even a cough or stutter, the engine suddenly died. The captain uttered some unintelligible but highly predictable words and leapt down the iron ladder to the engine room. I looked at my watch. Five-fifteen. It would soon be dark. I grew concerned that the boat wouldn't be freed before nightfall.

In the silence we heard the twitter of birds in the trees and the quiet voices of the Indian paddlers as they talked among themselves. I wondered what they were saying about our predicament! A few minutes later the engine coughed to life and the captain emerged with a triumphant smile.

I called out, "Look at the drums!" and pointed to a dozen or more which had started to float away down the channel. His smile quickly disappeared. A crewman commandeered an empty canoe to round them up. He was joined by the Indians in their canoes who encircled the drums so they would not escape again.

The sun dropped towards the trees at an alarming rate and painted the sky with splashes of orange and purple. Then darkness descended like a theatre curtain.

A long-hulled boat from the village materialized with a lantern on its deck. The captain welcomed this additional help and ordered his crew to transfer the crates of beer and soft drinks into the long-boat to lighten the weight even more. Oddly enough, the lantern didn't attract flying cockroaches but mosquitoes attacked us without remorse.

The Condesa's propellers continued to churn the water as the list increased to 45 degrees. We were in serious trouble and, although I didn't want to admit it to Penny, I was extremely worried. Penny gripped the railings so tightly her knuckles turned white. Trying to act casually, I steered her to amidships to be away from the propellers in case the boat capsized.

From the hold a crewman emerged with another long pole and threw it into the water. While the crates were unloaded, other crew-men rammed the pole under the hull and heaved upward with loud grunts and groans. By now, all the crates had been transferred. The captain ordered more drums to be raised out of the hold with the ropes and pulley and tossed overboard.

As the crewmen put their shoulders to the pole we detected a slight shift of the hull off the mud. The engine revved loudly. The crewmen heaved again, and again the hull shifted. Suddenly it floated free, straightening up until it was on an even keel.

We all cheered.

Next came the task of reloading the cargo. The crew and the Indians yelled directions to each other as they loaded the drums.

After the work had been completed the captain treated the crew to beer and gave beer and bank notes to the Indians.

We continued our journey in pitch blackness along the off-the-beaten track backwater channel then moored in a quiet cove near a village. When mosquitoes emerged from the scrub to persecute us we slapped on repellent. As I lay in my hammock, mosquitoes circled and buzzed me but didn't land. Eventually, helped by a chorus of crickets, I dozed off.

I awoke when we slipped our moorings and departed, engulfed in the early morning gloom, still navigating the meandering backwater. The crescent moon occasionally penetrated the canopy of leaves and threw down patches of light onto the dark ribbon of water. It was a witness to our progress.

The only sound I heard while I lay in my hammock was the rhythmic throb of the engine. I felt a breeze cool the air and brush against my face. I was awed by the deep stillness of the trees and riverside bushes whose dew-laden leaves were tinted with a faint, lunar blue. I often lost the moon behind the majestically tall trees and vines which kept the channel in a haunting half-light. I hoped the captain could see what was ahead so we wouldn't have another mishap.

Suddenly the captain shook my hammock. I jolted upright. Then he roused the others. He yelled to us in rapid Spanish. We got the message: get up quickly.

I heard another boat approach through the blackness. Our captain blew his whistle and we pulled alongside. The other boat sat low in the water with a box-like structure on the deck from bow to stern.

The two captains exchanged some friendly words. The Indian family collected their bags and bundles, a crewman did the same and indicated with hand signals that we should do likewise and transfer to the other boat. What was happening?

This new boat was going back the way we had come! We were puzzled. We hesitated. Even if we asked what was happening we wouldn't understand the answer. Then the other skipper yelled at us to hurry. I noticed the boats were drifting dangerously towards the riverbank where they could get stuck in the shallows.

The women, children and the crewman clambered over the Condesa's railing and dropped onto the deck of the second boat. Not having any choice, we quickly followed them, hoping the boat was going to Ramon Castilla. The boats parted and we headed back the way we had come.

We watched the Condesa ghost along the dark channel and fade into a smudge. Despite the problems, I had become attached to the ol' girl. Penny read my mind. "After it being our home for the past five days I feel abandoned," she said.

I soon realized that by returning along the channel we would reconnect with the Amazon River, and then head for Ramon Castilla. The crewman who transferred with us was a Chilean working his way around South America. He told us the captain had never intended going to Ramon Castilla. He preferred to pocket the fares, and give a few coins to another skipper to take his passengers downriver.

Eight hours later we arrived at Ramon Castilla, a town of wooden houses, government offices and a tavern – all standing on stilts. On the other side of the Amazon we could see Leticia, Colombia's southernmost city. We boarded a small boat for the ten-minute crossing and sat facing each other. I saw a smile cross Penny's face.

"What's up?" I asked.

"I just remembered something I said in Iquitos: That I was looking forward to a leisurely trip down the Amazon!"

Colombia

Different directions

Farewell at Leticia on the Amazon, December 1975
See map, page 10

December the twenty-ninth, the day after Penny and I arrived in Leticia, Colombia's riverport on the Amazon, was a day I dreaded. It started at eight a.m. when Penny bought her airline ticket to fly from Leticia via Bogota to Vancouver. Buying the ticket was the first concrete realization for both of us that the final curtain was about to descend on our four months of adventures.

Together we had shared fun, excitement, disappointments, discomfort and danger. I felt as if outside forces had conspired to test two people's compatibility. And we had passed the test. Over the weeks we had come to accept and respect each other's individuality and independence. This respect had grown into a deep friendship and, dare we say it, love. But we both knew that our present paths were heading in different directions.

It was hard for both of us to believe that the bond that held us together was about to be severed. In the airport terminal we stared at each other, neither wanting to say goodbye. I had a hollow feeling in my stomach; I was losing the company of someone I cared for. Penny was about to say something but tears rolled down her cheeks.

Her flight was announced over the intercom.

We embraced. She gathered her backpack, walked to the departure lounge then turned and waved goodbye.

I felt an emptiness consume me.

"One day," I silently vowed, "we will meet again."

I continued my travels, arriving in Australia three months later with only fifteen dollars to my name. I wouldn't be travelling anywhere else for a long time.

We corresponded for many months, then I received a letter asking what I thought of her coming to Australia to "check out the weather." I was ecstatic.

Penny was finally doing what I had suggested a year before on our blind date: "Leave your job, sell your car and quit your apartment."

I thought she was quite adventurous because I knew it was out of character for her to sever ties to embark on such a trip by herself, not knowing what the future held.

Within a few months of Penny's arrival in Melbourne, we married. Ten months later saw us embarking on a fifteen-month backpacking trip across Asia and Africa to Vancouver.

And the journeys continued.

Australia

In two worlds

Paranormal encounters in Melbourne, June 1977

A damp chill permeated the night air, typical of Melbourne in winter. I had spent many winters there; it being my hometown.

Penny and I checked the number then walked up to the house which, like many in the suburbs, was built with red brick. I knocked.

A woman opened the door. Her hair was coppery blonde. Wide cheekbones, narrow nose, deep set eyes fringed with long curving lashes. In her forties, I guessed. She greeted us with a welcoming smile, introduced herself as Pauline and led us into a warm living room where more than a dozen people stood chatting, having come in response to Pauline's newspaper advertisement. She wanted volunteers for an experiment.

The room was sparsely decorated. A crucifix hung on one wall and, on another, two scenic paintings of the Australian Outback featuring red hills and white-barked eucalyptus trees.

World newspapers were full of stories about Uri Geller, an Israeli psychic who bent spoons and other utensils without using any physical force. Geller maintained others could achieve the same results through belief, willpower and concentration.

In the 1970s he travelled the world, appearing on television and radio to demonstrate his abilities. His high profile attracted debunkers who devised ways to duplicate his metal-bending achievements by using stage magic. Many parapsychologists stopped taking him seriously.

Pauline, also a psychic, wanted to find out whether we could use our willpower to bend metal to prove Geller right. We sat on chairs in a circle. I counted ten women and five men in the age range of twenty to over sixty.

Pauline addressed the group. "I will hand each person a spoon. I want you to stroke it continually with your index finger and, at the same time, focus your mind on the spoon to coax it to bend."

She dimmed the lights to help create a meditative mood.

We all stroked our spoons. Minutes passed by. Occasionally someone cleared their throat or coughed politely. It surprised me how much noise a small group could make when trying to be quiet.

After fifteen minutes a woman whispered excitedly, "My spoon's bending." Another minute went by and someone else said the same thing. I stared at my spoon. Nothing was happening. I concentrated harder. I noticed the spoon of the man beside me was starting to bend. I lost my focus and watched his spoon curl back on itself as he continued stroking it. I congratulated him. Pauline was ecstatic. She had proved that metal could bend by willpower.

She collected the eight spoons that had not been bent. I was disappointed that our spoons were among them.

The experiment fascinated me. I wondered about the power of the mind that must be in all of us, waiting to be tapped. The success rate had been about fifty percent. Why couldn't we all bend our spoons? Weren't we serious enough? I know I was focusing as best I could. I figured we just needed more time.

The evening ended when Pauline announced the next week's experiment to which we were all invited. "We'll have everyone sitting in a circle in the dark and try to attract spirits or ghostly apparitions." It sounded unbelievable. She continued: "For spirits to show themselves to us they draw from our bodies a white mist called ectoplasm and mould it to form phantom physical shapes. For a spirit entity to materialize it is essential to have a darkened room because light waves have a destructive effect on the ectoplasm. In the darkness the naked eye won't see the ectoplasm but it is known that a camera can photograph it. It may have something to do with the sensitivity of the photographic film. This brings me to a question. Does anyone have a Single Lens Reflex camera who would like to take photographs of the sitters?"

Photography was a hobby of mine. This experiment intrigued me. Although not usually a volunteer, I raised my hand and got the job.

One week later, Penny and I arrived in the early evening, apprehensive but excited for the event about to take place. I had brought my camera and a 36-exposure roll of high-speed infrared film designed for night photography. I had realized during the week that I would not be able to use a flash bulb on my camera because, from what Pauline had said, light waves have a destructive effect on ectoplasm. With the infrared film I wouldn't need a flash bulb.

By eight-thirty there were twenty in the room. We had lost a couple of participants from the previous week but gained four new people. One woman, a single mother who had attended last week, couldn't find a babysitter for her eight-year-old son so she brought him along.

Pauline asked everyone to be seated in the circle of chairs and to place their hands on their knees, palms up. She announced that I would be taking photos but to ignore me as I moved around the room. Then she turned off the light and spoke into the gloom, asking that if there was a spirit entity present could it manifest itself. I walked clockwise within the circle, taking pictures of small groups of sitters until I reached my starting point. Then Penny came into my viewfinder, looking relaxed but as serious as everyone else. I wondered what she was thinking; it wasn't our usual Saturday night's entertainment.

I repeated walking clockwise, going around four times until the film was finished. This took about forty minutes.

Pauline switched on the lights. "Did anyone experience anything?"

No one had seen, felt, or smelt a ghostly apparition. Sometimes a spirit will produce a perfumed odour, she said.

Everyone agreed we reconvene the following Saturday night to view the slides.

During the drive home Penny confided she was somewhat sceptical and that the whole scenario was bizarre. I concurred but we both agreed we were curious to see the results.

A few days later I picked up the processed film and held each slide up to the light and looked for a ghostly person hovering over the sitters but saw nothing. "I'm afraid you'll be disappointed when you see the slides," I told Pauline by phone.

On Saturday night I put the slides into the carousel as the other guests made themselves comfortable. I clicked through the slides fairly fast, lingering just long enough so people could see there were no ghosts. When I had finished, Pauline asked that I go through them again. "I may have seen something," she said. When I got to the young boy she said, "Stop." There was nothing unusual, I thought. The boy was slouching in a chair too big for him, next to his mother.

"There's a cloudy mark near the boy," said Pauline, "but it may be a fault with the film. Keep going."

I showed the next few slides slowly but we saw nothing unusual until another slide of the boy, his mother and other sitters. "Stop," Pauline said. "Look to where the boy is sitting. There is an opaque mist covering his body."

I studied the slide. "It seems as if a drop of processing fluid was spilt on it."

I continued showing more slides. After six slides the boy showed up again. "There's that mist again," Pauline said. "It's definitely ectoplasm. It would be an impossible coincidence to have processing fluid spill on the boy twice, six slides apart. And there was a cloudy mark on the first slide of the boy. It's definitely ectoplasm. You can see a face starting to form. Spirit entities find it easier to draw ectoplasm from children because they are not long out of the spirit world. And they haven't been tainted by negative thoughts about the afterlife or spirit world that many adults have."

Everyone studied the slide.

The boy's mother spoke first. "This has opened another world for me. It's exciting."

The others nodded keenly, obviously sharing her enthusiasm.

A young man admitted it was an unusual experience. "I'm glad I participated, even though we will never know what the apparition finally looked like."

I was impressed by Pauline's in-depth knowledge of the paranormal but Penny summed up the experience when she said, "I feel like I'm in two worlds."

Indonesia

Let there be light

The light bulb caper in Yogyakarta, January 1978
See map, page 11

In Yogyakarta, Indonesia, Penny and I checked into a small, no-star hotel with a grand name, Hotel Indonesia, a popular haunt for travellers from Australia, Europe and North America.

A flight from Australia had dropped us on the verdant island of Bali, the first stop on our fifteen-month backpacking trip across Asia and Africa. After Bali, a boat and meandering buses carried us to Yogyakarta on Java's south coast.

The Hotel Indonesia was a one-storey building with a dozen or so rooms ranged around a spacious courtyard.

We were pleased to see in the middle of the courtyard four small cement tubs – the laundry facilities. We scrubbed our travel weary clothes in one of them. When Penny pulled the plug an unexpected deluge of water gushed out of a drain at ground level. We leapt back as water splashed over our feet before seeping into surrounding gravel. We still had to get used to local plumbing, or the lack of it. In our wet sandals we squished our way back to the room.

In the late afternoon we relaxed, wrote letters and updated our journal. As darkness fell I switched on the light. A pale yellow glow flickered from the little bulb in the ceiling – not enough light for reading or writing. I peered out the window at the other rooms around the courtyard and saw they were all as gloomy as ours. I unscrewed the bulb from its socket and examined it. Only 10 watts!

What we needed was a brighter one. Much brighter.

The next day we bought a 100-watt bulb. When evening came I exchanged the bulbs and flicked the switch. The room flashed into brilliance.

Angry shouts pierced the calm air. "What's going on?" someone yelled from the next room.

Across the courtyard rose a frightening frog-like bellow, "Why have all the lights gone out?"

I felt a pang of guilt. Did I cause the disturbance?

Penny parted our curtain an inch and we peeked out. All the other rooms were in darkness. Our 100-watt jumbo had syphoned all the current from their puny 10-watt bulbs. I grabbed the offensive bulb, unscrewed it with flying fingers and shoved in the 10-watt with a quick twist.

Peace reigned once again as each room regained its mellow yellow!

Thailand

Just travel lightly

A trek in Thailand's hilltribe region, March 1978
See map, page 11

Without warning the keel scraped the shallow riverbed of the Mae Kok, a ribbon of brown water in northern Thailand's hill country. The boat lurched. Someone shouted, "Get out!" I vaulted over the side and four others scrambled after me. Muddy water swirled around our knees. With its lighter load the boat floated free.

The previous day in the northern city of Chiang Mai, Penny and I had read a handwritten poster on our hotel notice board: Wanted – People to join Hilltribe Trek. This was the main reason we had come to Chiang Mai. We eagerly signed on for a three-day trip. Our group of eight men and seven women came from Canada, United States, Australia, Britain, France, Germany and Switzerland and were to be accompanied by two guides and two porters.

Our chief guide was Kiri, a short, vigorous type with an athletic build, in his mid-twenties. I asked him if there was anything crucial to take or important to know before we left.

"No," he said, "just travel lightly."

To get to the starting point of the trek we all travelled by truck from Chiang Mai to Tha Thon then boarded a boat to travel down the Mae Kok to a Shan village.

A crewman bent over the outboard motor and yanked on the starting cord. The propeller, bolted to the end of a long shaft, was lowered into the murky water and the boat, about ten metres long, surged forward. To the left and right of the river, hills rolled away, daubed with patches of green and brown. In the distance they lost themselves in a purple haze. The tropical sun, white hot in the blue sky, burned us with its heat.

We had heard tales from other travellers about a tribe that eats dogs, bubbling springs of scalding water, remnants of a Chinese army, lizards that live in village huts and tall grasses that reach three times a person's height. It all sounded very exciting; we could hardly wait to get there. Was it all true? We'd soon find out.

It was on the boat trip that, without warning, the keel scraped the shallow riverbed, causing four others and me to scramble over the side to allow the boat to float free.

"Hoy!"

I jerked my head up to see who had shouted. It was Kiri. He stood in the boat staring at the water. He jabbed his forefinger at the muddy river and blurted, "Maybe crocodiles are here."

Without a moment's hesitation I gripped the side of the boat and hoisted myself up. The others followed. I tumbled into the boat and landed at Penny's feet. Kiri laughed. I wasn't sure if he was joking or not about crocodiles. I squeezed in between Penny and a backpack as a crewman poled the boat from the sand bar towards deeper water.

An hour-and-a-half downstream we reached our destination. Bamboo huts of the Shan ethnic group were clustered near the river-bank. We disembarked and greeted the farmers who were carrying loads of garlic, corn, tobacco and rice. The Shan, we learned from Kiri, were agriculturalists and pastoralists whose ancestors settled in northwestern Thailand after migrating over the hills from Burma in the late nineteenth century.

We started our trek at the Shan village. Each of us carried a back-pack, holding not much more than a change of clothes and a sleeping sheet.

Dogs barked at our heels as we tramped in single file along the village lanes. The dogs were scrawny critters, their coats mangy and their bared teeth scary. Penny and I did our best to ignore them by keeping a steady pace and staring ahead. My mind roamed. I thought of being bitten, getting rabies and frothing at the mouth. Fortunately they got bored with us.

On the outskirts of the village lay terraces of empty rice fields. We passed by a farmer who trudged behind a wooden plough being pulled by his black-skinned water buffalo. On the farmer's skeletal frame hung brown trousers and a brown shirt. On his head perched a yellow hat made from rice straw. As he glanced up we caught the flash of a smile. We waved a greeting.

Ahead of us stood tall thickets of green bamboo, their tops arcing over the narrow ribbon of track that snaked ahead of us into the foothills. The only sounds were twigs snapping beneath our sandals. Teak trees with their rich brown bark rose majestically in the forest. We descended into a dry, dusty, river bed and picked our way over rounded pebbles and clambered up a barren hillside of red-brown earth.

Kiri reached the summit first and halted. He pointed down into a valley towards a copse of beech trees that partially obscured huts of bamboo and thatch. Villagers, looking like specks on the landscape, trudged to and fro, going about their work.

"The village of the Lahu people," announced Kiri. He explained that they migrated from Yunnan, southwestern China, more than one hundred years ago. The migration of the Lahu and other hill peoples was caused by racial disharmony in southern China. In the hills of northern Thailand the different groups maintained their own distinct cultures but lived peacefully in close proximity.

We trekked down the hillside along a trail of red earth past the tall grey trunks of the beech trees and entered the village. Children shouted gleefully as they played together. Dogs barked.

A woman wearing a green skirt and yellow blouse crouched on her haunches as she swept away leaves in front of her home. She raised her head. Her black hair was combed back from her brown face, revealing a high forehead, dark eyes nestling behind slanting eyelids, high cheek bones and a broad nose. She rose to greet us and waved her arm towards the other village huts as a way of welcome.

The huts sat on raised platforms one-and-a-half metres above the ground. The walls and floors were built with split bamboo and rice straw covered the roofs. A straw roof will last about three years before it needs to be replaced, Kiri told us. He was a knowledgeable guide who doled out snippets of information when he thought we needed them.

Pungent odours from the muddy barnyard taunted us. Grey-skinned pigs grovelled on the ground, grunting as their flat snouts sniffed at corn husks, rice stalks and heat-baked banana skins. Chickens clucked as they searched for rice grains.

Young children bounded around beneath the huts; some carried younger brothers and sisters on their backs. A little girl who was crouching behind a recumbent cow was spotted by a young boy who rushed over and tapped her shoulder. She squealed with excitement, jumped up and streaked towards the huts, looking for others who were playing the game. Kids at play are the same all over the world and it gave us a warm, homey feeling to watch them.

Late in the afternoon we mustered at the northern edge of the village and set off for the Lisu village. Our trail, etched out of the hillside, twisted through thickets of green fern and bracken. Penny and I observed our fellow trekkers throughout the day and couldn't help but categorize them into four types: the stragglers, who took photos of anything that moved; the plodders, who hiked at a slow, steady pace; the rubbernecks who didn't want to miss anything; and the jockeys who competed to be first across the line. Penny and I classed ourselves as rubbernecks.

Kiri forged ahead. He topped a rise, turned and called to us: "Lisu village."

I figured we had huffed and puffed up hills and down and around curves for four or five kilometres.

Kiri waited until everyone had caught up. I was impressed with his thoughtfulness for the group and with his guiding abilities.

Kiri and the other guide arranged our sleeping accommodation. Penny and I glanced inside a hut. It contained sleeping platforms of bamboo slats, about one metre above the bamboo floor, safely above any nocturnal crawling creatures such as snakes that may enter the hut. The accommodation definitely didn't rank a star but it was clean.

The rooms didn't have their own toilet or bathroom facilities. Nearby stood a bamboo fence which encircled an open air, communal toilet – a hole in the ground – partly covered by a platform of tree branches used for squatting on. The tree branches placed across the deep, dark, cavernous hole looked unstable. As I stepped on one to squat, another branch shifted alarmingly. I got a shock but steadied myself, fearful I would fall into the hole.

I couldn't imagine this being the village toilet. I fantasized that inside their homes they all had sit-down, flush toilets and that this communal toilet was set aside for visitors so they could have an experience of rustic living. I looked towards the village huts made of logs, tree saplings, split bamboo and grass and shook my head. No, I realized, this was the village toilet!

To have a wash we had to climb down a rocky embankment to a creek. From the top of the embankment a pipe protruded from the rocks, harnessing some of the creek water. A steady stream of water poured out of this pipe into a pool beside a huge boulder. The top of the rounded boulder stood about one metre above the pool.

Penny volunteered to be the first to try the washing facilities.

"This is quite a challenge," she said nervously as she balanced on the boulder, attempting to wash her face and hands and brush her teeth.

I couldn't believe this place was the bathroom, but Kiri assured me it was.

"My knees were knocking down there," Penny admitted as she climbed off the boulder and crawled up the embankment. "One slip and I could have fallen, twisted an ankle, or worse. I don't think I'll try that again."

I gave her a hug and assured her that I would have pulled her out of the pool if she'd fallen in.

Yellow rays of the setting sun bathed the surrounding hills with a golden hue. For a few quiet moments Penny and I watched in awe as the sun painted the sky crimson and the western hills purple.

In the evening Kiri lit our cooking fire. Red and yellow tongues of flame licked the black bottoms of the iron cooking pots. Our guides served a spicy meal of rice, pork, string beans, cucumbers and tomatoes which we ate heartily. A pot of water hissed and bubbled for tea, a refreshing drink after a day of hiking. The cooking fires died and darkness settled over the village.

A cool breeze swirled some dust. I expected mosquitoes but we were too high, about 800 metres, and the air too chilly. We all rose to go to bed but Kiri stopped us.

"The women and girls want to show you their dances," he said, as a woman lit a single kerosene lantern and hung it on a bamboo pole. The women and girls wore dresses of blue cotton with red, yellow and black braid decorating the bodice and sleeves. A man plucked and strummed a four-stringed instrument that looked like a mandolin. The dancers clapped to the beat and danced with a shuffling step in a conga line. The yellow light from the lantern cast moving shadows on the ground as they danced joyfully around a glossy leafed bush, chanting, their faces aglow.

Our group sat together on benches on the sidelines and were energized by their music and dancing. We clapped in appreciation. It was evident to us that even though they were entertaining us, they were also dancing for the sheer joy of it.

After the performance, eight of us shared a guest hut and lay in our sheet sleeping bags on a platform. With my flashlight I scanned the bamboo walls, and spotted lizards crawling up the slats. I watched these harmless little geckos stalk mosquitoes and flies, flicking their tongues at their prey to capture and swallow them, then I fell asleep.

The trail the second day became steeper and afforded views of distant blue hills. We rounded a curve and entered a heavily wooded area on the shoulder of the hill.

Suddenly someone pointed forward, yelling, "I see smoke."

Sure enough, smoke was billowing above the treetops a few hundred metres ahead.

We should have run from it but, instead, we all hurried forward through the forest and burst upon a patch of ground alive with bubbling hot springs.

It was steam, not smoke, that rose above the tree tops.

The rising vapour shone like silver pellets against the blue. Water boiled vigorously in pools the size of bathtubs. Any water that didn't rise as steam spilled over mud and rocks and cascaded down the hillside. This barren, muddy clearing, as large as a tennis court, was pockmarked with circular pools of boiling mud, many as big as a truck tire.

Hot underground gases rose, ballooning each pool of mud into a mound until it burst with a plop and spattered hot mud in all directions. The witches in Shakespeare's Macbeth would feel right at home here.

Grey boulders lay scattered throughout the area, tempting a German couple to use them as stepping stones.

Kiri bellowed: "Don't go near the water. It's boiling!"

They leapt from the boulders onto the hot, soft mud. It oozed over their boots. For a few moments they were stuck in the mixture of clay and mud but managed to take measured steps until they reached us.

We followed Kiri, pussyfooting past the cauldrons of death. So, the travellers' tale of bubbling springs of scalding water was true.

Bells tinkled in the distance. When the sound got closer we saw three young men leading a trio of packhorses with bells tied around their necks. We stepped off the narrow trail to let them pass.

"The men are from the Sukruthai village," explained Kiri. "Their fathers fought in China for the Nationalist leader, Chiang Kai-shek. When the Communists gained power in 1949 the army of Chiang Kai-shek fled China. Some went to Taiwan; others came to Thailand."

Encountering them was almost like finding a lost army.

Yet another travellers' tale was true.

"How do they earn a living?" someone asked.

"They collect bark," said Kiri. "That's what the packhorses are carrying. The villagers sell it in Chiang Mai for use as incense in Buddhist temples."

After we reached the village Kiri met an elder, a bald headed, handsome ancient with a narrow, wrinkled face. Wispy grey strands of beard poked out of his chin, accompanied by a drooping mustache. I tried to visualize him as a gun-toting soldier battling the Communists but I couldn't get a picture. After all, the man had aged considerably over the thirty years since the defeat of Chiang Kai-shek's Nationalist army.

Kiri made arrangements with the elder for us to leave our backpacks in a hut and to return in the late afternoon to stay overnight. In the meantime we continued our march. An upward climbing track sliced through silvery pampas grass, three times a person's height. Trudging along the trail, dead leaves and twigs crunched under my feet. The uphill climb was hard work. Perspiration trickled down my cheeks. I tasted its saltiness.

We tripped on exposed tree roots that grew across the trail but eventually emerged at the top of a rise and saw a tall gateway. It was built with four upright posts which supported two horizontal beams. Stretched flat across the beams lay the brown hide of a dog and its whitened skull with an open mouth. It was a macabre sight. I was bemused. Some of the local boys must have put this up as a joke.

Kiri tapped my shoulder. "It is to ward off evil spirits. This is the entrance to the Akha village. The Akha eat dogs." I shuddered. I couldn't imagine eating a dog, especially the fatherless mongrel I owned years ago. But then, I had become attached to it. Not all cultures consider the dog as man's best friend.

We trekked into the village built on a flat ridge. Bamboo huts stood on stilts. Vegetable gardens surrounded each home; bamboo fences protected the corn, beans and tomatoes from the pigs and cattle. The red earth around each house was swept clean so snakes couldn't lurk in bushes.

Women in knee-length black skirts stood at weaving looms, the frames of which were constructed of bamboo. They and other women wore elaborate headdresses as everyday attire. Their brimless black hats were artistically embellished with old silver coins, silver balls and plastic beads of different colours. Red woollen tassels attached to their hats hung down over their ears. The eye-catching ornate hats, which distinguished the Akha from other tribes, were like bright sparks among the earthy hues of green and brown that dominated their world.

We watched a woman stoke a fire beneath a cooking pot. On the ground near the pot lay piles of short, black, dog hairs. I assumed the dog was in the pot.

We greeted some village men who wore black baggy trousers and long-sleeved jackets of homespun cotton. Their hair was long, braided into a pigtail. They walked with an air of nonchalance, some of them smoking long-stemmed pipes. The women, meanwhile, continued weaving and doing household chores. The Akha, Kiri said, migrated from Yunnan, China through Burma to Thailand at the end of the nineteenth century.

From the mountaintop refuge of the Akha we descended to the Sukruthai village.

The women were bent over the vegetable gardens. Their conical straw hats bobbed up and down as they chatted and weeded around the cabbages and bok choy.

This was the second and final night of our three-day trek.

The building we slept in, constructed with poles covered by coconut palm thatch, consisted of one large room with an earthen floor. A bamboo platform accommodated all of us when we squeezed together.

The next day we passed through a village of the Karen whose homes were raised two metres above the ground on thick poles. At night they corralled their domestic livestock under their homes. On top of the gable of some of the houses a cross, fastened by rope or nails, identified the dwellers as Christians. The Karen, originally from the Thai-Burma border area had been converted by Baptist and Catholic missionaries. But many were Buddhists, and some were animists who kept their belief in nats, or nature spirits, which they say inhabit mountains, rocks, rivers and trees.

We continued our walk out of the hills towards the Mae Kok and passed through a village of the Shan where we hired the same boatmen for the return journey to Tha Thon. This time they steered away from sand bars!

During the past three days we had travelled back in time, all the while picking up gems of advice to add to Kiri's "just travel lightly."

Our gems:

Leave your alarm clock at home as it's not needed where time stands still.

Practise brushing your teeth with one foot on a boulder and the other in the air.

Carry a flashlight at night to visit the loo and avoid the void.

Don't take your dog if it's plump.

Burma *(today's Myanmar)*

Whisky and cigarettes

Surviving Burma, March 1978
See map, page 11

A local man scurried towards us. He had bright button eyes set in a round face and a sense of urgency in his manner.

"I'll give you 400 kyats (chats) for your whisky and cigarettes," he said.

I quickly calculated we would make a net profit of forty-three dollars, but I was not ready to sell and told him so. I didn't know who the guy was. For all I knew he was a government man placed there to catch us doing something wrong before we knew it was wrong, such as selling liquor without a licence.

Penny and I had arrived at Rangoon airport after a one-hour flight from Bangkok on a Burma Airways Fokker F28. We looked forward to our seven days in Burma – the maximum a visa would allow.

We strode across the hot tarmac, each clutching a conspicuous, clear plastic shopping bag with our tax-free purchases from Bangkok: a quart each of Johnny Walker Red Label whisky and a carton each of State Express "555" cigarettes. They were not for us to drink and smoke; they were for us to sell. We called this booty our survival kit.

You can live for a week in Burma from the profit made selling duty-free goods. We were amused to see most of the passengers who disembarked carrying similar purchases. It was a common practice for visitors to Burma to sell their duty-free goods.

Customs officers delayed us as they searched our backpacks and discovered our large caché of film. As photography was our passion, our backpacks were half full of movie and slide film. The senior officer suggested, loudly and incorrectly, we were going to sell the film without paying import duty. When Penny and I denied it he told us to take a few films for personal use and leave the rest in the Customs office 'in bond' until we left Burma. We were apprehensive about doing so but we had no choice. On a positive note, our backpacks would be lighter. (Upon departure from Burma a week later our films were returned.)

By the time we had gone through Passport Control and the Customs search an hour had passed and all the other travellers had vanished.

It was at this time that the local man with the bright button eyes scurried towards us to buy the whisky and cigarettes. After telling him no we visited the airport bank and changed five dollars for kyats. We strolled outside into an already humid, sunny morning.

Button eyes stood by his taxi-truck. "Four hundred kyats and a free taxi ride to town," he blurted.

"No," I told him again as we got into his taxi. We had no urgency to sell.

Ten kilometres down the road he stopped for another fare. The man got in, saw our whisky and cigarettes and said, "I'll give you four hundred kyats."

"No," I said. "I'm not ready to sell yet." I wanted more of an idea of how much the whisky and cigarettes were worth.

The taxi dropped us outside the Orient Hotel but it was full. A man, hair slicked back, a grin from ear to ear, ambled over to us and said, "I'd like to buy your whisky and cigarettes." There seemed to be no shortage of buyers. I told him we were not selling until we found a hotel. "The San Pya on Barr Street," he quickly suggested. We followed him and checked in.

Our helper's name was Henry. "Not my real name," he told us.

"My Muslim name is too difficult to remember. I'm married to a Chinese girl. Very unusual in Burma. She converted to Islam but my family refuses to accept her. They won't give me any financial help. That's why I buy things from tourists: cosmetics, shoes, clothes, films, calculators, ball-point pens, liquor and cigarettes. I make about one-hundred dollars a month which is enough to live on."

He went on to explain that if he made too much money, a rival buyer could bribe a policeman to pick him up and put him in jail. Because policemen's wages were low they used the power of their uniform to boost their income. A policeman had the authority to hold a person for fourteen days without laying a formal charge. If no charge was brought or there was no evidence of wrongdoing the detainee would be released.

We enjoyed Henry and his candor but his mind was not far from business. "I can take you to a street tobacconist to get you a good price," he said.

We followed him along a sidewalk that bustled with outdoor vendors standing under tiny lean-to stalls, or sitting on blankets, selling everything from betel quids, Buddha statues, chewing gum, watches, sun glasses, single cigarettes to throat lozenges. The street teemed with traffic. Cars, decades old, spewed blue exhaust fumes, and overcrowded buses honked their way through the ox carts and bicycles. The business district of Rangoon had not had a paint job since the Second World War and the once whitewashed buildings had a moldy look.

We reached a girl in her teens with long ebony hair and large, intelligent, dark brown eyes. She had yellow streaks of cosmetic paste across her cheeks which we later learned helped to protect her skin from the sun and keep it soft. She sat against a wall with a glass display case in front of her with an array of imported cigarettes. Henry hung around waiting to see if we made a deal with her. It was clear he would earn a commission for taking us there.

She looked into our plastic bags and in a take-it-or-leave-it tone said: "110 kyats for each bottle and 135 kyats for each carton if they are English-made, or 95 if they are Singapore-made."

"I'm sure they're English-made," I said. Passersby gathered

around to observe the negotiations. A gaunt man with a cigarette dangling on his bottom lip emerged from the crowd. "If they are English-made," he said with an authoritative air, "it will say so on the carton." He examined it. "It doesn't say Made in England so they are Singapore-made."

I took the carton and with a knife gently slit open the end to look at a packet. Unfortunately it said Made in Singapore. I bargained the price up to 110 kyats for each carton. I was satisfied with the transaction. It netted us almost fifty dollars, enough to live in Rangoon for a week.

While Henry waited for his commission we returned to the San Pya and went to our room. The walls were made of sheets of thin plywood with an added feature: small holes drilled through them at eye level. Thankfully the holes had been circled with pens and pencils by previous guests to warn others of possible Peeping Toms in the adjoining rooms. To dissuade voyeurs we stuffed the holes with paper.

Lying in bed that night I realized we weren't the only guests in our room. Cockroaches scuttled across the floor and rats scurried above the ceiling. But for one-dollar thirty-five a night for the room I didn't complain.

A few days later Penny and I were ambling past the Diplomatic Store, a shop that stocked Western merchandise and good quality Burmese goods, including Burmese-made Duya export quality cigarettes. The goods were sold for foreign currency to diplomats, tourists and Burmese government officials. The ordinary Burmese citizen, even if he had foreign currency, could not buy directly from the store. By chance we saw Henry near the store talking with friends. He introduced them, all wheeler-dealers like himself.

They had perfected a system to buy Duya cigarettes which they could sell to local Burmese at a profit. "We have used our system many times," Henry said, "but each time we need the help of a tourist. Can you help?"

Why he approached us I didn't know. Maybe he thought he knew us well enough after having found us a hotel room and helped sell the whisky and cigarettes.

Penny looked skeptical. She had a knack for detecting things that were out of the ordinary.

"What do you want done?" I asked.

Henry explained the plan. They would give me forty-five dollars in cash to buy fifteen cartons of Duya cigarettes at the Diplomatic Store.

I asked them where they got their American dollars. "From a monk in a monastery," a crony explained.

I laughed.

"It's true," he said.

Henry looked pensive. "There's one problem about buying fifteen cartons."

Penny leaned closer, frowning.

"According to Government rules a buyer can only buy a maximum of three cartons. Nevertheless, we've arranged with the girl at the cash register to sell fifteen cartons, and that she can keep one for herself."

Penny interrupted: "Is this legal?" There was a strong tone of doubt in her voice.

"Well," said Henry, "it's not illegal. We are just buying cigarettes. Buying and selling is one of the ways we survive in Burma. It is similar to your selling cigarettes and whisky. You did so to survive in Burma for a week."

I decided to do a dry run to make sure the store had enough cigarettes and to see if the cashier would agree to the sale. Penny reluctantly followed me into the store and up the stairs to the cigarette section. I found the Duya cigarettes, and spoke to the cashier. "I would like to buy fifteen cartons of Duya. Can you sell them to me if I give you a carton?"

She nodded with a knowing smile. We left without buying. It was going to work.

Penny and I returned to Henry and his cronies, took their forty-five dollars into the store and returned with fourteen cartons. They were ecstatic. After they had sold the cigarettes for a profit and split the proceeds, one crony said, their families would be able to survive another week. Henry offered me a cut for our involvement but I declined. I was pleased I could help increase their income in some small way even if the method was a bit shady.

We all shook hands, and I told them Penny and I were heading to the Strand Hotel for lunch. Henry insisted on getting a taxi for us and paying the fare. We appreciated his benevolence and accepted.

The Strand, a three-storey, late-Victorian hotel built in 1901 was a national landmark. At the Strand, we walked into a colonial era world of white-jacketed waiters and tables with white, starched table cloths. In the high-ceilinged dining room fans whirred, cooling the air.

For four dollars each we enjoyed a four-course meal of mulligatawny soup, fish fillets with chips and salad, and bread and butter pudding. I topped off my meal with a large bottle of Mandalay beer while Penny settled for a cup of tea.

We were surviving Burma quite well.

Bangladesh to India

Day of endurance

The border crossing at Biral, April 1978
See map, page 11

We froze.

A strange noise had woken us. Someone was in the room.

It was early morning, still pitch black.

I felt for the flashlight on the chair by the bed and shone it towards the table. A cat!

It leapt onto the window sill, squeezed between the steel security bars and disappeared. We were relieved it was only a cat. Now wide awake, I checked my watch. Five o'clock. We decided to get up and have some breakfast as we had an early train to catch.

"Where's our loaf of bread?" Penny asked. "It was on the table last night."

We looked around and discovered chunks of bread on the window sill and the floor. The cat had stolen our breakfast!

We were staying in the Government Rest House, a hotel in the northern Bangladesh town of Pachagarh. Not far away was a convenient border post we planned to go through to get to Darjeeling in northern India. The previous day, however, we had met a Bangladeshi customs official who advised against crossing in the north. He said the Bangladeshi officials would allow us to cross the border, but the Indian officials would not permit us to enter India because of civil unrest in the area. He suggested we take the next morning's six-thirty train via Dinajpur to Biral, a border post in southwest Bangladesh.

We packed our belongings and in the semi-darkness strode to the town square, expecting to replace our stolen breakfast. But it was too early for bread shops to be open or street vendors to be selling food.

In the town square we spotted a lone pedal rickshaw with the driver curled up on the seat. He lived in his rickshaw as so many of them did. Penny gently shook his shoulder, not really wanting to disturb his sleep; but we needed a ride. He rubbed his eyes and smiled, pleased to get work so early in the day. He pedalled quietly through the empty streets to the train station. Only the crunch of rickshaw tires on the gravel road broke the stillness.

Being on the streets of a town before it awakens evokes a special calming effect on a person. The silence was a pleasant contrast to the ringing of bicycle bells, honking of car horns, vendors calling out for customers and people scurrying here and there once the town came alive.

We caught the train at six-thirty and four hours later reached the border town of Biral. There had been no time to search for food so we sustained ourselves on two thermos flasks of water and a few candies. The train station at Biral consisted of a platform and a small office building. People stared at us curiously as if we were oddities. We guessed that few travellers used this route.

The station master and two government officials led us into the Customs and Immigration room where there was a table and half-a-dozen chairs. The natural light beaming through the door and windows was blocked by the heads of curious men and boys who crowded around outside the building, all craning to see the two foreigners in their midst.

The senior official told us that the last foreigners to cross the border at Biral were a Dutchman six months earlier and a German traveller one year before him. Biral was normally only used by Bangladeshi and Indian traders, the station master added. The senior official checked our passports for Bangladeshi visas but was baffled when he found a visa in my passport but not in Penny's. I explained patiently that Penny did not need a visa, being a Canadian, but I needed one, being an Australian.

After deliberating with the other two men and shaking his head, the senior official told us we would have to return to Benopal in the south where we had entered Bangladesh and leave by that same border post. I objected saying it was not possible, and argued that the Dutchman and the German had passed through. I couldn't imagine retracing our steps just because these officials were unsure how to process our documents.

The junior official stepped forward and searched for something in a cupboard. He found it – the Register – a large book in which he wrote our names and passport details. I was relieved to see some positive action. Junior blew the dust off a rubber stamp, inked a dry stamp pad and, with a flourish, stamped our passports. The whole exercise took one-and-a-half hours.

Now we were officially out of Bangladesh.

I turned to the station master. "What transport can we get to the Indian border town?"

"There is nothing," he replied. "The train line between Bangladesh and India is not used any more. It is a six-mile walk."

"We could go by ox cart," Penny suggested.

"The farmers don't go that far. You'll have to walk," he said. "But it is too hot right now; wait until it cools down. The Indian train leaves at four from the border."

It was now midday with the sun blazing down on us but we were determined to catch that train. We filled our thermos flasks with boiled water (to kill the bacteria) at the train station and slung our backpacks over our shoulders. We spotted a street vendor and bought his last packet of crackers then started along the disused railway track.

The countryside around us was flat, brown, parched and inhospitable. We passed by a small rural village of square, squat, mudbrick huts packed tightly together like a jigsaw puzzle.

Curious men and women looked up from their garden plots

and stared, but children screamed and took refuge indoors.

Penny looked at me. "If we are only the third and fourth Westerners in eighteen months to pass this way we may be the first Westerners the children have seen."

I nodded. "With our big backpacks we must look as if we're from another planet."

Beyond the village the terrain stretched to the horizon like a bumpy brown carpet. The sun pursued us with relentless ferocity, its heat oppressive and dry, much like the heat that blasts from an open oven door. Every ten minutes we stopped to rest and sip water from our diminishing supply.

After a further half-hour of trudging in the heat we arrived at the rim of a gulch with a gently flowing river of reddish brown water. The steep slope down to the river was sparsely vegetated with clumps of hardy grasses and scrub, but not enough to stop erosion of the reddish brown earth.

Spanning the gulch was a wooden trestle bridge more than one hundred feet long and thirty feet above the river.

This was a challenge I hadn't expected. The single-track railway line ran over metal ties spaced widely apart. To step from one tie to the next we would have to stretch our legs to the maximum. Between the ties was nothingness – a space big enough to fall through.

Penny turned to me, her eyes wide open in fright. "I can't cross that," she blurted. " My legs won't stretch that far and I can't stand heights."

I, too, was apprehensive and scanned up and down the river for a possible place to ford, but it looked too deep.

"We have to cross the bridge," I said. "There is no other way. I'll hold your hand."

Penny hesitated, looked up and down the river for a crossing point, then agreed to tackle the bridge.

We set off. I looked down between the ties and saw the deep brown river. I got a lump in my throat, my heart skipped a beat.

"Try not to look into the river," I told Penny as I gripped her hand tighter, not only to reassure her but to boost my own nerve.

At each step we stretched our legs in rhythm to the next tie.

About a third of the way across the bridge I noticed her knees knocking. It was too late to go back. I stopped for a breath and looked around at the pastry coloured landscape. We were two cherries on top of the pie.

"Let's not stop," Penny said, as she wavered on a railway tie, "otherwise I'll lose my balance."

"If one of us falls," I said, "we need to slip our backpack off before hitting the water so we don't get dragged under."

Penny's legs suddenly wobbled uncontrollably. Had I said something wrong?

"Relax. Try to stay calm," I said.

"I'll be all right. I can do this."

"You're doing fine," I said as we continued.

Penny's backpack suddenly shifted. She tightened her grip on my hand. I held hers tighter. I had to keep my balance. Felt a rush of adrenalin. Took a deep breath and waited until the butterflies in my stomach folded their wings. I calmed down, glanced at Penny. She was taking quick breaths.

"Take deep breaths," I said.

Her breathing slowed.

At each step I coaxed both of us forward. "Stretch your leg farther. You're doing great. Now, another step. Not far to go. Keep up the rhythm. We're nearly there. Just one more step. We've made it."

Penny's legs had turned to rubber. She collapsed onto the ground, emotionally and physically a wreck.

I didn't feel too great myself.

We sat for a while to rest and regain our strength but we couldn't escape the burning sun. Our water was running low and we only had a few candies left. The crackers we'd bought were stale and inedible. How far did we still have to go? We weren't sure. We'd been walking for three hours. Maybe two more to go.

A grove of trees appeared in a haze ahead of us on the track. It gave us hope we were nearing the station, but as we got closer they faded away. To our disappointment they were a mirage.

Finally, after rounding a curve we saw far ahead a shimmering building and tried to quicken our pace. It must be the train station. Or a mirage. Then we saw, in the distance, puffs of black smoke rising in the blue sky and heard the faint whistle of a train. It was leaving right on time, four o'clock.

Eventually we staggered into the station so exhausted we just lay flat on the platform trying to gain some strength. I was half aware of several people coming to look at us. After a short rest we checked around and found a water tap. We splashed water onto our faces to cool down but we didn't dare drink it. We had been so careful to purify our water during our travels that we didn't want to take a chance and drink carelessly.

The station master, a tall stoop-shouldered man, appeared and told us the next train was at seven and that an immigration official would come to inspect our documents.

At dusk the official arrived carrying a coal oil lamp. He was a skinny man of about thirty-five with nicotine-stained teeth and fingers. He thumbed through our passports.

"Where are your visas for India?" he asked in a gruff voice.

"We don't need visas for India," I said.

"Do you have a permit to enter India at this border control?" he asked.

We presented our Darjeeling Entry Permit which expired today and hoped that would satisfy him although it had nothing to do with this border control. He glanced at the permit with a disapproving look and tried to make a telephone call, but without success. He appeared unsure what to do with us and seemed to be relieved when the station master and an assistant arrived. They discussed what they should do in loud animated voices and a lot of arm waving. Then the official tried to make another call but he didn't get through.

He asked where we had been and where we were going, took a large book from a shelf, blew off the dust and started writing.

Because Penny's maiden name was in her passport along with her three given names and her married name, it perplexed him, causing him to spend about one hour to write all our particulars in the book. His next job was to stamp our passports. Fortunately he found the rubber stamp quickly. Now we were officially in India.

During our travels we had crossed many borders but we'll remember this day's experience as the most gruelling.

The whistle blew as the seven p.m. train entered the station; we were the only passengers getting on.

We stretched out on the seats, thankful to be horizontal, but it lasted only fifteen minutes. At the next stop throngs of people poured through the doorways. Some even climbed through the windows.

After a long, crowded, sleepless five hours we arrived at the town of Katihar tired, hungry and thirsty. It was midnight but the dark streets were noisy and crowded with people meeting the train and others haggling for rickshaws. We were about to look for a hotel when a man appeared out of the darkness and said he would take us to one around the corner.

Whether he was just a helpful bystander or a representative of the hotel we never found out. It was not unusual for people to materialize from nowhere, give help when needed then fade away.

The Hotel Ashok was mostly used by train travellers with next-day connections. Our small room had a ceiling fan, side table and two charpoys – beds with mattresses made of woven rope. Our noses told us the toilet and shower were down the hall.

At the check-in desk I asked the clerk if there was anywhere we could get some food and boiled water. He offered to bring something.

He returned with bowls of meat in a sauce, stale chapattis and a large bottle of beer.

I tasted the meat and sauce. Hot! Spicy! It shot me into orbit, scorched my tongue, sizzled my amalgam fillings. I grabbed the beer and poured it down my throat to douse the fire in my belly.

Neither of us could eat it, nor the chapattis. Our thermos flasks had been filled with odd tasting hot water which we weren't able to drink.

At the end of an exhausting day that had started twenty hours earlier with the sound of a noisy cat stealing our breakfast, we dozed off. Still hungry.

India

Chai, the elixir of life

At Katihar Junction, April 1978
See map, page 12

Thirst and hunger wracked our bodies. The previous day's journey from Bangladesh by train and foot had weakened both of us.

It was April, the start of the hot season, and the early morning sun was already white-hot over eastern India.

We arrived at the Katihar Junction train station to buy tickets. A couple of diesel locomotives sat at different platforms with their engines idling, puffing vile smelling toxic fumes into the air. All of a sudden Penny's body started shaking from head to toe as if she were freezing.

"What's wrong?" I said as I put my arm around her shoulders and led her to a bench.

"I don't know, but I can't stop," she said, her voice trembling.

Near the ticket office a flurry of people scurried in all directions. Coloured hats and turbans, white dhotis (long loin cloths that are gathered between the legs) and the greens, blues and yellows of saris all blurred together. Babies whimpered, older children whined, tea vendors at their carts shouted incessantly for customers, and porters yelled over the din, offering their services.

From the melée an unusually tall Indian, head and shoulders above the crowd, approached and, in impeccable English, introduced himself as Lucas.

He came because he saw Penny shaking and wondered if we needed help. He asked if she had a fever. I told him we didn't know what the problem was.

"Have you been drinking enough water?" he asked Penny, but she was shaking too much to respond.

I told him she had drunk very little over the past couple of days.

"It's dehydration. You're suffering from dehydration," he said. "I'll get you some *chai*."

That was how we were introduced to Indian tea, called chai, a sweet, thirst quenching drink made with tea leaves, boiled water, hot milk and many spoonfuls of sugar. It stopped Penny's shakes almost immediately. We were amazed at the fast result of this simple life-saving elixir. We bought thermos flasks and decided we would never travel without tea.

Lucas helped us buy second class train tickets from Katihar Junction to Siliguri, and found a compartment. For his services we tipped him, as is the custom.

We relaxed in our comfortable seats, waiting to leave. However, prior to the train's departure a Ticket Examiner checked our tickets and asked us to leave the compartment because it was a second class sitting compartment for which the seats had already been sold. He said we held second class ordinary tickets. Dutifully we left the compartment and walked along the platform looking at the second class ordinary carriages with dismay. We were appalled at the overcrowded conditions: people hung out the windows and crowded the doorways.

"How on earth are we ever going to get on this train?" Penny said. I detected a hint of desperation in her voice.

We watched men swarm up the sides of the carriages to sit on the roof. With our backpacks that wasn't an option. Even without our backpacks that wasn't an option!

A young hustler who earned his money by helping travellers, offered to get us on the train for a tip of two rupees (twenty-five cents). He tried the carriage door. It had been locked from the inside by other passengers who didn't want anyone else to enter because the corridor and the compartments were already congested. Despite this drawback the hustler took Penny's backpack and pushed it through the door's open window but a passenger inside pushed it back. Our hustler pushed it in again without success. Pushing and shoving continued until I grabbed the pack and placed it on the platform. Everyone relaxed.

I saw another open window, unguarded.

I glanced at Penny and said, "Go for it!"

She dashed to the window, hoisted herself up, swung her left leg over the sill and dropped into the corridor, scattering stunned passengers.

In a flash, our alert hustler grabbed her backpack and thrust it through the window after her. Before the bewildered passengers could mount a defensive action I rammed my backpack through the same window, heaved myself up and tumbled head first onto the floor.

The startled looks on the other passengers' faces quickly reverted to one of acceptance. Typical of India. Life in the corridor went back to normal, that of keeping other passengers out. We both survived intact. I leaned out the window and gave our smiling hustler his well-earned rupees.

I was surprised at Penny's agility considering her uncontrollable shaking an hour before. After the excitement, we quenched our thirsts with chai from our thermos flasks.

A carpet trader sitting in the corridor kindly made space beside him and let Penny sit on his rolled up carpet. I perched on my backpack next to her in the crowded corridor. I expected the journey to be an uncomfortable four hours. The whistle blew and the train pulled away.

I went to check the toilet facilities at the end of the carriage, stepping gingerly around bags, bundles and bodies of corridor squatters. Most of them were men who wore the cool, cotton dhoti, but there was a sprinkling of women in their brightly coloured saris. I arrived to find the toilet door wide open and three passengers crouching inside. To my dismay they had claimed it as their compartment for the journey.

An essential requirement for second class ordinary passengers was a strong bladder!

While the train clattered and rumbled through the countryside, a warm wind blew in through the open windows. As I stared out at the endless green fields of wheat and rice I was spellbound by the scene.

Suddenly a whiskery face popped up in front of mine. It belonged to a man clinging to vertical bars on the outside of the carriage. He gave me a start. We stared at each other, our noses just inches apart. He grinned, revealing a mouthful of teeth blackened by the betel nut he habitually chewed. Instinctively, I pulled back.

As the train rattled onward and lurched around a bend he lifted a basket up to the window to show us the food he was hawking. Penny selected a couple of boiled eggs and a packet of glucose biscuits. After accepting her rupees he took off with the agility of a chimpanzee, swinging from bar to bar to the next open window. He easily could be jolted from the carriage. I was astounded by the way the Indian entrepreneur risked his life to sell his goods.

The train continued to hurtle along the tracks, swaying from side to side.

A few minutes later another grinning face appeared at the window.

"Chai?" he asked. While he gripped an outside iron bar with one hand he raised his kettle to the open window and poured hot chai into our thermos flasks.

The elixir of life! We couldn't live without it.

India

Second class ordinary

On the Madras express, June 1978
See map, page 12

The evening departure of the Indian Railways' express from Rameswaram, in southern India, to Madras was delayed.

The delay meant we would have enough time to visit a cobbler near the station for a quick fix of our well worn sandals. We were pleased to see he resoled them with tread from an old car tire. This made our sandals good for many more miles even though the tire's 5,000-mile warranty had expired! His meticulous job took longer than expected, cutting down our time to get to the station's ticket office.

We planned on buying first class tickets to the intermediate town of Pondicherry, just eight hours away. There should be plenty of seats available because the train was starting out empty from Rameswaram.

As we hurried along the platform the buckle of my left sandal snagged my lightweight, thin-with-age cotton trousers and ripped the right leg from my knee to my ankle. The torn leg flapped like a flag as I ran. Feeling conspicuous, I detoured into the Railway Retiring Room and changed into a spare pair of trousers.

This took precious minutes. The train was due at the platform at any moment and we still hadn't bought tickets.

Reaching the ticket office, we asked for first class but unfortunately they were sold out. We had to settle for second class ordinary.

In first class we would have had the luxury of reserved seats. In second class ordinary, seating was on a first come, first served basis which was often a challenging experience. It wasn't a practice in India to line up in an orderly fashion. You needed to be aggressive and force your way through the crowds like the locals did. We didn't look forward to getting on the train.

The station was densely packed with families: women in saris of every hue of the rainbow, men in their dark slacks and white shirts or the traditional dhoti and the children in dresses or shorts. Some family members sat listlessly on piles of suitcases, others occasionally erupted into loud animated discussions. Porters in their red caps with carts of luggage in tow yelled warnings as they pushed through throngs of waiting passengers. Small-goods vendors sold combs, mirrors and perfumes. Tea vendors did a brisk business filling passengers' thermos flasks. At the fruit stand we bought a couple of bananas for the trip.

A young hustler approached and offered to find two sleeping berths in second class for a tip of eight rupees ($1). It was worth paying him to save us battling the crowds. He needed something to lay on each berth to claim them for us.

"Two towels," he suggested.

I had a sudden vision of our towels disappearing with him into the throng, never to be seen again.

Penny came to the rescue. She ripped my worn out trousers in half. "Take these," she said.

It was a brilliant idea.

When the train arrived he scurried aboard with the two legs trailing behind him.

He returned wearing a smug grin of success and escorted us quickly to our compartment. He proudly pointed up at our berths.

We stood stunned but amused at our accommodation: two overhead luggage racks on either side of the compartment, each of which he had claimed with a trouser leg. The racks were wooden shelves about seven feet long, as wide as our bodies, and suspended about two feet from the ceiling. How were we going to survive the next eight hours on those narrow shelves?

Passengers pushed and shoved their way down the corridor into the various compartments, calling excitedly to family and friends as they found seats and overhead storage. We had to act fast.

Penny quickly tipped our helper as I heaved the backpacks up onto our two shelves. We had to hurry as the compartment was being invaded by more passengers. We grabbed the edges of our luggage racks and swung ourselves up, escaping the wave of humanity swirling beneath us.

They glanced up at the luggage racks, expecting to put some of their belongings overhead. Their faces showed no surprise when they saw us peering down. Obviously, luggage rack travel wasn't that unusual. We flashed them friendly smiles.

I looked across at Penny who was trying to get comfortable. "I wish I had more meat on my bones," she said. "This wooden shelf is not going to get any softer over the next few hours." Without head space, we couldn't sit upright but we were happier up top than down below.

From my perch I watched passengers fill every inch of space. The compartment should have held only eight but I was amazed to count seventeen people crammed together. The women, with their bright saris and matching headscarves, made the compartment look like a painter's palette.

A couple of the men slipped out of their sandals and sat, yoga-like, with their feet tucked under crossed legs. I couldn't help but notice that their footwear lacked long-wearing car tire treads. Obviously they hadn't been to our cobbler.

Eventually the whistle blew and I felt a shudder as the powerful diesel-electric locomotive pulled out of the station.

As the train swayed and rattled over the tracks we braced ourselves. One wrong move could send us falling onto the crush of people below. Getting my customary forty winks would be a problem.

In spite of the discomfort of lying on a board, I felt fortunate that we had these luggage racks. We were above the crowd and close to the ceiling fan which created a welcome breeze.

A disadvantage was our inability to get down without stepping on someone. I had to put aside any thought of using the washroom; it was probably occupied as a compartment anyway.

As the journey progressed into the inkiness of the night, hunger gnawed at my stomach. We only carried the two bananas bought at the station. But we were out of luck. Neither Penny nor I could reach into our backpacks from our cramped positions.

The people below chattered amiably and soon opened their food baskets. Aromas of curry and other spices filled the compartment and drifted to the ceiling to tease our nostrils and tantalize our taste buds.

We were tempted to drop in on them, literally.

Pakistan

Ahmad's hospitality

Lahore to Okara, July 1978
See map, page 12

In the walled courtyard of Ahmad's home in Okara, Pakistan, Penny and I consumed a breakfast of chappatis, coconut milk, curd and tea.

Ahmad, our host, was a chunky man in his thirties with a caramel-coloured face, wavy black hair and a neatly clipped mustache. He introduced his young son, Babar, a dark-eyed shy boy of about ten wearing a blue kaftan. Then he introduced his daughter Rehana, a pretty seven-year-old with long, dark hair, wearing a red dress.

"And here is my baby daughter," Ahmad said proudly as he unwrapped the bundle in his arms and showed her smiling face.

"Would you like to meet my wife?" Ahmad asked, directing his question towards Penny. Both Penny and I said yes and rose from our chairs. But Ahmad held up his hand in front of me and said, "Not you."

Our journey started the previous afternoon when Penny and I stood at the ticket window of the Lahore train station.

"Two tickets for the two-forty-five to Sahiwal," I said. From Sahiwal, our plan was to go by bus to Harappa, an old Indus Valley city that dated back to 2500 BC.

The ticket seller studied the train accommodation charts in front of him and said he could sell us two first class tickets but there was a restriction. "You cannot be in the compartment after nine p.m.," he said, "because it becomes an overnight sleeper, and four men have booked it to Karachi. But you will be off the train by then because you reach Sahiwal at six p.m."

Right on time the diesel-electric locomotive with six carriages pulled out of Lahore station. The overhead sky was moody with angry dark grey clouds. The four men occupying the compartment acknowledged us with nods. They were businessmen in dark trousers and white shirts, jet black hair, clean-shaven, coasting into middle age. Two read their newspapers while the other two looked out the dust covered windows. No one spoke.

The terrain was flat, dotted with the occasional village with flat roofed homes built of mud brick. We passed whitewashed Muslim shrines, flocks of sheep and fields of rice and maize.

The train clicketty-clacked at about twenty-five miles an hour along the ribbons of steel and the carriage swayed gently. Rain drops spattered the window panes, causing the dust to streak.

At five p.m. we stopped at Okara but still had thirty-seven kilometres to go before we reached Sahiwal. Half-an-hour went by and I wondered when we would be leaving the station. Penny poked her head into the corridor and said people were milling around, chatting, while others stood on the platform. She couldn't see anyone in authority to ask what was happening. If this was a scheduled stop it had not been mentioned to us. I asked the men in the compartment the reason for the delay but they shrugged, showing no concern.

Time ticked around to seven o'clock. Vendors from the town arrived with curried chicken, tea and soft drinks to sell to passengers. Because we were foreigners another passenger came to us and explained the reason for the delay, that another train had derailed down the line, and that workers were at the site.

Eight o'clock passed. Nine o'clock came.

Penny leaned over and whispered: "It's nine o'clock. We shouldn't be here."

"I know," I said. "But let's stay a little longer. The rain is now coming down in torrents."

I looked at the men and felt uneasy. They probably wanted to lower the two top bunks so they could all stretch out. Now past nine, we had overstayed our welcome but they were too polite to ask us to leave.

Time ticked on to ten. The rain finally stopped. Penny looked outside and said there were little groups of people with luggage walking away from the train. That did not look promising.

What a dilemma. Should we wait a little longer to see if the train would move? Should we stand in the corridor and let the men have their compartment or should we get off the train? We decided to wait a little longer.

Promptly at eleven, we decided to leave. We grabbed our bags, thanked our fellow passengers and said goodbye. I detected their collective sigh of relief.

We headed into town, trying to step over large, deep puddles in the road that were difficult to see in the dark. As we splashed along, our feet slipped around in our sandals. Ahead, a sign on a building said Standard Hotel. We went inside but it was full. Obviously, passengers who left the train earlier had taken the rooms. There was only one other hotel in the town, the desk clerk told us. He pointed down the road. When we got to it, after walking through ankle-deep water that now covered the main road, we learned that it also was full.

We wandered out of the hotel into the night to ponder our next move. We watched people riding bicycles along the watery main road. Others walked, carrying luggage on their heads.

I was thinking about asking at one of the hotels if we could sit in the lobby overnight, when at that moment three men appeared out of the darkness, and stopped.

"What are you doing here?" one of them asked.

"We're from the train," I said, "looking for a place to stay."

"Wait," he said, and disappeared into the hotel.

"It's full," he confirmed. "Would you like to stay at my home?"

"You're very kind," I said. "We'd like that very much." I was thankful that a complete stranger would offer hospitality so spontaneously.

He hailed a tonga – a horse and cart taxi – for the five of us which included his two friends. We all climbed the single step to the canopied cab behind the driver and pressed together. At the driver's crack of the whip, the horse strained for a moment then pulled forward. As we headed along a paved road that was above the floodwaters the rhythmic clip-clop of the horse's hooves on the blacktop resounded through the balmy night air. Then the tonga sloshed through flooded, unpaved side streets.

We got off at the entrance to a dark alley and plodded along, skirting the puddles and stepping on occasional bricks and boulders where water covered the width of the alley. The alley was flanked by high walls with gates that led to individual courtyards of homes. Presently we reached a gate which our host pushed open.

We stepped into a courtyard paved with cobblestones, illuminated by two light bulbs. A long verandah ran the length of the building, and about half-a-dozen doors led into what we assumed were living quarters. Like many homes in the area, the adobe brick had been whitewashed.

Our host introduced himself as Ahmad, and showed us into one of the rooms off the verandah. The room with yellow, stuccoed walls was just large enough for two single beds and two chairs. The cement floor was strewn with straw mats and, in a corner, stood an electric fan. In the ceiling, a naked light bulb dangled from protruding wires. "This room is for you, for as long as you want to stay," he said.

It was hard to believe that a person would offer shelter for an indefinite period to people he had just met, and with whom he hadn't had a chance to have a conversation. Nevertheless, he then added, "I'll go get some mangoes. You must be hungry."

The five of us squeezed into the room and ate sweet, juicy mangoes and talked. Our host was a road contractor, another man was Ahmad's brother and the third was the town barber. At midnight they rose to leave. I realized when Ahmed's brother settled down on a cot outside to sleep, that we had been given his room. A portable fan whirred over his bed cooling the hot, humid air.

We closed the door, thankful for the beds, and slept soundly.

Morning came quickly. There was a knock on the door. It was

Ahmad with breakfast. This was when he introduced his children and suggested meeting his wife, something he would only allow Penny to do. He drew a hand over his face to indicate a veil. *"Purdah,"* he said. I understood this to mean that because his wife was not wearing her veil she could not be presented to another man. So, only Penny went with him.

After about fifteen minutes she returned to say she had met his wife, Afzal, who was dressed in a black cloak. She had also met young female members of the extended family who giggled shyly during the visit. Ahmad had placed a straight-backed chair in the middle of the room for Penny to sit on. She felt conspicuous and wanted to join the women and girls who had gathered on the floor around her, but they insisted she sit on the chair. For the girls, and even the mother, it could have been the first time they had seen a white foreign person so close. She felt they scrutinized her every movement. Penny told me she did a lot of smiling and sign language in her attempt to communicate.

When the time came to leave, Ahmad told us that the trains were still not running according to a passerby in the muddy lane. He directed us to the town centre from where we could catch a bus to Sahiwal. The rain had stopped, the sun was shining and our spirits were high.

"Come back one day," Ahmad said, "so I can show you Okara when it is dry."

But we did not want to see Okara when it was dry. We preferred to remember Okara with its flooded streets, clip-clopping horse and Ahmad's hospitality in time of need.

Pakistan

Gunsmiths and drug dealers

Among the Afridi at Darra, July 1978
See map, page 12

Mud clung to our sandals, making the walk through the streets a slow slog. We were in Peshawar, Pakistan, where a monsoonal rainstorm had just drenched the city.

At the bus station we bought tickets to the town of Darra Adam Khel in the Northwest Frontier tribal region. It was known for its gun making, not that we loved guns but we were curious about the town and the people who lived there.

The bus proved to be an eye-opener. Every part of its exterior was painted with colourful flowers. A luggage rack, the full length of the bus, had been built on the roof to carry not only passengers' baggage but sheep, goats, and extra people when the inside of the bus was full.

The bus lumbered along a rough mountain road and groaned through loops and bends, passing villages whose clusters of mud-brick huts were surrounded by defensive walls of mud and tree limbs. All the passengers were men, either clean shaven or with long beards. They all wore tribal garb of beige cotton robes, black vests and either a knitted cap or a loosely wound, dirt-stained beige turban with one end hanging over the shoulder.

After a forty-kilometre drive south of Peshawar we passed a weathered billboard-sized sign. It warned that visitors proceeding beyond this point were entering an autonomous tribal region where the Pakistani government was not in control. It was inhabited by the Afridi, the most infamous tribe of the fiercely independent Pathan ethnic group.

"Should we really be coming here?" Penny asked with uncertainty. "What if something happens to us, no one will know where we are."

I tried to reassure her: "Nothing has happened to us in the last six months of our travels; we'll be fine." I hoped I had disguised my own flicker of self-doubt.

The bus rumbled into a short valley with steep brown hillsides, following the dirt road into Darra. We drove down the main street lined on both sides with one-roomed shops and one- and two-storey ramshackle houses, all built with sundried mud bricks. Some storekeepers rested on charpoys (beds with rope mattresses) that were set out on the sidewalk in front of their businesses.

Men with rifles slung over their shoulders strolled casually to and fro.

"They all look like a rough bunch of characters," Penny said. "We haven't been in a town like this before. And have you noticed there are no women on the street?"

A few sheep roamed aimlessly, giving the town a rural atmosphere. They scattered when the bus bore down on them. Power poles lined the street. Some stood upright, others leaned drunkenly. Drainage ditches on either side of the road still carried rainwater from the early morning monsoonal downpour which left the ground muddy. Most shopfronts displayed a large sign with a painting of rifles, hand guns and machine guns and the name of the shop owner in Arabic and Western scripts.

We drove by a little shop with a banner that boasted "International Arms and Hashish" then pulled up near a garishly painted sign with rifles and hand guns and the name Rabnawaz & Bros., Arms dealers. Through the bus window I saw two men sitting cross-legged on the floor of their shop amidst an alarming array of rifles and pistols stacked around them and hanging on the walls. I was eager to get out and explore.

As soon as we stepped off the bus a young man approached, directing us to a small shop which made gun parts. He was looking for potential customers. Suddenly I heard a rifle shot. I spun around and looked over the road to where a couple of men stood with a rifle.

"It's okay," the young man said, "the shop owner is only proving that the rifle really works. We hear gunshots all day."

As time ticked by we got used to the gun blasts as men stepped into the street, aimed skyward, pulled the trigger and shot at nothing.

We soon discovered that ninety percent of the businesses in the town were dedicated to gun making. The only other shops we could see sold clothing, plastic ware and pots and pans and a shop that sold pharmaceuticals and medical supplies. Medical supplies? That was pertinent, considering the shooting accidents that could happen. In another shop a tea vendor was stoking the charcoal fire under his 100-cup urn in readiness for thirsty gun shop workers.

We wandered along alleyways and watched the craftsmen, both men and boys, at work sitting on the ground or on their haunches in dark, dingy workshops. They were replicating weapons from Russia, China, the USA and Israel. For decades, buyers of their weapons have been Afghan tribesmen; the Afghanistan border was only forty miles to the west.

We were in another world. Not being gun lovers, we suddenly found ourselves overwhelmed. Men called to us in friendly tones, inviting us to come and see what they were doing. We watched as they pumped bellows to heat the mud-brick furnaces, hammered heated metal rods on anvils, operated primitive lathes and bow drills, bored gun barrels, filed firing mechanisms and polished wooden stocks of rifles. One young boy was filling cartridges with gunpowder for Lee Enfield rifles, the rifle that has been a favourite since World War One.

We left the workshops to visit the cemetery on the side of a hillock above the main road. Numerous white gravestones were carved in the Arabic script. Because of all the guns in the village I wondered how many people had been shot accidentally? Or deliberately?

Guns were regarded as part of a man's attire. Disputes often concerned women and property – especially land. The Pathans, and by inference the Afridi, lived by their code of ethics, the *Pashtunwali*, which promoted hospitality, demanded revenge for a wrongdoing, and specified that family honour be upheld.

From the graveyard we spotted half a dozen men in their turbans, vests, long tunics and baggy trousers striding purposefully along the main street with their rifles slung over one shoulder. Each man carried a bandoleer of bullets draped over the other shoulder. They were involved in an animated discussion and appeared to be heading somewhere with determination in their step.

Although apprehensive about so many guns casually displayed, our curiosity got the better of us. We followed the men to the outskirts of town, a five-minute walk down the road.

Small, rugged sandstone hills, the colour of toast, were smudged with little green thorny bushes and stunted trees. The hills swept away into the distance to meet the blue-grey sky. This tranquil setting was soon disturbed. On a small hillock close by, a man tied a plastic bag to a thorny bush. Then he joined the others about 200 paces away. They took turns shooting at it, testing rifles.

They didn't mind us being there nor were they bothered by our taking photos. Their gunshots pierced the air and reverberated off the hillsides. We covered our ears to muffle the blasts. Penny switched on our tape recorder to record live sound to go with the Super-8 movie I was shooting but the high pitch of the gunshots blew a fuse in the machine.

Because the high decibel blasts were hurting our ear drums we headed back along the main street where we were interrupted by "come and have a cup of tea." A man standing in the doorway of a pharmacy was beckoning. It was one of the few shops that was not selling guns.

"My name is Faizullah Afridi," he said. "Please sit down and take tea with me."

We joined him, a dignified, clean-shaven, melancholy man. Drinking tea is a relaxing past-time no matter where you are in the world. Often it is used to open discussions about family or business.

Faizullah asked the standard question common throughout Asia: "How many children do you have?"

"We don't have any," Penny said.

"I don't have any either," Faizullah said with a tone of disappointment. "Everyone seems to have a son. The drug dealers here teach their sons about the quality of poppies and the opium smuggling routes, the gunsmiths teach their sons all about guns but I have no son to teach."

Penny changed the topic as he was becoming wistful. "Where are the women?"

"They are all at home in the villages," he said. "You may know that from puberty they must be hidden from men who are outside the immediate family. If they leave the house they must wear the burka." We had seen women in Peshawar draped in this tent-like cloak with only a crocheted mesh screen to look through.

"What about the guns being made? Is it legal?" Penny asked.

"Yes. It's legal because there are no laws banning the making of guns. Selling them, however, is illegal. Since the days of British rule we have run our own affairs. We have no government except our tribal councils. We have no police and we pay no taxes.

"The problem the gunsmiths have is to get the guns out of here to Afghanistan or Iran. That's the illegal part. Same thing with drugs. They are trucked illegally to Quetta in the south then through Iran and Turkey to Europe. Or they are trucked to Karachi, then shipped to Europe. Drugs are sold openly here in Darra, as you have probably seen."

"No, we haven't seen drugs being sold," I said.

"You should see more of Darra. Across the road is a shop selling drugs. It is run by Munawar Afridi. You should look. It is near the clothing store."

Both men used their tribal name as their family name, a common practice in Pakistan.

After thanking Faizullah for the tea and conversation we rose to leave.

In the shop across the road Munawar, a jolly, voluble, robust man welcomed us and offered tea. In this warm climate we had a great capacity for tea. His offer of tea, as well as being a social custom, was possibly one of his marketing ploys to get us to buy his products. He handed a thermos flask to an assistant who headed down the street to the tea vendor.

While we waited for the tea we looked around his little shop. The walls were lined with shelves of jars and plastic bags containing powders, and bricks or cakes in shades of white and brown. On the floor in a corner, two large sheepskin bags, open at the top, held a dark brown powder. The man caught us looking at it. "Raw hashish. I also have it in cakes which makes it easy to carry." There was an unpleasant odour in the air; we weren't sure if it was coming from the sheepskin bags or their contents.

Munawar looked at Penny and pointed to her thin arms. "You need hash to make you strong."

"No thanks," Penny laughed. "I might be thin but I am already strong."

The tea arrived and he showed us some small brown tablets. He had not caught on that we were not in the market for his drugs but we were enjoying his tea.

"Heroin," he said. "Only twelve thousand a kilo."

"Twelve thousand what? Rupees?" I said.

"No, dollars. American."

We gulped at the price while he went on to show us various drugs: morphine for $6,000 a kilo, opium for $170 a kilo. We had never seen any of these drugs before. We were amused by his casual attitude as if he was selling various kinds of flour.

We were interrupted when an elderly man shuffled in, his long beard reddened with henna and his body hugging a walking stick. Without any conversation Munawar immediately sold him a small packet of powder for a couple of heavy coins, then turned his attention back to us. "He is a regular, always buys the same thing."

We weren't giving him any business and didn't want to waste his time. We thanked him for the tea and apologized for not buying anything. He didn't seem to mind. As we were leaving another man walked in with a couple of coins.

"Munawar probably has a steady clientele," Penny said as we

passed the customer on our way out.

Outside the sun was shining and the air, fresh. We agreed that Darra ranked highly on our list of unusual places we had visited. Gunshots fired in quick succession confirmed this. We swung around to see a teenaged gun maker shooting at the sky, his face a study in grit and determination.

Half-a-dozen sheep followed a shepherd along the middle of the street. One day they'll just be sheepskin bags holding hashish, I predicted.

Across the street Faizullah stood in front of his shop and called us over. "Please come in. I have a gift."

He opened the drawer of his desk, fumbled around and came up with a ring. It was bright red and shiny. He held it for a moment as he gazed at Penny.

"I want you to have this precious stone. It is a ruby." He handed it to her.

She admired it, smiled warmly and slipped it on her finger. It fitted snugly after she squeezed the expandable tin band.

"Thank you, it will be a wonderful reminder of our visit here."

In the late afternoon we boarded the bus for Peshawar under a grey slaty sky. As I lolled comfortably in the seat my mind wandered over the harmless shotgun blasts that had rung in my ears and the refreshing tea that had settled in my belly. As the bus passed the sign which warned of the lawless tribal region I looked at Penny's new ring. "Nice piece of glass," I said, thinking kindly of the soft-hearted Faizullah, and wondered if all the 'fierce' Afridi tribesmen were out of town.

Afghanistan

Tea break

With Kochi nomads near Kabul, July 1978
See map, page 12

The sun had been up for three hours, warming the land and generating farmyard odours which mixed with the aroma of freshly cut hay. It was about nine o'clock at the Puli Charhi open-air animal market just five kilometres outside Kabul.

Camels chewed their cud and belched, cattle lowed, and goats and fat-tailed sheep bleated as bearded Afghan farmers inspected them.

The dress code was strictly casual: baggy, beige trousers partly covered by a long, dirt-stained whitish shirt that reached below the knees, and a long dark coat to protect against the early morning chill. Headgear consisted of a sweat-stained beige turban with one end that hung loosely over the shoulder, handy for wiping away perspiration and covering the face when dust blew off the land.

Penny and I had taken an early bus from Kabul to Puli Charhi but it was not early enough. When we arrived the market was winding down. Nevertheless, we saw half-a-dozen transactions. Buyers bargained with the sellers for the best price. Money changed hands. Handshakes cemented the deals. Cattle, goats and sheep waited dutifully to be led away while camels stood proudly, displaying a look of aloofness as they waited for their new masters.

In the distance, beyond the market, loomed the brooding

immensity of a stark, bluish-grey mountain range, its folds discernible as a deeper blue. Along its shoulders was draped a shawl of cloud. At its base I could just make out white triangular specks – tents – in an ocean of golden wheat.

A trader saw us looking across the plain and said, "Kochi."

His one word explained a lot. The Kochi tribe was the dominant nomadic group in the region. The people often contracted their harvesting services to landowners in return for products such as tea, coffee, sugar, flour and kitchen utensils.

Deciding to visit them, we set off across the parched, cracked earth which hadn't seen rain for a couple of months.

Puffy cumulus clouds in the deep blue sky hid the sun every now and then, causing light and shadow to sweep back and forth over the land. As we drew closer the sunlight illuminated the dark specks of workers who were slashing at the stalks with scythes.

As we neared a harvested wheatfield we saw an open space where a cow, harnessed to a horizontal pole, trudged around and around in a circle, threshing the sheaves of wheat. To keep it moving, a young boy walked behind, goading it with a stick.

Nearby, men with practised skill winnowed the wheat, throwing it high into the air from flat trays, allowing the chaff to blow away in the soft breeze while the grains of wheat dropped to the ground. Young girls in ankle-length red dresses – which meant they were not married – quickly gathered the grains into baskets. They stared at us quizzically.

There were about thirty people working. About five families, I guessed. As we watched them toil they all shot sideways glances at us but kept their rhythm. Everyone, it appeared, wore dirty clothes and their hair was matted and unkempt – a result of their lifestyle when on the move without much water. Kochi is a Farsi (Iranian) word for "those who move."

A man with a sunbaked, wind-scoured face and an air of authority put down his winnowing tray and said, in a questioning, friendly tone, "Chai?"

He was inviting us to have tea with him. What unexpected good fortune for us. We smiled our acceptance. I added *"shukran,"* Arabic for thank you, not knowing any of the Kochi language. The man wore typical Afghan garb: a short black vest over a knee-length, off-white shirt which hung down over large baggy, once-white trousers.

A group of curious children scampered behind us as we followed the man to his white canvas tent – commercially made, probably from Pakistan. The more traditional tents were made from black goat hair. Products of the modern world were slowly becoming popular among the nomads.

Outside the tent three goats were tethered. He waved us inside which was high enough to stand in. A kitten and chickens scurried around excitedly when we inadvertently disturbed them. Hand-woven carpets covered the ground. We followed the man's example and sat cross-legged on the carpet. I wondered how long I would last in this unfamiliar position. Penny groaned quietly; I knew she'd soon be stretching out her legs.

As my eyes grew accustomed to the dim interior I saw a large wooden trunk along one wall. At the back of the tent a teenaged boy lay among wicker baskets and bundles of clothes which were piled in a disorderly fashion. The man rubbed his stomach to indicate his son was ill but with a wave of his hand he brushed off the illness as being minor. We met his other teenaged children – two sons and a daughter. The boys wore ragged but warm jackets over their thin trousers and the girl, who had long, black wavy hair and big, dark eyes wore a long red embroidered dress.

Presently his wife arrived from the wheat fields, having been summoned by one of the children. A black cloak partly covered an old dark red skirt. Unlike the Afghan women in the towns, Kochi women didn't wear veils. Her weathered face had been exposed to many years of sun and harsh winds. When she welcomed us her eyes twinkled and her warm smile displayed a few isolated teeth.

She started a fire nearby in a small pit and perched a blackened kettle on rocks over the orange flames. The water boiled and steam hissed. She added tea leaves and sugar to the kettle then carried it to the mother goat tethered nearby. She squeezed a teat; milk spurted into the kettle.

Penny whispered: "That's what I call fresh milk!"

While she prepared the tea her young daughter scrubbed cups in a basin of water on the ground.

From a stained cloth in the tent the woman unwrapped a plate-sized piece of flat unleavened bread which she placed before us on the carpet. She then fumbled among the clothes and baskets and proudly presented us with a freshly laid egg. She smiled and pointed to the fire, indicating she would cook it for us.

We were humbled by this generous gesture but shook our heads and protested with our hands. They had so little; we couldn't eat their precious egg. As we drank our piping hot sweet tea, the man constantly waved a cloth over the bread to keep off the persistent flies. He did not drink with us, nor did his wife who stayed outside the tent. We thought it odd, but it may have been their custom with strangers.

The children who followed us must have spread the word about outsiders in their midst. Before long, the doorway of the tent darkened with many young people staring at us. We smiled and greeted them with hello but they looked back at us with blank faces. We conversed with the man by hand signals, shaking and nodding our heads and smiling a lot.

We gathered that this group of Kochi was doing contract work – harvesting wheat – for a local landowner. We were in a warm and friendly atmosphere and wished we had come prepared with a small gift. But who were we to know when we left the hotel in Kabul earlier in the morning, we would be enjoying the hospitality of nomads?

As we continued our mute discourse with the man, his wife kept filling our cups with more tea. I glanced at Penny. She, like me, felt comfortably at home in this unfamiliar setting.

Penny suddenly remembered she had candy in paper wrappers in her shoulder bag. She put them on the mat in front of the man but he waved them away. Either he didn't know what they were or we had committed a cultural taboo – by a woman offering them to him.

We didn't want to overstay our welcome or keep the family from the fields. It was time to head across the plain to the main road and return to Kabul. Penny left the sweets on the mat for the children.

We bade our farewells. I watched the woman clasp both of Penny's hands in hers and look into Penny's eyes with a friendly, warm smile. She held Penny's hands for a few extra seconds; it was as if a bond was being sealed.

It is a memory Penny cherishes.

Jordan

A chance meeting

With Hussein's family near Petra, October 1978
See map, page 13

Petra, in Jordan, so impressed the Romans that they bullied the inhabitants into submission and annexed their city in 106 AD. What they got for their efforts was a beautiful city carved from rock in a valley surrounded by mountains of pink, yellow and purple sandstone. It was a city of twenty to thirty thousand residents.

Who inhabited the city?

Nabataeans. This semi-nomadic people migrated from northern Arabia in the sixth century BC and hammered their tent stakes into the ground in this hidden valley. From this humble beginning a city developed. Over the centuries they filled their coffers through trade and by the collection of tolls from camel caravans. The tolls ensured their safe travel across Nabataean controlled lands. The city prospered and stone masons carved temples, palaces, homes and tombs in the hillsides.

When the Romans moved in they expanded the city by adding many free-standing stone buildings and hewed an amphitheatre out of a hillside to seat seven thousand spectators. The Romans were big on pomp and circumstance!

Unfortunately, a series of earthquakes in the fourth, sixth and eighth centuries toppled many of the buildings.

Crusaders arrived in the thirteenth century, settled down for a few short years until shown the exit by a Muslim army. Then Petra lapsed into silence for six hundred years until a Swiss explorer rediscovered it in 1812 and leaked the news to the world.

It was in this hidden valley that Penny and I spent a full day.

Upon reaching Petra in the morning by passenger truck we saw that men from local farms had arrived with donkeys and horses to transport visitors into the valley.

We left our backpacks at the Visitors' Centre and decided to walk rather than ride through the *siq*. This narrow chasm was just over one kilometre long with natural rock walls that soared straight up to 100 metres. The siq, which varied from three to sixteen metres wide, was the way in and out of the valley where Petra was hidden.

Because sunlight never touched the bottom of the narrow chasm, the path remained in perpetual shadow. We followed the trail through the gloom and rounded the final curve. A pinkish glow emanating from the end of the chasm intrigued us.

We hurried forward then suddenly stopped, spellbound. Before us loomed an imposing temple-like structure carved out of the rose-red cliff face. Slender stone pillars stretched skywards. Rays from the blazing sun bathed the facade in a pink light. We edged closer and gazed up at pillars whose capitals boasted intricate clusters of stone leaves. Panels on the lintels were carved with delicate friezes and the second level was adorned with statues. We stared, overcome by the magnificence of this hand-carved edifice whose height was that of a twelve-storey building. Earlier visitors dubbed this architectural masterpiece the Treasury although it may have been a shrine, or a tomb.

Penny stood transfixed. "How can we fully describe to anyone else what we've seen here?" She spoke with a tone of reverence. "I'll never forget this sight as long as I live."

We ventured into the valley. A trail led us past stone rubble – the remains of homes, storehouses, stables and shrines brutalized by earthquakes. The trail that skirted around hardy, green acacia bushes led us towards a valley wall of sandstone, pockmarked with Nabataean tombs. As we got closer we saw elaborately carved pillars and lintels on the facades of the palace-like burial chambers. Inside, we discovered spacious rooms carved into the hillside. Outside, pinnacles of eroded sandstone stood like silent sentinels guarding the empty tombs.

Towards the late afternoon we climbed an arduous pathway of 1,045 stone steps to the eminence of an ancient altar and king's throne. It had been a grind but the view from the high point was worth every puff and wheeze.

We flopped on the king's throne in the oven-like heat of the white-hot sun, took a swig of water and gazed into the valley. Most of the ancient man-made cave homes, carved into the cliffs, were empty. Bedouins occupied some of them in defiance of the government who didn't want them there in case they offended the sensibilities of tourists. Personally, I appreciated the life and colour the nomads brought to Petra. The city was built by humankind. With people missing, the site would be sterile.

I looked towards the blurred line where dusty, deeply creased hills met the sky. The immensity of this eroded landscape will forever be etched on my mind.

The sun slipped towards the horizon and bathed the sky with hues of pink and gold. A cool wind began to blow, kicking up dust. We watched visitors leave the valley below on foot, horseback and donkey, being led by local guides. We followed the stone stairway down to the valley floor and re-entered the siq. Twenty minutes later we emerged at the Visitors' Centre and to our dismay discovered all buses, trucks and cars had left the parking lot.

Already exhausted from a day of climbing, we retrieved our backpacks and started to walk to Wadi Musa, the nearest town. The surrounding terrain was rocky with scrubby vegetation. We had walked only about 200 metres when I heard the clip-clop of a horse approach from behind. I turned to see one of the guides riding his horse home. He drew alongside and looked down at us. "You look very tired," he said. "Please put your bags on my horse. My name is Hussein."

We thanked him for his kindness which came just when we needed it.

He gripped the bridle to hold his horse steady while Penny and I lashed our backpacks together and hoisted them over the saddle. It was a relief to have the horse carry our bags because we knew there were two or three kilometres of ascending, winding road to Wadi Musa.

Hussein was a bone-skinny man with kind, dark brown eyes, two similarities he shared with his horse. Like other Jordanian men he wore a kaffiyeh, a black and white checkered headscarf. For his job as a guide at the ancient city of Petra he wore slacks, a loose fitting shirt and sandals.

As we walked in the twilight he told us he was twenty and lived in a farmhouse with his parents, two brothers, a sister and a cousin who had a young baby boy. He asked if we would like to stay overnight. We accepted immediately, thankful for his hospitality.

In this desert terrain all was quiet except for the sound of the horse's hooves on the paved road. We veered off and followed a trail that led to pasture land. Ahead lay a farmhouse built of small boulders. The building was about fifteen metres long, five metres wide and two metres high. Hussein explained there were four rooms. His parents slept in the first one, everyone else in the second one, the third was a kitchen and the fourth a barn for the animals: the goats, sheep, chickens and the horse. There was no mention of a bathroom and we didn't think to ask.

In the living room a low wattage light bulb cast a mellow glow. Against one wall lay a stack of foam mattresses and blankets. Against another stood a cupboard of dishes with clothes piled on top of it. Hussein's younger brother carried in a low table and three chairs – for Penny, Hussein and me.

Their mother walked in – a woman with a big smile and a bigger girth. Her girth was expanded by the numerous skirts she wore. "Ten skirts," Hussein told us, when he caught us staring, mesmerized by her massive size. "And she never takes them off!" That explained her strong body odour. When I asked Hussein why she wore all those skirts he shrugged.

His father was a bright-eyed man, lean and bent forward. He clasped my hand when I offered it. When Penny held hers out he covered his hand with his cloak and then shook hands. His Islamic cultural tradition forbade making physical contact with the wife of another man.

Although Hussein had a smattering of English the rest of his family did not. Instead of struggling with conversation Hussein introduced us to the "Toss the Matchbox" game. We took turns tossing two matchboxes into the air and guessing how they would fall: label side up, blank side up or on the edge. We scored points for correct guesses. It was rather tedious but it filled the time. Hussein appeared enthusiastic from the way he deliberately put fast spins on the matchboxes and the way he spoke to the boxes, coaxing them to fall a certain way. We were relieved when interrupted by a call to dinner.

The seven family members gathered on the cement floor around a large bowl of yoghurt, a dish of olives and some unleavened bread. The mother beckoned us to join the family circle on the floor but I saw that their meagre amount of food was to be shared among seven people. I declined cordially, saying we carried our own food and didn't want to deprive them of theirs.

From our backpacks we took our pot, the propane stove and a packet of dehydrated chicken noodle soup. Hussein fetched water for us, watched with interest as Penny fired up the stove, then joined his family.

After we had all eaten Penny offered to wash the dishes. Hussein showed her to the backyard where the dishwashing was done. One of his young brothers poured cold water over them after Penny had done the scrubbing. Because the family ate out of a communal bowl there were few dishes to wash.

In the living room the parents rose, nodded and left. Hussein and the others pulled foam mattresses and blankets from the stack and laid them on the floor. There were enough for everyone.

I looked around the room to see if anybody was changing into night attire. Hussein's cousin, still in her dress, settled on a mattress with her baby. His brothers lay down in their farm clothes. Hussein bedded down fully dressed; he even kept his headscarf on. His sister lit a coal-oil lamp and placed it on the window ledge, then switched off the electric light.

Penny leaned towards me and whispered, "Do you know where the toilet is?"

"I've no idea," I said quietly. "I'm not sure they have one in the house. It's probably outside somewhere. I'll look later. Can you wait?"

"Sure," came her answer from the darkness. Fortunately we were blessed with strong bladders.

I slept soundly. At about five in the morning I felt the call of nature. I crawled out of bed, groped for my shoes and tiptoed over slumbering bodies to the door and pushed it open.

It creaked alarmingly as I stepped into the gloom.

Within a few minutes I was back beside Penny. "If you want to go, go now," I suggested, "while it's dark." She rose quietly and glided over the other occupants. Only the creaking door betrayed her exit. Moments passed before the hinges squeaked again.

"That was quick," I said.

"Yeah. It was dark and spooky out there. Lots of big rocks all over the place."

An hour later the golden rays of the new day streaked through the window panes. Rather than be an inconvenience and a burden to the family at breakfast time we decided to leave early. Outside a rooster crowed; inside, blanketed bodies started to stir. Hands appeared from beneath the blankets to push them back and rub their eyes.

"Hussein," I whispered, "we will go now."

"As you wish," he said. "Will you be all right?"

I assumed he was asking if we would be all right for onward transport.

"Yes," I answered, "we will go to the bus station. Thanks for everything."

"Okay, *Salaam*." (Peace.)

I took Hussein's hand and pressed a couple of bank notes into it. "Buy something for the horse." He smiled.

Penny and I emerged into the early morning sunlight. The surrounding rocks, bathed in dew, glistened. Our nocturnal ventures weren't far from our minds.

"Where'd you go?" Penny asked.

"In the field. How 'bout you?"

"In the front yard," she said, pointing, "by those big rocks."

"You're kidding!"

"No. Why?"

"That's the family graveyard."

Penny stopped, her face flushed. "How awful!"

I couldn't help but laugh.

We chuckled with a twinge of embarrassment all the way up the hill.

Near the top I looked back at the farmhouse, gilded in a rose-gold warmth, and beyond to Petra where the sun was painting the sandstone mountains in soft watercolour shades of pink and mauve.

It would not be long before Hussein was saddling the horse to begin a new day in the hidden valley.

Jordan

In search of the map

With George and family in Madaba, November 1978
See map, page 13

We stepped off the bus.

Nothing stirred.

The orange sun slipped behind the low-rise apartment buildings. The temperature dropped dramatically, common to desert terrain at night.

A quiet place. Eerie.

This was Madaba, just 25 kilometres south of Jordan's capital, Amman.

A bulky figure lumbered towards us out of the gloom. It was a man clothed in a long white robe and a black and white checkered headscarf.

"What are you doing here?" he asked in a soft, polite voice.

"Looking for a hotel," I said.

"There are no hotels around here. It is late. You are welcome to stay at my house."

We weren't surprised at his quickness to offer hospitality. Jordanians are generous like that. "My name is George," he added.

We expected a Mohammed, Ahmed or Abdul, but not George. "I am an Arab Christian," he said, to explain his name.

His face was lined with grooves and his chin covered with short, grey stubble. Bright and friendly grey eyes smiled at us when he spoke in his gentle manner. I felt a quick connection and trust as we followed him along a dirt road. He told us he had three sons and five daughters, that he was 56 and a retired school principal.

We told him that we had been backpacking for the past eleven months in Asia and the Middle East. He didn't seem to comprehend the concept of overland travel. He couldn't relate it to his lifestyle of raising eight children.

"Why have you come to Madaba?" he asked.

"To see an ancient map of Palestine on the floor of a church," I said.

"I will show it to you tomorrow. It dates back to the sixth century AD."

After our walk along the quiet road we arrived at the gate of an impressive three-storey home. Built with cement blocks, it stood in the middle of a large tract of land.

"My house," he said. "I know it is much bigger than other houses around here but I have studied more and worked harder to provide for my family." He sounded almost apologetic. "My neighbours are envious of me and dislike me because I have a big house."

Lights shone through the windows of the ground floor. The door swung open and a large woman, covered from neck to toe in a black robe, stood in the doorway. "My eldest daughter," said George. We said hello and stepped into the living room and got a surprise: a cement floor completely littered with discarded orange peels, peanut shells and apple cores. Half-a-dozen men and women in their twenties – some of his children – sat cross-legged on the floor despite the empty sofas and chairs. They were a jovial bunch, chatting and laughing. One of the men offered us chairs.

A plump older woman draped in black entered. Her face had smooth skin, a bright smile that showed two rows of white teeth, and a soothing voice when she said hello.

She beckoned Penny follow her into the adjacent room where two robust daughters bent over sewing machines. I watched through the doorway as the mother introduced them. They looked concerned when the mother took one of Penny's thin wrists in her hand and said "hungry." Penny was telling her we weren't hungry as they re-entered the room.

"You must be hungry," the mother insisted. I also told her we didn't need anything, not wanting to cause her any work. But we must have looked hungry because we hadn't eaten since noon, nine hours earlier. Within minutes she carried in a tray with two bowls of mildly spiced lentil soup. We savoured every spoonful. This was followed by a platter of sticky rice, tomatoes, onions, olives, boiled eggs, stuffed green peppers and creamed cheese. She placed these on a low table for everyone to share.

As the others had already eaten, they made only token gestures at sampling the food, just to be polite. The meal was accompanied by a large slab of flat bread. We ate in the traditional Middle Eastern way, with our fingers. For each bite we tore off a small piece of bread, wrapped it around the food and popped it into our mouths. After the first mouthful I realized how ravenous I was.

When we finished feasting, two daughters swept all of their orange peels, peanut shells and apple cores into a corner, then carried in thick foam mats and blankets and put them on the floor for us. Because the house wasn't heated we were pleased to have the warm blankets. The sweet, pungent aroma of discarded orange peels and apple cores lingered in the air as we drifted off to sleep.

In the morning when the house began to stir we got up. George offered to show us his property. We ambled among young olive, plum, apricot and lemon trees and passed many rows of tomato and squash plants which were starting to wither. Water was scarce, George said. We re-entered the house through a basement door and disturbed about ten pigeons that leapt off their perches and flew around in the basement while some grey rabbits crouched quietly in a hutch. Fresh food, George explained.

After we climbed steps to the roof where chickens pecked at scattered grain, we looked out over the arid property and noticed a barbed-wire fence around the perimeter.

"It keeps out thieves and other enemies," George said. His statement surprised me. Other enemies? At that moment a man strolled by the house, raised his arm and called out a cheery greeting. George waved without enthusiasm.

"My neighbour. On his way to the mosque," George said. "He hates me. The man is showing off by waving to me when I have guests, just to appear friendly."

I was perplexed. Why would the man hate George? Was it because of religious differences or because of George's large house? Maybe, I mused, the man didn't hate George at all but that George was just paranoid.

While we stood on the rooftop we talked about Jordan's early history. We discussed the Crusaders from Europe who arrived in the 12th and 13th centuries to wrest the Holy Land from the Muslims and the possibility that one of George's ancestors may have been converted to Christianity at that time. He said it was possible but he didn't sound convinced. He added that about half of Madaba's population was Christian, mostly Greek Orthodox, and the other half, Muslim.

We left the roof and went downstairs where we enjoyed a breakfast of milk, bread and fruit. We thanked George's wife who, as we were leaving, generously loaded us with fresh bread and bananas.

George accompanied us to the Greek Orthodox Church of St George, famous for the fifteen-hundred-year-old map on the church floor, the reason we were drawn to Madaba. The church was dusty from renovations in progress, as evidenced by some interior scaffolding and lumber scattered about, but no one was around.

George pointed to the map which lay between two pillars. It was a masterpiece comprised of thousands of coloured mosaic tiles embedded in mortar. We were impressed by the intricate workmanship required to put it together. It featured the region from Egypt to the Phoenician cities of Sidon and Tyre.

The lack of security precautions to protect it surprised us because this was the oldest map of the Holy Land in existence. It had originally been part of the floor of a 6th century AD Byzantine church and was discovered when the present church of St. George was under construction over the same site.

We could make out the oval-shaped, walled city of Jerusalem which had survived almost intact. A recognizable building was the

Byzantine Church of the Holy Sepulchre whose tower appeared to rise above the other buildings because of the three dimensional effect created with the tiles.

The map originally covered a floor space of fifteen by six metres and depicted all the important biblical sites, including Jericho, Bethlehem and the Jordan River. Because of loss and damage to many tiles it is now about ten by five metres. Estimates suggest about 750,000 mosaic pieces are in place. Originally there were about two million.

We felt privileged to see the map but when we think of our visit to Madaba we think of George – and his hospitality to two strangers in the night.

Egypt

Anxious moments

Ahmed's taxi, Cairo to Alexandria, November 1978
See map, page 13

"Alex. Alex!" yelled a taxi driver.

"Alexandria?" I queried to confirm his destination.

"Yes, get in."

Penny and I had come to Ramses Square in downtown Cairo to find a share taxi – a long-range taxi which leaves only when all seats are sold. The dry midmorning air was full of honking horns, fumes from cars and buses and the shouts of drivers who bellowed out their destinations. Our plan was to visit Alexandria, 225 kilometres to the northwest on the Mediterranean coast. We hoped to visit catacombs almost 2,000 years old.

We slung our backpacks on the roof rack and slipped into the two remaining places on the back seat. Painted on the dashboard was our driver's name, Ahmed. He was an expansive toad-like personage whose dark brown face had narrow slits for his quick little eyes.

With the taxi now full, Ahmed flopped into the driver's seat. His dirty gallabiah, a blue cotton robe similar to a long night shirt, billowed over his large frame.

In the front with him sat two passengers who stared straight ahead. Four of us sat crushed together in the back seat, suffering from the cramped quarters and the 30°C temperature. This was going to be a long two-and-a-half-hour drive. Beside me sat Penny and crammed beside her a man with a thin, hawk-like face. The man next to him gazed out the window. To breathe fresh air I lowered my window, but hot air, thickened with diesel fumes and dust, poured in, mixing with the sour smell of sweat. I quickly rewound it.

Ahmed nosed the car into the slow stream of Cairo traffic and honked his horn in unison with other drivers. It is customary in Egypt for drivers of any vehicle to constantly lean on the horn to warn donkey carts, buses and other vehicles of their approach. From the way he muttered to himself I could tell he was impatient to get onto the open road so he could speed. The traffic thinned, his chance arrived. He pressed the accelerator pedal to the floor; the car shot forward. Penny clutched my arm.

Ahmed dodged potholes and overtook everything: cars, trucks, donkey carts and camels. The speedometer registered a steady 110 kilometres an hour, too fast for the narrow, paved road with crumbling shoulders. Ahmed's reckless speed continued. Nothing daunted him, not even the smashed taxis and private cars that littered the roadside. Rusted hulks rested in peace alongside the newly departed whose bodies had been stripped of parts and sheet metal.

We sped by flat-roofed farmhouses with hay stacked on their roofs, out of reach of farm animals. We glimpsed a black-robed woman on a donkey herding goats and hurtled by sugarcane fields, some harvested, others still with tall green stalks waving in the breeze. And we streaked by roadside vendors whose stalls were piled with oranges. They were a blur. We were disappointed we couldn't enjoy the scenery because of the speed, but we wouldn't ask Ahmed to slow down. This was his job. The more trips he made the more money he earned.

A powerful stench unexpectedly wafted through the driver's open window. The man with the hawk-like face turned to us and wrinkled his nose. In the mirror I watched Ahmed's face contort and his nostrils twitch. He took a hand off the steering wheel, squeezed his nose and rammed his foot to the floor to escape the odour. We bolted past the source – a dead donkey with its belly ripped open. I had never smelled such a putrid odour; we gagged as we sped by.

Ahmed had no choice but to slow down when we reached

Alexandria, a city jammed with cars, cargo trucks, blue buses, yellow street cars, horse drawn hansom cabs and masses of people. We drove along a narrow, treeless street strewn with garbage. An old man, or a man made old before his time, was tossing rags and cardboard into a donkey cart. Supposedly for resale. Everything had a value.

Ahmed became visibly agitated when he had to stop for a funeral procession that crossed the road in front of us. Pall bearers tried his patience as they slowly carried the coffin. I thought it ironic that while the procession was winding its way to a modern cemetery we were heading to an ancient one.

Our destination was the Kom el Shugafa catacombs, underground tombs quarried out of the local sandstone in the 1st and 2nd centuries AD, during the time of strong Roman influence. It is the largest Roman burial site in Egypt. Our map indicated the catacombs were nearby. Somewhere.

Ahmed dropped us off in a narrow residential street of old apartment houses in a poor section of the city. The homes we passed were square, flat roofed and joined together by common walls. Their front doors opened onto a street strewn with rags, corn stalks, sugar cane stalks and broken bottles. Women gossiped in the doorways, seemingly oblivious to the mess.

Behind us shrill laughter erupted as children played. A young boy yelled something and the laughter stopped abruptly. I glanced back just in time to see about ten urchins pick up stones and pitch them at us! They screamed – most likely yelling profanities. Their actions unnerved us; we were used to being surrounded by curious youngsters who asked: What is your name? How are you? Where are you from? But we had never been attacked before. Most stones fell wide of their mark but a couple of them hit our legs.

I was concerned the situation would worsen if we turned and acknowledged them. We didn't want them to see us run otherwise it would encourage other children to join the pursuit. We quickened our step and turned a corner into a narrow alley, then blundered along it, picking up speed. Our hearts pounded as we shook off our adversaries. Penny, breathing heavily, blurted out that we had been safer in Ahmed's taxi! I readily agreed.

In the alley we leapt over a dead rat and a dead pigeon and finally arrived at the Kom el Shugafa catacombs. I was relieved that the children had lost interest.

Back in 1900 a donkey cart had fallen through the layer of sandstone that covered the catacombs, exposing the interconnecting passages which had long been lost. In recent years a rotunda had been built over this archaeological site to protect it.

A downward spiralling staircase carved into the sandstone descended through three storeys of underground funerary chambers. We passed some of the many coffin-sized recesses once used for the dead. They now lay empty due to centuries of decomposition of the bodies.

Greece's favourite son, Alexander the Great, founded the city around 330 BC. The Greeks, and later the conquering Romans, paid homage to the gods of Egypt.

Dim light bulbs illuminated the Egyptian gods carved into the sandstone walls by the Romans. Notable among them was Anubis, the jackal-headed god of the dead whose image was carved as a Roman soldier.

We were alone in the catacombs and agreed we felt like archaeologists discovering long lost tombs. The air became cool and dank as we descended the sandstone stairway in semi-darkness. Farther down, the string of light bulbs petered out. As darkness started to close in on us we gingerly felt with our feet for the next step. I was leading the way through the gloom when suddenly I stumbled into water. I sprang back in shock. It was surprisingly chilly. Later we learned we had reached the water table in the bottom chamber of the catacombs, about thirty metres down.

I turned to Penny. "I can't go any farther. I think we should go back." My voice bounced off the walls with an eerie echo.

"To think that three hundred people were once buried in this confined space is a bit daunting," Penny said.

Masons must have spent hours at a time in this damp, cold environment, chipping away at the sandstone rock, working by the light of flickering oil lamps.

I envisaged a burial in progress: a coffin being lowered by ropes and then placed in a recess. I imagined how the family of the deceased would come and sit in one of the underground guest rooms to help the spirit on its journey to its next life.

We climbed up the steps, passed through the empty gallery and emerged into the sunlight. The children had gone. Ahmed wasn't around. It seemed so peaceful.

We headed to the bus and taxi station.

"Cairo. Cairo!" yelled a taxi driver.

"Cairo?" I queried to confirm his destination.

"Yes. Get in."

Penny and I looked at each other and headed for the bus.

Egypt

A helping hand

With Jimmy in Cairo, November 1978
See map, page 13

Office workers streamed out of nearby buildings and stampeded along crowded overhead walkways to the empty buses at the station in Cairo's El Tahrir Square. The evening rush was on. Big red buses quivered as commuters clambered aboard.

Departing buses spewed thick, black, diesel smoke into the balmy air and drivers sounded their horns to scatter commuters who drifted into their bus lanes.

It was in this chaos that I tried to find a hotel on the outskirts of the square. Penny remained behind, standing by a ticket office at the bus station with our luggage. After searching in vain for a hotel I returned along an overhead walkway and spotted Penny talking to a man – possibly another traveller.

"Meet Jimmy," she said.

I shook his hand. He was a short, stocky man about 55 years of age with fair skin. I took him to be a European. "Where are you from?" I asked.

"Cairo. I was born here. My real name is Gamal. But call me Jimmy. Can I help you find a hotel?"

"We would appreciate that," I said. "Do you know which bus goes to the youth hostel?" I read the address from the hostel handbook.

Jimmy found the bus and we climbed aboard. He insisted on

coming with us and carrying Penny's backpack.

"I feel like a traveller," he said with a good natured grin.

During our travels many people approached us to practise their English, sell something or offer their services for a tip. Some people were genuinely friendly without seeking anything in return. This is how I thought of Jimmy.

The horn honked, the engine belched and we lurched away. Cairo doesn't have enough public transport for its burgeoning population. Not everyone was able to get on the bus.

"I'm pleased we're inside," Penny said, nodding towards the window where I saw the heads of people who were hanging onto the outside.

We had seen many freeloaders cling to the outsides of buses. Six or seven men at a time would travel precariously with one foot on the bottom step, the other leg dangling, and a hand gripping one of the vertical, chromed bars on either side of the doorway.

We travelled for half-an-hour standing in the aisle crammed against other passengers.

Soon a cry went out, "Next stop." It was Jimmy's voice. We forced our way through the crowd to the exit, not wanting to lose sight of him.

We gathered together on the sidewalk and made our way to the youth hostel. This was Jimmy's first time in a youth hostel. He waited while we checked in; he wanted to make sure there was space for us.

"Would you like to come to dinner tomorrow night?" he asked. "I would like you to meet my wife and daughter."

We readily accepted the invitation from this helpful stranger with whom we felt so comfortable. It was always a rewarding experience to be invited into a home. It gave us a feeling of being in a culture rather than looking at it from the outside through a window. We have found that people everywhere have basically the same wants: a place to live, enough food, a life of peace, respect from others. But the differences were the things we found interesting: the religion, language, customs, etiquette, interaction between themselves and with us, the interior of their homes, the way food was cooked and presented, and their occupations.

"I will meet you at the bus station tomorrow to show you the way," Jimmy added.

Jimmy, his wife and teenaged daughter lived on the ground floor of a six-storey apartment building in the sprawling suburb of Heliopolis. As we passed through their front door we were greeted with cooing noises. About ten pigeons were perched in a wire cage. We eat them, Jimmy told us.

On the living room walls hung posters of Egyptian and American pop stars. "My daughter likes to decorate," Jimmy explained. His daughter came into the room, an attractive sixteen-year-old with a quick smile and bright eyes. "Anna Maria," Jimmy said proudly.

In the kitchen doorway stood an older attractive woman. She smiled, laughed and began to giggle uncontrollably.

Jimmy explained quickly. "This is my wife, Janet. Her mind is a bit ill. It started when I went to the war. She worried too much about me and became emotionally unstable." Then he added: "Isn't she beautiful? She is pure Coptic, you know." Jimmy took her hand and squeezed it gently. We were touched by his concern for her and immediately felt at ease with this warm, welcoming family.

The family intrigued me. Jimmy looked European, his real name was an Egyptian one and he fought in a war. But which one?

Janet called us to the dinner table as Anna Maria brought in chicken and rice with potatoes covered with a spinach sauce. Dining in a foreign household is an adventure because you don't always recognize the food and you don't always know what eating utensils you'll get, if any. However, in this instance we used knives and forks and the food was recognizable and tasty.

I turned to Jimmy. "Please tell us about your family."

"Of course. I'll start with Janet and Anna Maria. They are both Coptic Christians, a Copt being a native Egyptian descended from ancient Egyptian stock. Janet's ancestry can be traced back to the fourth century when many Egyptians were converted to Christianity. Her family line never converted to Islam when the Muslims arrived from Arabia in the seventh century."

I glanced towards Anna Maria who was listening lovingly to her father. I think she was impressed by his command of English. Janet meanwhile stared into space and made an occasional noise in her throat.

Jimmy continued by saying he was a Muslim whose mother came from Lebanon and whose father, from whom he inherited his European features, from Iraq.

He asked about us. He couldn't understand how an Australian and a Canadian could meet and marry when their countries were so far apart. Did our parents arrange the marriage? Penny said no, we met on a blind date. He was intrigued when she explained what it meant but the concept was foreign to him.

Janet laughed nervously and continued to giggle. Anna Maria dutifully served the cake and oranges.

I asked Jimmy which war he fought in. The war against Israel in 1967, which only lasted six days, he told us, then added he was an officer and spent just two days at the front.

"It was a terrible defeat," he said. "On the first morning the Israeli Air Force destroyed more than 300 of our planes in three hours – almost our entire air force. I was in the Sinai with 100,000 infantry without air cover. The soldiers didn't obey us and ran away. Thousands were captured by the Israelis. I, too, had to run."

There was a moment of silence as Jimmy reflected. Then his face brightened.

"Let's talk about something pleasant. I have a hobby; I paint on wood."

He showed us a painting, ten by seven inches, of a camel in front of the pyramids painted in muted tones of blue, yellow and green. We both exclaimed how wonderful it was. Next, he showed us a painting of an Egyptian woman pouring water from an urn.

"Which one would you like?" he asked.

We protested that we should not take his craft work from him.

"If you cannot decide which one you want, I would like you to take both."

He handed them to us. To refuse would have been extremely hurtful to him. We accepted them graciously.

The clock in the dining room struck nine. The time had passed quickly. I suggested it was time to leave because the hostel was two bus trips away and we weren't sure whether its front doors were locked at ten or eleven.

Jimmy, Janet, and Anna Maria accompanied us to the bus stop.

The light of a bus cut a yellow swath in the darkness. We stepped aboard, clutching our mementos of an evening with a special family. We waved to them as the bus drew away, enroute to Tahrir Square where, just a day before, Jimmy had given us a helping hand.

Sudan

Sand and silence

Desert trek to Meroë, December 1978
See map, page 13

Seven of us were trekking across the brown, sandy wastes in northern Sudan. We were probably the most ill-equipped group ever to hike in a desert. Only half-an-hour into our trek Mike sidled up to me and asked: "Can you spare some water?"

I was taken aback. "Finished yours already?"

"No, I didn't bring any."

Penny and I had been travelling in Egypt from north to south, exploring the pyramids and other archaeological sites. At Aswan on the Nile River we boarded a ferry – a twin-decked, flat-topped barge powered by a diesel engine, with two barges lashed to either side. This strange looking hybrid carried about 700 Sudanese and Egyptians, and fourteen Westerners, along Lake Nasser for forty-three hours.

Our destination, Wadi Halfa, came into view – a desolate, dusty little Sudanese town surrounded by desert and pyramid-shaped sandstone mounds. A railway line ran from there to Khartoum, Sudan's capital. Our loosely knit group of independent travellers boarded the waiting train.

Penny and I had read about an ancient city in the desert called Meroë, pronounced Merro-way, which had more than fifty pyramids and some ruined temples. We hoped to visit it and wanted others to join us. Evi, from Germany, laughed and said the place couldn't exist because she had never heard of it. Some travellers were sceptical but others wanted to hear more.

I explained that back in the fifth century BC, the city was doing all right for itself. It had iron ore deposits and a small iron smelting industry. There were lots of trees and pasture lands on the plain of Meroë and well-watered crop lands. There was plenty of food to feed the population.

Then the power brokers decided to make Meroë the new capital of the Kingdom of Kush, doing away with Napata, the then-current capital which was in ruins after a battle with Egypt. The success of Meroë's productive iron industry probably helped sway the vote. Developers moved in, took over some prime real estate and started to build homes, government buildings and pyramids using local sandstone and granite. Workers flocked in, looking for jobs. Times were good. The iron ore smelting industry boomed and Meroë exported the manufacturing technique to other parts of Africa. This helped put Meroë on the map, making it a cultural link between Egypt and the rest of Africa.

Artists developed goldsmithing techniques, fashioning their own style of jewellery, different from that of Egypt which had some cultural influence over Meroë. Agriculture prospered. They had water wheels on the Nile to irrigate the land.

The prosperity of Meroë caught the attention of the bigwigs in Rome who sent a small army along the Nile to check them out. The army gave Meroë a couple of jabs in the side and then went home.

Meroë continued along its merry way.

Then environmental mismanagement reared its ugly head. To feed the iron smelting furnaces all the trees were eventually cut down. Even the puny, thorny acacia bushes didn't escape the axe. Business dropped off but the people hung on. But they had another problem – a lingering border dispute with King Ezana of Axum in Ethiopia. The dispute dragged on, trying the patience of Ezana who raised an army in 350 AD and sent it off to fix Meroë once and for all. "Lay waste to the place," he said. And they did.

With their city destroyed, the inhabitants fled, and with the trees gone the desert took over. All that's left today are the pyramids, slag heaps and foundations of some temples.

"Well," I concluded. "That's about the whole story. Is anyone interested?"

Five people were intrigued enough to join us. There was Donn, a tall American with a long, fiery-red beard that reached to his chest. He was an artist who had switched his palette and paint brush for a backpack. His companion Karen, a slim, self-assured American was always ready for any adventure, she said. Next was Mohammed, a Lebanese-American who called himself Mike. His face was covered by a bushy black beard and his eyes by thick glasses – enormous circles rimmed with dark frames. He was partially blind, he told us. I admired his desire to travel with this challenge.

Also in the group was Paul, medium height and trim with a mound of dark, wavy hair, accompanied by Jude, a spirited, rosy-cheeked woman with blonde locks. They had only recently married in England. "It was too cold to go to Blackpool for our honeymoon," Paul explained, "so we came to sunny Africa."

Our mixed bag of people got off the train at Shendi and found accommodation at the National, the only hotel in town. According to our Michelin map Shendi was the nearest big town to Meroë.

The next day in the market place we found a five-tonne cargo truck heading north to Kabushiya which would take us close to our destination. We climbed up the tailgate to sit on top of bales of cotton. About a dozen Sudanese Arab passengers, dressed in their cool white robes, were already sprawled on top of the cargo. We flashed friendly smiles and hoped they didn't mind our joining them as they shifted to make space.

No real road existed, just a sandy wasteland of old ruts. As the wheels rolled along them and churned through desert sand the truck swayed dangerously. We clung tightly to the ropes around the bales, fearing if we relaxed we would bounce off the top. The roar of the truck's engine and the rattling of its wooden sides made conversation impossible. I glanced over my shoulder at another fully loaded truck following in our tracks, edging closer. It pitched and rolled over the ruts like a drunken dinosaur.

Ahead stood a ramshackle building – a truck stop where tea was sold. The shack had a thatched roof held up by tree limbs. The two trucks arrived together and the drivers cut their engines and raised the hoods. Steam hissed from both radiators, obvious signs that the trucks weren't going farther.

We were in the middle of nowhere. I felt responsible. I had hoped we would all be dropped off near the pyramids.

We scanned the horizon for signs of Meroë. To the northeast on the distant horizon, Paul pointed out some hazy triangular bumps. Meroë?

Mike strolled over to our truck driver, chatted with him and confirmed it was Meroë, and that the way to get there was by foot.

The driver warned him about little flying insects in the desert which attack the ears and once they are in they are hard to get out. "They keep buzzing and can make you crazy," Mike said. "We should wear a scarf over our ears. Also, watch for scorpions."

I was surprised at all this information. "The driver's English must be good," I said.

"No," said Mike, "I understand some Arabic."

We bought boiled water for our canteens at the truck stop and, as we intended completing the walk to Meroë and back the same day, we intentionally carried only meagre provisions: bread, biscuits, grapefruit and dates. We started out in midmorning. The sun was high in the blue sky and the air, dry – comfortable for walking. The only sounds were the crunch of sandals on the small stones and patches of sand, and the swish of knapsacks on our backs.

No one spoke. I imagined everyone was contemplating the stark beauty around us, or maybe wondering why they agreed to come to this desolate place. A few hardy shrubs with shiny green leaves the size of a person's hand poked up through the sand. Surface water was nonexistent. The plants got their nourishment at night when wind carried moisture from the Nile River.

Occasionally a breath of wind scooped up dry tumbleweeds

and rolled them along the ground, bringing some semblance of life to the quiet terrain. I watched for scorpions but didn't see any. I guessed they were under rocks or in holes to escape the heat of the day.

My thoughts were interrupted when Mike approached me for a drink of water. He didn't own a canteen. I realized what a reckless bunch we were: ill-prepared and not knowing each other's strengths and weaknesses. I gave him a swig from my canteen.

Suddenly Jude screamed and smacked the side of her head.

"One of those insects flew into my ear."

Paul ran to her side. "Is it still there?"

She thumped her ear. "I'm not sure."

Mike yelled out, "Can you hear a buzzing sound?"

She stood quietly. "No." She sounded relieved.

Quickly, we all pulled scarves and handkerchiefs out of our knapsacks and covered our ears.

Ahead of us the pyramids of Meroë were slowly getting bigger. Another hour or so and we'd be there. As we pressed on, our sandals stirred up puffs of fine sand. It seeped through our clothes, blew up our noses and settled between our toes.

When we got closer we climbed over old slag heaps, the tailings of the iron-smelting process which helped bring fame to the city. As we neared the closest pyramid we passed hardy desert bushes eking out their lonely existence, then we struggled up a golden sand dune which had blown up against the stone blocks of a pyramid.

We broke up to explore at our own pace. Penny and I wandered among rows of pyramids clustered together and discovered we could stand between two pyramids and touch them both at the same time. The pyramids appeared to be miniatures of Egyptian ones but with noticeable differences in the construction, dimensions and angles.

Meroë's pyramids, constructed with small sandstone blocks, rose to a height of only fifty to one hundred feet, rather small when compared with Egypt's highest at almost 500 feet. And the angles at which the buildings rose were steeper than those of Egypt.

The peaks had been destroyed by overzealous treasure seekers in the 1800s who had dislodged blocks of masonry in their vain search for jewellery rumoured to be at the top of each one. From ground level we saw that the pyramids were built by placing two layers of stone blocks over a mound of rubble.

A unique feature of Meroë's pyramids was the funerary chapel attached to the front of each pyramid. We had seen nothing like this in Egypt. We examined the exterior walls of one of the chapels and discovered a sculpted relief which depicted men from the south (they had negroid features) being paraded as slaves or prisoners of war. The men were linked to each other by ropes or chains. Another chapel's wall depicted Egyptian gods, proving a cultural link with Egypt. I was fascinated seeing what I had only read about.

Archaeologists who excavated here reported that each pyramid was a solid mass of rubble and stone built over a burial chamber cut out of the bedrock to provide a tomb for royalty. The pyramids therefore were not tombs, but tombstones.

We snooped around the exteriors of two dozen pyramids; there may have been more scattered elsewhere but we didn't search any further. Instead, we stumbled upon the foundations of a temple about the size of a tennis court. Only two or three layers of stone foundation blocks showed above ground. A combination of Ezana's army and erosion had most likely reduced the temple to rubble.

After exploring Meroë for two hours we regrouped and discussed what we had seen to make sure no one had missed anything important. Donn said: "Until a couple of days ago I didn't even know there were pyramids in Sudan. The trip has definitely been worth the effort to get here." He seemed to have spoken for everyone, because they all agreed.

Karen remarked that she found the place haunting, then switched her conversation to a more practical matter. "How much water do we have?"

Our canteens were almost empty. And we had a desert to cross. We were all sharing our water with Mike who apologized and said he'd figure out a way to make amends. Penny and I only had enough water for an occasional sip from the canteen's plastic cap but we made sure Mike got his capful.

From a vantage point on a rise near a pyramid we surveyed the desert plain. I found it hard to believe the land stretched out before us once supported trees and green pastures. On the western horizon we made out a blurred grove of trees along the banks of the Nile. We shuffled down the sandy incline to the flat ground. As we did so the trees disappeared from sight.

We trudged across the desert. The wrath of the sun bore down on our heads like a broiler and melted the horizon into shimmering mirages of lakes and trees. I hoped that the grove of trees we had seen from the vantage point on the rise was real.

We stopped often to sip water. When Jude gave Mike a drink he remarked that we'd soon be at the Nile and wouldn't have to ration water. With that said he set off.

Paul yelled: "You're going in the wrong direction."

Mike turned. "Are you sure?"

It was a good question. We all looked around . . . and around. We saw neither Meroë nor the grove of trees.

Karen suggested we vote on which direction to go. From the sun's position we figured we should be heading southwest. Then we voted to go in that direction.

After an hour we came across a dark angular man in a white robe sitting under a lone acacia tree, the only tree visible in the brown, dry expanse of desert. From the branches hung a couple of goatskin bags of water. He eyed us with curiosity and delight and offered to fill our canteens. We squatted awhile under the tree. What a relief to be in the shade. We offered to pay for the water but he refused to accept anything. We thanked him for his kindness and bade goodbye. It seemed strange to leave him alone in the wilderness.

The afternoon sun beat down, warming the sand beneath our sandals. After two hours Donn, who had ventured ahead, turned and yelled, "I can see a couple of huts."

The sighting invigorated me. As we approached I glimpsed a woman disappear into her abode – a dome-shaped hut covered with woven reed mats and rags. A goat was tethered near the doorway and at her feet a newborn kid – curled up with afterbirth still attached. The dutiful nanny goat cleaned the moist skin of her newborn. It touched us to witness the beginning of a new life in the desert.

The woman emerged from her hut. Dark-complexioned, gaunt and draped in animal hides and a sheet of dirt-stained cotton fabric, she approached with a wary smile and handed Penny a tin bowl with enough water for all of us. I felt humbled that she would share her precious water for which she likely had walked a long way.

The water was cool and refreshing. We all took turns drinking from the bowl and expressed our thanks by saying *shukran*. A smile illuminated her face every time we thanked her.

In the far distance we saw the grove of trees along the Nile. We bade *salaam* (peace) and continued our trek to the road beside the river. The memory of her desert hospitality will stay with me forever.

Because of our diversions in the desert we took three long, hot hours to trek from the pyramids to the river. We waited under the blazing sun for an hour before a cargo truck stopped. It was already full with Sudanese passengers in their flowing robes, and sacks of empty bottles.

We climbed up the tailgate and greeted them with *salaam aleikoum* (peace be with you). They made no effort to move aside and didn't look pleased that we would be taking up some of their space. We smiled to let them know we were friendly. They relented and we all found places to settle.

The truck hurtled along the sandy track, pitching and rolling. We were perched fifteen feet in the air with nothing to shield us from the hot, dry wind. Sand blew up my nostrils, into my lungs. We bounced around on the lumpy cargo. Dust billowed from the wheels; black diesel belched from the exhaust pipe. Every time we slowed, the foul smelling mixture caught up to the truck and blew into our windburned faces. It caused us all to gag. I glanced at Penny. Her face, like everyone else's, was covered in a layer of fine desert dust, giving her a ghostly look.

Mike's black beard turned a powdery white. And he looked parched. I handed him my canteen which he accepted with a guilty nod. Then he faced the rest of our group and shouted above the rattling bottles and noisy engine. "When we reach Shendi, I'm buying the drinks!"

Sudan (part one)

Man overboard!

The White Nile: Kosti to Bor, December 1978
See map, page 13

"Man overboard!" a Sudanese man yelled in English.

I saw a man's head bob up and down as he struggled to grab hold of reeds that lined the river, but he couldn't get to them through the floating water hyacinths. No one volunteered to jump into the river to help – it was infested with crocodiles.

Our journey along the White Nile River in Sudan started in Kosti, a river port of sandy streets and square, squat, stuccoed buildings, located south of Khartoum.

Penny and I had booked a two-berth cabin in second class to go upriver to Juba, a journey of about eleven days on a paddle steamer called the Marra.

Two other couples also booked second class cabins: Paul and Jude whom we knew from our trek to Meroë, and Reiner and Quem, a German couple we had met in Egypt. With our student discounts for which we all qualified (we all went to the University of Life!) each cabin was $60 for the journey. Third class, by comparison, consisted of deck space without any privacy, but for half the price.

Travelling was made easy by our being able to converse with Sudanese Arabs and blacks in English. Once known as Anglo-Egyptian Sudan, the country had been controlled by the British who introduced English – which is still taught in schools in the predominantly Muslim north. In the south, Christian missionaries introduced English as well as religion.

At the dock Penny and I found the Marra, due to leave the next day. To our dismay the paddle wheel lay dismantled on the dock. The chief engineer stood staring at the iron frame and paddle boards laid out in front of him. He looked concerned as he stroked his chin, but he assured us he'd have it put back together in time for tomorrow's departure. With parts scattered about the dock we hoped he was right.

The entire superstructure had been painted white but that was many years ago, judging from the peeling paint. Tied up nearby sat six barges for second and third class passengers which would be lashed to the paddle steamer. The engineer told us about some of the features of the Marra. It comprised crew's quarters, toilets, a restaurant that served rice and beans, a lounge room and a couple of first class cabins. It was fifty years old and ran on diesel fuel. He added it had been due for retirement thirty years ago. This news didn't give us much confidence. However, hundreds of people in the town were waiting to board, so we could only assume it would be safe.

To buy supplies for the eleven-day journey we headed to the local market. Our first purchase was a small fifty-cent charcoal-burning stove, a common cooking appliance among the Sudanese. Made from a four-gallon oil can, its sides had been cut out to insert the charcoal. We also bought a bag of charcoal, candles, insect spray, matches, a water canteen, water purifying tablets and two plastic buckets.

We stocked up on food: packets of macaroni, spaghetti and cheese, cans of baked beans, sardines, mackerel, tuna, and jars of jam. Fresh produce included potatoes, onions, cucumbers, tomatoes, green peppers, lemons, bananas, grapefruit, dates and peanuts. Finally, at the bakery we bought more than a dozen flat loaves of unleavened bread.

We joined the other four travellers in hiring a man with a horse and cart to transport all our backpacks, equipment and food to the steamer. Fortunately for the skinny horse whose brown hide stretched tightly over its rib cage, the trip took only ten minutes.

Penny and I found cabin number 10 on barge number 693 and started to make the grubby little place livable. We swept up the thirty-odd dead cockroaches and tossed them overboard, wiped down the walls which had a buildup of oily diesel fumes, placed brown paper over the two greasy bunk beds, strung a clothes line, stashed food in a cupboard, laid a plastic table cloth over the tray-sized table, spread blue cotton sheets (which had been provided) on the bunks, placed our stove and bag of charcoal in the passage-way and finally snipped coloured pictures from a *Time* magazine and taped them to the walls to give a homey feeling to the cabin. We were ready to leave on our river journey.

The next day six barges, already loaded with passengers, were assembled for departure. The two second class barges with cabins were lashed to either side of the paddle steamer. Three third class barges were placed together in front of them, and another in the forefront. We estimated there were about one thousand Sudanese passengers, including about seventy soldiers in khaki uniforms. Our route along the White Nile to Juba, almost 900 miles upstream, was going to take us through the largest swamp in the world, the Sudd, a fearsome, watery area of papyrus reeds, hippopotamuses and innumerable crocodiles. It covered an area the size of England and Wales.

In the 1800s, boats of explorers, and slave and ivory traders, were lost in the Sudd. They became trapped by tenacious grasses and floating islands of reeds. The region is called As Sudd in Arabic, meaning barrier – an apt name.

Just two hours out of Kosti the engine coughed and died. We were defenceless against the current; it rammed the barges against the riverbank. And that is where we moored while the engineer tinkered late into the afternoon without success.

Near the equator the sun descends quickly to the western horizon. I watched it go down and was struck by a feeling of reverence as the sky changed from blue to yellow to scarlet. Silhouettes of people on the barge roofs were etched against the reddish sky. The river was awash with a pink sheen.

By five-thirty, the sun had gone. An hour later a half-moon rose in the east, casting a pewter light on the river.

Passengers on the barges bent over pots that steamed on their charcoal stoves. My stomach growled as aromas wafted across the decks towards us. It was time to prepare our stew.

Throughout the night the metal hulls of the barges scraped against each other. We slept fitfully because of the noise.

We woke early to a sunny day and the sound of tinkering in the engine room. Whether that was good news or bad, we didn't know. Finally, at lunchtime the steamer vibrated when the engine started, the horn blew and the steamer dragged us away from the muddy bank.

Penny and I explored the cluster of barges and met eight Westerners who had staked their places with their sleeping bags on the deck of a third class barge. Among them was Mike from our trek to Meroë. That evening Mike, Paul, Jude, Penny and I shared a stew cooked on our charcoal stove. The meal rated five stars compared with the meagre rations of bread, biscuits, grapefruit and dates we shared on our trek to see the pyramids.

Penny discovered that some of our flat bread had developed small spots of green mould caused by the humidity. She suggested we dehydrate the bread by toasting it over our stove. Later, to make it edible, we could sprinkle water over it and toast it again.

She sliced all the flat loaves in half. I stuck a fork into the first piece of bread and held it over the glowing embers until completely dry and hard. I removed the hot fork from the toast and noticed some tasty crumbs on the tines. Without thinking I raised the fork to my lips. WOW! My lips sizzled. I rocketed forward in shock and just missed the hot stove. I finished up with bulbous, scorch- marked lips that took more than a week to heal.

On the third day we climbed up the boat's framework of roof supports and sat on the flat top to enjoy the warm sunshine. The rooftop had become a place to gather, not only for the Sudanese, but also for the Western passengers. For miles around, the flat grassy plains were studded with stunted trees and enclaves of circular, thatch-roofed huts. At the edge of the riverbank we were thrilled by the rare sighting of three hippopotamuses wallowing in grey, sleazy mud, their bodies out of sight and only their eyes, nose and twitching ears visible. Moments later we spotted crocodiles lazing on the bank, their jaws wide open, cooling their bodies.

A cool wind skimmed along the river and the sun painted the sky red as it disappeared below the horizon. We discovered the only light bulb in our cabin had blown so we had an evening snack by candlelight and turned in for an early night. A mistake!

Within a few minutes we heard footsteps and men's voices in the passageway that ran beside our cabin. The sliding wooden shutter of our window was open. (There was no glass.) All of a sudden one of the men shone a flashlight through the window into my eyes. Startled, I jumped off the bunk, leapt to the window and shouted at him to take his flashlight and move on. Someone laughed as they left, which annoyed me.

"What's happening?" Penny said in a frightened tone.

"Whatever it was I think it's over now."

But five minutes later the men returned. Another flash of blinding light shone through the window. I sprang off the bunk and, as I reached for the sliding shutter, I caught a glimpse of a face with three-day-old stubble and bloodshot eyes. I rammed the wooden shutter along its track but the madman outside clenched his fist and drove it into the shutter with such force that he cracked the wooden slats. Some of them flew into the cabin; one hit my forehead and drew blood. I yelled at the man outside and he roared at me, his breath a blast of whisky.

The noise attracted numerous onlookers who hung over the railing of the neighbouring barge. My adversary eyed the remaining slats and clenched his fists but his colleagues grabbed him. He started ranting: "Tickets, tickets."

He's a ticket collector, I realized. I explained to him and his colleagues in a rational tone that I had shown my tickets earlier. The madman then countered, "Passports, passports." A polite official said to him, "Tomorrow." The officials shuffled away with the violent man.

The polite one stayed behind and asked if his colleagues had knocked on the door to ask for tickets, and I told him no. He apologized and followed the others. I fixed my head wound with ointment and a band aid. I guessed the ticket collector would be resting his head and knuckles over the next couple of days.

On our fourth day we arrived in Malakal just as the sun was rising over the mosque, the hospital, town council offices and Resident Magistrate's Court. We watched passengers disembark and new ones walk up the gangplank, including half a dozen shackled prisoners wearing prison garb – beige linen shorts and collarless smocks.

With Paul and Jude we went ashore and discovered the open air produce market where we stocked up on pumpkin, aubergines, tomatoes, and peanut butter sold by the spoonful out of a bowl. At the bakery we bought small loaves of bread. After returning to the steamer Paul cut into a loaf and discovered dried bugs inside. Obviously they had not been fast enough to escape when the baker kneaded the dough. I borrowed his knife and cut into a loaf and discovered a cockroach in the middle of it, contentedly nibbling the newly baked bread. Cockroaches really are among the world's longest surviving species if they can survive being cooked in an oven.

Some of the local passengers found the animal market and bought a sheep – probably for a festive occasion, a common thing to do. A young man carried the sheep up the gangplank while others followed with armloads of grass. Then they tethered it to one of the railings near the bow of their barge.

We watched the engineer as he tightened nuts and bolts on the paddles and iron framework. This was his last chance to ensure the machinery was in working order before entering the infamous Sudd. After five hours in Malakal the engine emitted a throaty roar and the paddles swirled mud. The barges shook, shivered and bumped together. Slowly we continued the journey upstream.

We returned to our cabin and discovered that three of the prisoners who had boarded were sitting directly across from our door, but on an adjoining barge. They sat on their haunches, their arms and legs shackled with chains to a railing. One of the men stirred their lunch – a pot of beans – over a charcoal stove.

A Sudanese passenger told us one was a murderer and the other two, thieves. They were allocated deck space near the public toilets which became blocked on the first day on the river. Some of the one thousand passengers using the facilities daily left the deck area in front of the toilets a minefield of excrement. Twice daily a ferry employee hosed down the deck but it was difficult to keep clean. Despite their crimes we sympathized with the prisoners for being chained so close to the reeking loos.

Some of the Western travellers arranged with the two first class passengers to use their locked toilets. Preferring to be independent we used one of the buckets bought in Kosti as our chamber pot. My domestic duty was to empty it over the side each morning before daylight.

Immediately after a golden sunrise on the fifth day, Penny and I hoisted ourselves onto the roof and saw that we were now steaming slowly through the Sudd. Our assembly of barges had entered the Sudd some hours before, travelling with the aid of a searchlight. From the wheelhouse, the searchlight had swept the river in search of drifting vegetation that could block the channel. The current carried rotten vegetation downstream, compacting it into floating islands fifteen to twenty feet thick.

We found ourselves lulled by the sea of waving papyrus reeds and grasses which stretched as far as the flat horizon. The stalks grew ten or more feet high with arcing fronds. Along the waterway they appeared as impenetrable walls of interlocking reeds. Water hyacinths, many with mauve and purple flowers, floated against the thickets along the edges of the channels. The swamp attracted numerous species of water birds including herons which swooped gracefully over the water in search of fish.

When we returned to our cabin from the roof we met a local man waiting for us with his five-year-old son who had a problem – a slashed arm. The man showed us a razor blade the boy had been playing with.

We were unsure why the man came to us. Maybe he thought that the chances of Western travellers carrying a medical kit were good. He was right.

Blood oozed steadily from his son's arm which someone had   crudely bandaged. Gingerly Penny and I unwrapped the blood-soaked bandage and were repulsed by a quarter-inch deep gash about two inches long. It required immediate first aid. We needed boiling water and we needed Jude, a registered nurse.

Penny climbed to the roof and called her while I lit our charcoal stove. I gave a candy to the boy to soothe him. Within no time we had bathed the gash and added ointment. From her comprehensive first aid kit, Jude took suturing tape and placed it tightly over the gash to bind the edges together, then bandaged it. She tried to explain to the father that his son must rest his arm and not play. What five-year-old boy would understand that? Within five minutes the boy had escaped and with his brother was swinging on the railings, undoing Jude's medical work. So, we repeated the procedure.

As we drank tea with the father in the second class common room we heard a commotion and saw passengers arriving from the other barges. They climbed over our railing and lined up outside the door of the common room. Word had spread like wildfire that there were doctors on board. They came with headaches, stomach aches, cuts and sores on their arms and legs, imagined ailments and plain curiosity.

We were overwhelmed and, other than Jude, felt inadequate and ill prepared to be administering first aid and, in some cases, false hopes. We treated as many as feasible from our meagre supplies of aspirin, ointment, band aids and bandages until we were down to what we needed to keep for ourselves. Someone of authority must have realized this and ordered people to leave us alone because the number of patients suddenly diminished.

In the morning of the seventh day we approached Adok. We looked westwards over the swamp towards some low mounds and saw roofs of huts peeping over the green reeds.

We watched as villagers, mainly women, streamed along a narrow trail that had been hacked out of the reeds from their village to the river's edge. These slim, straight-backed women balanced large rolls of yellowing reeds on their heads. The reeds could be used for walls, roofs and mats and were a valuable trade item.

Because there wasn't a dock the steamer pulled up as close as possible to the riverbank so a crewman could lower a couple of gangplanks. But some eager traders jumped off the boat with their wares and sloshed through the shallow water to get an early start with the trading process. In exchange for the reeds the villagers received cloth, cooking pots, charcoal stoves, sacks of millet and stalks of sugar cane.

The scene we witnessed belonged to an earlier century. Time seemed to have stood still for these people whose only contact with the outside world was by paddle steamer. I felt privileged to be able to visit this small pocket of Africa.

Fishermen in dugout canoes paddled eagerly to the barges and offered for sale their four-foot-long Nile perches. Unfortunately they were still trying to sell their fish by the time we pulled away from the reeds and continued upstream.

Penny and I went to check on the young boy's arm and were thankful to see it was healing. His mother, a cheerful, round faced woman with short ebony hair and soft brown eyes that matched her skin sat on the floor, the family possessions piled around her. Her feet were propped on a stool, after being beautified with henna. She had to stay still until the henna mud dried. Using sign language, she insisted Penny sit beside her and have a henna treatment on her right hand.

We had seen henna applied before, in the Middle East, where it was used as a solid reddish paint on the soles of the feet and palms of the hands. Obtained from a bush, the green leaves are crushed into a powder then mixed with water. The result is a reddish mud mixture.

In Sudan the use of henna has developed to a high artistic level. The woman drew flowers and leaves and geometric designs on Penny's hand with a ballpoint pen, then used a pointed stick to spread the reddish mud onto the lines of blue ink. After an hour or so her hand was dry, ready for the mud to be washed off. Penny was delighted to have the henna applied but as the days wore on and the pattern didn't fade she became self-conscious as her hand looked dirty. Three weeks passed before it faded.

The next morning started like any other. I lit the charcoal stove, sprinkled water on our dehydrated bread to soften it, then toasted it over the embers with a fork.

A local man came by wanting to light his cigarette from our fire. He was coal black and slender and, like many Sudanese, stood over six feet, had curly hair, full lips and a nose which was flat and splayed – all characteristics of the Dinka tribe. Of the 596 tribes in Sudan, the Dinka is one of the main ones. His forehead scarring indicated he was a Dinka. In early childhood, cuts had been made in a horizontal line across his forehead and filled with gunpowder, resulting in a series of grey beads, or bumps.

He bent down over the stove and, with his long black fingers, plucked out a red hot ember and lit his cigarette. He didn't flinch or utter a sound. We were shocked. "That's hot!" Penny exclaimed.

"Me African," he said, and smiled, implying it was no big deal.

How did he do it? Had he lost his sense of touch? Why weren't his fingers burnt? We remained mystified.

All of a sudden, above the sound of the Marra's engine, we heard yells coming from the back of the boat. Passengers on the roof immediately dropped down onto our deck, leapt over the railings and dashed to join the throng gathering at the stern. I was right behind them.

"Man overboard!" a Sudanese man shouted in English.

A passenger stood ready to throw a rope. Someone warned him about the crocodiles.

In the river a man's head bobbed up and down as he thrashed his arms at the water, desperate to reach the green wall of papyrus reeds beside the river channel. But water hyacinths blocked his way. He lashed wildly at the hyacinths. They came away in his hands. He began to flounder. To my horror the current swept him away.

The skipper reversed the engine and we steamed down the river after him. Everyone was looking over the railings, hoping to spot him in the hyacinths or the reeds. We spent forty-five minutes going up and down the river but could not find him. I heard someone say he was the man who had carried the sheep aboard. He had bought it for a special occasion: his wedding. Someone else said he fell in when he leaned over the edge of the barge to collect water in a bucket tied to the end of a rope.

His sheep grazed nonchalantly on grass at the bow. A Sudanese man told us it would be taken care of by the man's relatives who had been travelling with him to the wedding.

Although we didn't know the man we felt an emptiness. His relatives and friends on board must be in shock. A pall settled over the passengers who were close to him. At the end of a sad day the sun went down, seeping into a morass of darkened reeds, draining the colours from the sky and showing the river as a faint ribbon of black glass. Then the clammy air turned cold.

On December the twenty-third, our supposed second last day on the Marra, we arrived in Bor which was linked to Juba by road. We had a choice: travel by passenger truck to Juba – a five-hour trip – or stay on the steamer. The Marra would take two or three more days because of the shallowness of the river and the profusion of weeds that prevented travel at night. After ten days the barge felt like home so we decided to stay on board. It would be comforting to be in familiar surroundings on Christmas Day with our travelling companions.

Sudan (part two)

Run, whitey, run!

The White Nile at Bor, December 1978
See map, page 13

The Marra stopped in Bor to unload some of its cargo. Dock workers carried off a variety of building materials on their backs – cement, lumber and corrugated iron sheets. The stop allowed time for passengers to disembark, new ones to board and enabled foreigners like us to fan out and explore the village.

One of the main cattle-raising tribes in this area were the Nuer, distinguishable by tribal scars of three or four parallel lines on their foreheads, administered with a hot spear tip when they were boys.

Near the dock Penny and I watched Nuer skinners scrape meat and fat from cow hides stretched between large wooden frames. Meat was eaten on festive and religious occasions, and the fatty grease used as healing ointment. Nothing was wasted. The hides provided sleeping mats, drum skins, rope, and roof coverings for their huts. The humped, long-horned zebu cattle also supplied them with milk, their horns for utensils, bones for weapons and ornaments, and dung for fuel.

We wandered away from the dock to a street lined with mud-walled shops selling cooking oil, candles, soap, tomatoes and metal spear heads. The women in the street wore long dresses of colourful, printed fabric. Some men wore shirts and shorts while the more traditional men wore bright red robes like Roman togas.

We passed a shop selling imported sherry. At that moment we heard the horn of the paddle steamer call everyone aboard.

I turned to Penny. "You'd better go back. I'll be along in a few moments."

While Penny hurried back to the boat I entered the liquor store and stared at the sherry. With Christmas only two days away, I decided to surprise the other travellers with a bottle we could share. Behind the wooden counter stood a beanpole-of-a-man in his twenties with tribal scars on his face.

"How much?" I asked, pointing to a bottle.

"Eighty-five piastres."

The horn sounded again. There was no time to bargain. I handed him a 100-piastre note and he plunked a bottle on the counter.

"My change?" I asked.

"No change," he replied.

The horn sounded again. I felt edgy; I should be going.

"My change," I insisted.

He shook his head. He knew I had to rush away. I could forgo the change, after all it was only worth thirty cents but I decided not to let him cheat me. Why was I concerned about thirty cents? We were on a fifteen-month backpacking trip and every cent was important.

To get my change I decided to embarrass him. I didn't know which tribe he belonged to because his tribal scars were not distinctive. I had to guess.

"Dinka no good," I said.

He smirked and replied: "Me not Dinka. Me Nuer."

"Well, Nuer no good. Give me my change."

The horn sounded again. I heard an urgency in its throaty call.

I stood my ground.

Finally he put my change on the counter.

I grabbed the coins and the sherry, spun round and dashed along the dusty street as fast as my legs would carry me.

The horn bellowed again!

I put on an extra spurt and ran full tilt, puffing and wheezing and tasting sweat as it trickled down my cheeks. My feet pounded the dirt road through the village. Thatch-roofed huts and tin-covered shanty shops appeared a blur as I hurtled past. Young village boys yelled "Run, whitey, run!" and "Go, go, go!"

I streaked around a curve, saw the boat and spotted Penny on the gangplank, waving frantically. She leapt aboard. I glanced up, saw our friends on the steamer's roof, held the bottle of sherry high and loped across the gangplank. Then I heard three resounding cheers!

I looked over my shoulder and saw two crewmen quickly drag the gangplank aboard.

Our fellow passengers told me how Penny had stood stubbornly on the gangplank, not letting the crewmen pull it aboard. The crewmen kept badgering her to get on board.

"We called to her to hang in there and not to move off the gangplank," one of them told me.

I glanced at Penny who had a look of relief on her face. She told me she tried to ignore the crew at first, then pretended not to understand them. She added that all the time they were yelling at her she was trying to keep her balance on the narrow gangplank as it bounced gently up and down over the water.

I felt dreadful for causing her so much grief.

She continued: "My heart was thumping. I thought you may have had an accident. I was scared the boat would leave you behind."

I felt rotten.

Was the bottle worth the trouble?

I'd have to wait to find out.

Christmas was almost upon us. I hoped we could all celebrate together with a toast of sherry on the Nile.

Sudan (part three)

A Christmas to remember

The White Nile: Bor to Juba, December 1978
See map, page 13

As we steamed south against the current from Bor to Juba, our progress was slowed by the shallowness of the White Nile and the interminable weeds. The scenery changed gradually from reeds and grassland to stunted trees and scattered villages.

We approached Terakeka village, a huddle of rectangular and circular huts crudely constructed of sticks and millet straw. They stood on a flat, desolate area of grey sand above the river. Small trees struggled to survive in the sand between the huts.

The skipper maneuvered the barges to the riverbank, crewmen lowered a gangplank and looped hawsers around trees.

We stepped warily along the rickety gangplank, and followed the traders who disembarked with reed mats for sale. These merchants looked cool in their flowing cotton gallabiahs – collarless white or beige full-sleeved shirts that reached below the knees. Village men who wore rough, loosely woven togas approached the traders to buy the reed mats. Village boys watched the trading process to learn how to bargain. We looked forward to the stopovers at villages because they gave us a glimpse into the lives of these riverside dwellers.

I assumed the women were working in the millet fields in the hinterland because we didn't see them in the village. Their basic household wares lay neatly arranged beside their huts: stools, baskets, cow-hide mats, ropes, gourds, clay pots and a mortar and pestle for pounding grain.

The steamer's horn sounded twenty minutes later and, while the stern paddles churned the mud, passengers hurried up the gangplank.

Farther upstream another village came into view, a cluster of straw huts under leafless trees. Dust swirled over the barren land and swept down to the riverside. This was the dry season so the water level was low. These village huts were temporarily built on the riverbank to be close to a source of water and for fishing.

We steamed by, blowing the horn, but didn't stop. Villagers, particularly young men and boys, appeared on the riverbank. They were stark naked, spears in their hands and covered from head to foot with white ash which made them look ghostly and warlike. We were about thirty feet from the riverbank, travelling through territory inhabited by the Dinka and Nuer tribes. They often went naked; the white ash protected them from mosquitos and other insects.

Some Sudanese passengers shouted to them and they responded with whoops and a brandishing of spears. As the paddle steamer forged upstream we witnessed recycling in action, an important part of the African way of life. Passengers hurled empty tin cans, bottles and plastic containers to the young boys who sprinted along the riverside trail, scooping them up. The discarded containers would be used in their homes.

A few of the seventy soldiers on board almost went berserk when they saw the other travellers and us raise our cameras. One of the Germans was pounced on by a particularly aggressive private. An officer stepped forward to intervene and explain they didn't want us to take photographs.

"Why?" someone asked.

"We don't want you to show pictures of our naked people to your friends at home because they will laugh at us."

We denied we would do that. He was not convinced. He ordered his men to keep their eyes on us.

One of the soldiers accused Mike of taking a picture and wanted to destroy the film. When Mike denied the accusation the man backed down. Another eager soldier wanted to confiscate Reiner's camera but Reiner also denied taking a picture and was let off with a warning. Whether or not they took photos remained their secret.

We passed close to the riverside where small herds of long-horned zebu cattle were cared for by naked herders, some of whom were also covered in white ash to repel insects. Cattle were perceived as currency and a man's wealth was determined by the number of cattle he owned. When a man married it had to be to someone outside his own clan. Marriage was expensive. A bride was bought with an offering of cattle from the man's clan to the woman's clan.

On Sunday afternoon, December the twenty-fourth, we stopped at Mongalla. Tomorrow would be Christmas Day, the day we were due to arrive in Juba, but our arrival time was unpredictable. To ensure being together for Christmas, we Westerners decided to celebrate a day early and arranged to use the first class lounge room for our gathering.

As the sun set, draining colours from the sky, fourteen travellers took their contributions of peanuts, dates and sweets to the meeting room. We carried our own candles and flashlights because there were no light bulbs in the sockets of first class. Paul and Jude boiled water for tea on their charcoal stove on the deck, then cooked a large batch of drop scones. The aroma reminded me of my mother's home-baking. When I produced the bottle of sherry, Reiner tapped a drum roll on the table. I poured a ration into everyone's mug. We stood and wished each other Merry Christmas, good health and safe travels.

I looked around at our fellow travellers whose spirit of adventure had brought us together. A feeling of camaraderie was welling up in this small group on the riverbarge in the middle of Africa.

Penny suggested we sing some carols. The eight English-speaking travellers sang Joy to the World with gusto. The six Germans followed with Stille Nacht (Silent Night). Our carol singing drifted through the calm night air, attracting Sudanese Christian children from the town. They arrived in twos and threes, glided over the railings and stood quietly in the lounge room to listen. They clapped enthusiastically when we finished and we asked them to sing for us.

In the half-light of the candle-lit lounge all we could see of them were the whites of their large dark eyes as they looked out warmly from their raven-black faces. When they opened their mouths to sing Michael Rowed the Boat Ashore their faces lit up. The flash of their white teeth illuminated the room with goodwill. We listened to the perfect harmony of the almost thirty children. It stirred our hearts.

I glanced around the room at our group and caught burly, bearded Mike wiping a tear from his cheek. When the song ended we all jumped to our feet and applauded. They wanted us to sing again, so we gave them a rousing rendition of Rudolf the Red Nosed Reindeer, sung in English and German simultaneously.

The memorable Christmas Eve ended when the voice of a village elder summoned the children. They heeded his call, smiled their goodbyes and faded into the night.

We all agreed that the memory of this inspiring evening would stay with us forever.

My wish to celebrate Christmas on the Nile had come true.

Zaire (part one)
(today's Democratic Republic of Congo)

Heart of gold

Juba (Sudan) to Watsa (Zaire), December 1978
See map, page 13

Loud blasts from a bugle woke us with a start. The bugler was playing Reveille. I sleepily checked my watch; it was only five o'clock. For a brief moment I forgot where we were. The sky was changing from pink to mauve as Penny and I got up and watched a dozen or so policemen amble onto the parade ground, stand at attention and salute the Sudanese flag.

We had slept fitfully on the cold cement floor of the verandah of the police station at Yei, a border town in southwestern Sudan.

The previous day we had left Juba, a river port on the White Nile River in Sudan, and travelled for three hours with fifty locals in the back of a truck from there to Yei. The sky was black and moonless when we arrived at about eight-thirty, stopping outside a small, low building. Inside, a coal-oil lantern emitted a pale yellow glow which silhouetted the figures that moved inside the room.

With the other passengers we headed for the dimly lit room and found it was the immigration and police office where we had to show our passports and have them stamped. I asked the policeman in charge if there was somewhere to sleep at the police station as we planned on leaving early the next day. He guided us along a cement verandah crowded with bodies. Each body was covered from head to foot, wrapped in a blanket – the traditional African way of sleeping. We stepped gingerly over heads and feet until the policeman pointed to a vacant space on the floor where we could put down a plastic sheet, a blanket and our sleeping sheets.

In the morning I realized that the people we had almost tripped over in the dark were the same policemen who now stood on the parade ground. We felt quite safe on Sudan's wild west frontier.

Yei was a police and military town only forty kilometres from the Zaire border, and one hundred from Uganda. For many years weapons have been transported illegally over the borders, destined for the Southern Sudanese insurgents, the blacks in the south who want self-government.

Since the mid-1950s Sudan has had on-off civil strife based on the north-south distinction: Northern Sudan's language and culture is Arabic and the religion, Islam. The south is peopled mainly by blacks who have their own languages and culture and are either animists or Christians.

In 1969 I attempted to travel to Southern Sudan but had been denied a permit because of the fighting. The insurgents and the Sudanese government signed a peace accord in 1972 which lasted until 1983. Penny and I took advantage of peace in the region in 1979 to travel through Southern Sudan towards Zaire, known today as Democratic Republic of Congo.

On the verandah we boiled water for tea on our portable stove. Bread and jam fortified us for the next leg of our journey from Yei to Aba in Zaire. We searched for onward transport, aware there wasn't a bus service in this part of Zaire and that few people owned cars. We would have to find a truck to take us farther.

Parked near the police station was a green Toyota pickup truck. The driver, a Sudanese man with a pleasant smile and dressed in a cool, beige-coloured cotton robe told us he'd be going to Aba. He didn't know when but we could join him – for a fee, of course.

A policeman nearby overheard our enquiry. "The truck that brought you here from Juba is leaving soon for Aba; there is room for you," he said.

Thankful to get a more certain departure time we climbed into the back of the truck and sat on the floor to wait with a dozen or so locals. Within half-an-hour we were bouncing along a dirt road of red earth that snaked across an undulating plain past villages of thatch-roofed huts and fields of tall, green sorghum stalks. For three hours red dust billowed behind the truck until we finally climbed down in the village of Aba.

Houses were built with locally made bricks – a mixture of mud and straw baked in the sun – and roofed with corrugated iron sheets held down by rocks. A few dozen houses were scattered along wandering dirt lanes. The village lacked any trace of beauty. We didn't see any other Westerners; Aba was simply a transit point to somewhere else.

We were pondering where to start looking for accommodation when a young boy approached us. He led us to a row of small, old and neglected one-roomed brick cottages. In their earlier life the exterior walls had been painted but today the paint peeled like diseased skin. This was once an important coffee growing area so I presumed the buildings had been accommodation for the plantation workers. Later, we learned that some plantations closed because of mismanagement.

A short, dark man who described himself as the manager took over from the young boy and showed us to the nearest cottage. The windows were dirty, one of them was smashed. He pushed open the door. The room was furnished with an old iron bedstead. I flicked the light switch but it didn't work.

Through an open door we saw the bathroom. Ah! The chance to have a bath. But the room was dark and smelled of mildew. The sink's drainpipe was missing and the bathtub was black as if a fire had been lit in it. My dream of soaking in the tub had just gone up in smoke. The toilet wouldn't win any hygiene awards either. The water tank was missing so the bowl would need to be flushed with a bucket of water.

The manager told us the room was five dollars per night. We were aghast at the price and asked to see the other cottages. They turned out to be in worse shape with broken doors and windows, but were only four dollars. We agreed to rent the first one. The young boy went away and quickly returned with a coal-oil lamp and drinking water for our canteens. Then he brought two large plastic buckets of murky water to wash ourselves, our clothes and to pour down the toilet. The drinking water came from a rainwater tank while the murky water was drawn from a well. We were pleased with the room service and tipped him.

We fired up our portable propane stove and used the good water to cook a meal of spaghetti, onions and canned mackerel from our survival rations. We sat on our bed to eat and tried to figure out how to get out of this place. The truck we arrived in was going back to Sudan. We had seen only one vehicle in Aba and that was a truck with flat tires, obviously going nowhere. There seemed to be no immediate solution.

As the sun went down we noticed wasps with bluish bodies fly in through the broken window, and head for their nest in the corner of the ceiling. Penny watched them for a while. "They're doing their job, keeping down the bugs and insects." We decided that if we ignored them they would ignore us.

As we got ready for bed we heard a bizarre sound – like faint crackles from a dying fire. We ventured outside to listen but realized the mysterious crackling was in our room. I shone a flashlight on the walls and ceiling but saw nothing. Intrigued, I listened intently and traced the sound to the door frame. Some paint had cracked and peeled off the wood. I stripped away more paint and discovered the source of the noise.

"There are thousands of termites eating the door frame," I exclaimed to Penny.

She came and looked and, as if this was a common occurrence said, "Oh, well, as long as they don't eat the walls tonight we should be all right."

I liked her attitude.

Having solved the mystery, we went back to bed and were lulled to sleep by the sound of chomping termites.

The sun had risen and the temperature was already making us perspire as we strolled to the small open air market to buy food for breakfast. Only a handful of people were there. The few vendors' tables stood bare, except for one which had a few bananas on it. The prospect of finding anything else looked pretty grim.

A young boy in his school uniform, white shirt and blue shorts, approached us and said *petit déjeuné* and beckoned we follow him. I recognized the French words as "breakfast" but was baffled as to why we should follow him. Nearby stood a tall thin man neatly dressed in a yellow shirt and black slacks.

"The boy wants you to follow him for breakfast," he said in French. The man's bright eyes and white teeth lit up his ebony face when he spoke.

We were used to the friendliness of local people and their eagerness to help without being asked but this puzzled me. We followed the young boy to a large brick house, a mansion compared with the little huts in the town. A wide, shaded verandah extended around all four sides. In front of the house was parked the same green Toyota pickup truck we had seen the day before in Sudan. What was the connection between the truck and the house?

A teenaged girl in a blue and red wrap-around skirt appeared on the verandah and pointed to two cane chairs for us to sit in. Within minutes she placed two large cold bottles of beer and two glasses in front of us. Penny pushed her bottle towards me as she isn't a beer drinker. Next, a mouthwatering breakfast was served: omelettes, corn pancakes, a couple of oranges and half a dozen bananas. This wasn't the kind of breakfast we were used to while backpacking; it was usually bread, jam and maybe a carrot or two.

While Penny savoured every bite I wolfed mine down with gusto and wondered who our guardian angel was. Before we had finished our last banana the man from the market in the yellow shirt arrived.

He told us his name: Nyelemabe I'mande. And that this was his house.

He must be someone of importance, judging from the way the young girl deferred to him. She could be a house servant, or maybe one of his children.

I'mande told us he was leaving in three days to drive to Watsa, and that we could join him for free. We thanked him for his kindness. I had never heard of Watsa so I whipped the map out of my shoulder bag and learned it was 150 kilometres southwest of Aba. I'mande then wrote a note addressed to the hotel manager telling him to give us free accommodation until our departure. As we left the house he loaded us with a pineapple, six oranges and a bunch of bananas. We were even more bewildered. Who was this generous man?

The next morning after the hotel boy brought us three buckets of well water, we washed the red dust from our clothes and hung them to dry. As we sat on the porch studying the map and writing letters, young men passed by the cottage, waved and greeted us with *bonjour*. A few shook our hands and asked what we were doing here. We often asked ourselves the same question, because to get from place to place in Africa often meant long detours and unscheduled stops.

From Cairo we had journeyed south by trains, river boats and trucks in uncomfortable conditions. We had unlimited time but limited funds so we often chose the least expensive transport and accommodation available. Our journey in northeast Africa was not planned in detail. Actually it wasn't planned at all. Our original idea had been to travel in Egypt and return to Europe. However, after I told Penny about my travel experiences in Africa eight years earlier she itched to see more, especially the so called 'Darkest Africa.'

I had already travelled through Zaire and was familiar with routes we could follow. One way was to head east by land to Kisangani and travel by steamer on the Congo River to Kinshasa. From Kinshasa we could make our way overland to West Africa.

Women strolled by nonchalantly, some with their hair braided in intricate designs, others with half a dozen or so little braids wrapped in black thread that made their hair stick out from their head. They brightened up the landscape with their friendly smiles and long, colourful wrap-around skirts in yellows, reds and greens. We were relieved we could relax for three days to enjoy this small community before I'mande drove us south. However, within the hour we were unexpectedly interrupted by the boy who had met us in the market.

"Come, come," he said urgently. "The truck is about to leave."

We were stunned. This change of plan meant we wouldn't have our three days to relax but we didn't want to miss the only transport in town. In a wild panic we stuffed our wet laundry into plastic bags, rammed them into our backpacks and dashed to the house. The green Toyota pickup truck was still there, and beside it stood the driver we had met previously in Sudan. He told us he was a trader from Sudan and was giving the truck to I'mande in exchange for coffee beans. He added that I'mande owned the hotel cottage we stayed in. That explained why he could write a letter to the manager to give us free accommodation. But why?

The front door of the house opened and I'mande emerged with a man in a pale blue robe.

"Who's he?" I asked the trader.

"A friend of I'mande. He's an official with the Ministry of Information and Culture in Juba. He is coming with us to Watsa." He pronounced it Wadja.

Penny and I tossed our backpacks onto the back of the truck and hoisted ourselves over the tailgate. I'mande sat behind the wheel and the two men squeezed into the cab beside him.

The narrow dirt road twisted around small jagged brick-red hills. The sun was a stark, burning white. We passed many roadside thatch-roofed huts and a few people on bicycles, but we never saw any cars. Tall grass often flanked the road, growing higher than the top of the truck's cab.

After two hours I'mande turned down a bumpy track that wandered through a corridor of thorny acacias and electric light poles. After a few minutes we rolled into a village of two dozen huts built with a framework of saplings covered by mud, and roofed with thatch. I'mande pulled up at one that was larger and stood higher than the others. Orange and pink bougainvillea grew over its conical roof. I'mande disappeared inside and beckoned we follow.

It was a bar.

Before we sat down the barman plunked five tall, cold bottles of STANOR beer on the table – one for each of us – compliments of I'mande.

"I'm sorry," said Penny, "I don't like the taste of beer," as she pushed the bottle to the middle of the table.

I'mande, who did not understand English, frowned. Had he

misinterpreted Penny's action as a rejection of his hospitality?

The trader realized something was wrong because he said a few words in the local dialect which brightened I'mande's attitude.

I was perplexed. I'mande may be the type who always needed to be in control and wouldn't tolerate anyone who questioned his decisions, or he may fear rejection and to avoid it he showered people with hospitality, or perhaps he was a genuinely sincere guy with a heart of gold.

Penny regretted she had upset I'mande and sipped the beer.

"This isn't bad," she said. "It's thirst quenching and isn't as strong as I expected." She ended up drinking half of the bottle.

I'mande smiled, pleased she had tried some.

In the late afternoon we left the village.

As we approached Watsa the sun reddened and the distant hills took on a bluish haze.

At the top of a small hill we pulled up outside a large brick house with a pillared verandah. Purple bougainvillea covered the fence, pink magnolias and bright red flame trees filled the yard. This house, like the house back in Aba, was a big contrast to the huts we had passed along the road.

As Penny and I climbed down from the truck the trader told us this was I'mande's other house.

"How many does he have?" I asked.

"Two, or maybe more."

I'mande led the four of us to the house and into the main room. My eyes settled on the highly polished heavy table, chairs and wall cabinets crafted from reddish brown mahogany. The richest furniture we had seen in Africa. I tried not to stare. I'mande motioned for us to sit in front of a huge television set. The stern face of Uganda's president, Idi Amin, appeared on the screen preaching from a church pulpit, imploring his people to work hard to build the country.

I'mande explained the program was broadcast from Uganda, then he left to attend to some business. Amin's homily was followed by a Christmas church service with a choir singing carols.

Being in this palatial house was all too surreal. It was unsettling to know that all around us, villagers lived in thatched shacks without electricity or running water.

A robust woman in a pink and blue *pagne*, the popular wrap-around skirt, entered and invited us to be seated at the dining table where she had placed dishes of beef, pork, chicken, boiled potatoes, mashed potatoes, and potato chips. I could not help but think to myself that I'mande was doing very well for himself.

The trader leaned towards me. "I'mande's second wife," he whispered. "She's the sister of his first."

"How many wives does he have?" I asked.

"Three. Two in the house in Aba, and one here. His newest wife is a teenaged girl."

I realized we had met his newest wife. "She served us breakfast in Aba," I said. Then I asked if I'mande was a Muslim, knowing that Islam permits four wives.

"No," said the trader, pointing up to a large picture of Jesus Christ on the wall, "he's a Christian."

We had just finished the meal when I'mande returned. He led the four of us down the hill to a vacant home and said we could all sleep there. Penny reminded me it was New Year's Eve when we heard drumbeats vibrating through the still air. "I'm bushed," I said, "it's been a long day," as I flopped onto the bed. "Let's celebrate when we're outta here."

Frenetic drumbeats throbbed throughout the night. It must have been quite a party.

We rose before sunrise and strolled arm in arm into the blackness of the verandah. The drums had stopped. The only sound was a cock crowing. The night sky became alive with flame as the sun soared above the hillocks, sending shafts of golden light through the tall eucalyptus trees to the neat village huts on the hillside. Within minutes the valleys and hillsides were bathed in light.

Rather than impose on I'mande for breakfast we started towards the village market. Villagers, in a festive mood, greeted us with *Bon année* (Good year). Most of them were still inebriated from the all night party.

In the marketplace we found a girl selling bananas, a man slaughtering a sheep for the ongoing party and a woman rhythmically pounding sorghum in a mortar with a pestle. Sorghum stalks, which look somewhat like corn stalks, grow just over two metres high and produce heads of grain which are pounded into flour to make beer. Bananas, and sometimes pineapples, are added to give it taste. The homemade hooch has a shelf-life of only a couple of days before "going off" so it must be drunk as soon as possible. At this festive time that wouldn't be a problem.

The sweet-tasting sorghum stalks aren't wasted; they are fed to the goats, sheep and cattle.

We had heard that the soil was fertile and the rainfall sufficient to grow all types of vegetables: potatoes, carrots, onions, cabbages. But eighty percent of the villagers suffered from malaria and bilharzia, leaving malnourished women and children who had become lethargic and disinterested in attending their vegetable gardens.

This situation had created a circle of malnourishment. A girl born to an undernourished mother would likely be born stunted in height and weight and have a weakened immune system. If the child survived she'd be susceptible to infectious diseases and her learning ability would be seriously affected. If she became a mother she would bear low-weight babies, and so the cycle of ill-health would continue.

Many of the men from this and other villages had left to dig and pan illegally for gold in the bush. By selling the gold on the black market to traders from Kenya, the men earned good money, but their affluence pushed up the price of any surplus food they could buy from productive villagers.

At lunchtime we headed for I'mande's house on the hill and were taken aback when we saw the dining table laden with another feast: plates of roast chicken, boiled chicken, lamb cooked with onions and tomatoes, pork chunks, potato chips, sweet potatoes and bread buns.

Before we started eating, the house boy arrived carrying a box of Omo laundry detergent and a bucket of water. He sprinkled Omo on everyone's hands, then held the bucket for us to wash and rinse off the suds. The suds felt good on my grubby hands.

I'mande joined us and said he would speak to the manager

of Kilo Moto, a local gold mining company, to see if he could arrange onward transport for us to Bunia, a town 300 kilometres to the south.

In the late afternoon he returned from the Kilo Moto office to say the manager, Lutete, had agreed we could go to Bunia for free in the company truck.

Great news!

In the late evening I'mande drove us with our backpacks in the green Toyota to the mining office where the driver's helper told us the company truck would leave at three in the morning. This ungodly hour didn't bother us; nothing surprised us anymore. I'mande suggested we leave the company office and return later but we decided to stay. We wanted to be at the office when the manager arrived. I'mande climbed into his green truck and drove away into the darkness.

I marvelled at the coincidence of meeting this benefactor – how he appeared in the Aba market one morning and now had disappeared into the night.

Who he was remained a mystery.

But one thing we knew: he had a heart of gold.

Zaire (part two)

Trail of confusion

Watsa to Goma, January 1979
See map, page 13

The journey continued...

For five-and-a-half hours Penny and I sat on a wooden bench outside the mining company office of Kilo Moto in Watsa. Because the town sits on a plateau about 1,500 metres above sea level we anticipated a cool night. It was two-thirty in the morning and chillier than we expected. We huddled together waiting for the manager, Lutete, who knew we wanted to reach Bunia.

In the darkness we watched a steady stream of men, women and children gather outside the office. They carried their belongings wrapped in blankets tied with rope. We assumed they were mining families who, like us, were waiting for a truck to Bunia.

In this part of Zaire there was no public transport. Privately owned cars, of which there were few, rarely made long journeys because the roads were in appalling conditions with potholes the size of trucks.

A man in a heavy, long, black overcoat, wearing a woollen hat pulled down over his ears, appeared out of the darkness. From his purposeful stride I sensed he had some authority and that help was on its way.

"Lutete?" I asked, and he muttered something in response. He showed a surly face and gabbled at me in French: "You cannot go on the truck because you haven't signed the registration form."

"Registration form?" I queried. "I'll sign it now."

"No," he said angrily and stalked away into the night. I hoped he would return in a better frame of mind because he appeared to be the key to our getting out of Watsa.

I turned to Penny. "This is serious. If we don't get on the truck we could be stuck here for who knows how long."

However, about fifteen minutes later a company employee approached and motioned that we pick up our bags and follow him. He led us through a gate into the dark parking compound of Kilo Moto and pointed to the only vehicle in the yard – a 5-tonne truck. We thanked him, hurled our bags onto the flatbed and hoisted ourselves up.

There were no benches as in other passenger trucks we had travelled on so we sat on our backpacks and made ourselves comfortable for the journey. I felt relieved we had got on. A few minutes later the gate opened for the other passengers. They surged forward in a panic, probably fearful they may be left behind. They scrambled up the tailgate in a frenzy. Hefty men and women started to fill the entire flatbed. Penny and I quickly stood up, otherwise we could have been crushed by the weight of bodies if they lost their balance.

Women still on the ground yelled for assistance as they handed up babies to whoever could grab one. Penny leaned forward and reached for a baby boy but in the melée he slipped out of her grasp.

"I've lost him," Penny called to me, panic stricken. "He may get trampled." She peered in vain through the moving mass of legs and arms before her, knowing that somewhere in the confusion was a defenceless child.

People pushed and shoved as they jockeyed for floor space. Penny stood only an arm's length from me but I couldn't help her look for the baby because I was unable to move. Only my left foot touched the floor. My right leg was almost horizontal, pinned between the bodies of two huge women. When I pulled hard to extricate it my sandal fell off. I hoped to retrieve it when the furore died down.

Fifteen minutes later most people were settled. The engine growled and puffed black diesel fumes out of the tailpipe. A couple of men raised the tailgate and locked it with iron pins.

The baby must have survived because all the passengers except one seemed content. The big mama nearest me couldn't sit still. She looked perturbed. She rolled her buttocks from side to side then reached under to remove something: my missing sandal!

The truck laboured along the deeply rutted narrow dirt road that led to Bunia. The vehicle bucked and swayed through hilly terrain, passing many enormous car-sized boulders that showed the grey nakedness of granite rock. We sat on the metal frames of our backpacks but every turn threw us against the side of the truck. Our bodies became battered and bruised, particularly our arms and legs. Our rear ends grew numb from perching on the metal frames but there was nowhere else to sit.

The night was pitch black but the headlights briefly illuminated village huts beside the road and the hundreds of oil palm trees which provided cash to the local economy. Palm oil was extracted from the pulp and kernels of the nuts which grew in profusion at the base of the five-metre high trees. The oil was used locally as cooking oil, and the rest exported to make soap and margarine.

Everything was quiet except for the rumbling of the noisy engine. The swaying of the truck continued until daybreak when we pulled off the road for our first rest stop. We were exhausted. It was good to get off the truck to stretch our legs after the three-hour ordeal.

Around us a lush, dark greenery of grasses and shrubs hugged the edge of the red dirt road. Birds fussed and chattered in the short, scruffy oil palms as the sun filtered through the fronds. Some of the men climbed down to relieve themselves but none of the women did so. The trick was not to drink before a long trip. My guess was that the men didn't keep this rule, whereas the women did.

The babies on board were uncannily quiet – they neither cried nor whimpered. We watched as the mothers spoon-fed them a thick, grey paste that looked like glue but may have been boiled manioc, popularly called cassava. The tall plants grew to over two metres and had edible roots which the women boiled to a mush.

The sun climbed higher and the temperature increased. We were thankful for our hats. Just after midday we rolled into the small town of Mongbwalu and stopped for people to buy bananas.

In this country of uncertainties and changeable schedules and where people tell you what they think you want to hear, I asked the driver if his destination was Bunia. He told me it was.

In the late afternoon, after a gruelling fourteen hours, we arrived in Bambu, a town forty kilometres short of Bunia, and the driver announced he was going no farther. We weren't surprised.

"What time are you leaving in the morning?" I asked the driver.

"I don't know," he answered in an aggressive tone.

I think he resented our being on his truck. Maybe he didn't like foreigners.

Another passenger interjected by saying, "After seven."

The other people from the truck just seemed to evaporate. I assumed they had friends to stay with or went to stay in Kilo Moto's mine workers' accommodation.

The town consisted of a few mud-brick buildings with their walls covered in stucco and painted white. Every wall had spatters of red earth over the paint work, caused by heavy monsoon rainstorms splashing up red mud. A young man with a dark shiny face wandered out of one of the buildings and offered to show us to the hotel.

It was full.

We were exhausted and dirty and craved a hot wash to get rid of the sweat and red dust ingrained in our skin. The young man – he said his name was Odipio – offered to take us down the hill to find another place to sleep. The dirt road was rough with long, shallow channels caused by erosion when the monsoon rains fell. We stopped at a shop on a ridge where Odipio told us the owner had rooms to rent in the back. A tall, gaunt man, his face like black shoe leather, stood behind the counter.

"Do you have running water?" I asked. He nodded and led us past the rooms which were thatch-roofed huts and pointed down the hill to a small creek almost hidden by trees and scrub.

"Running water," he said.

I smiled inwardly. It was definitely running water, but with darkness virtually upon us I didn't relish groping down a dark, slippery path to get water.

Odipio then told us we wouldn't find accommodation with piped water. He took us to another place which he said had hot water, then left us. We walked through a compound where women stirred a pot of mushy manioc over an open fire. Beside them sat large pots of water waiting to be heated. Things looked promising. This must be the hot water Odipio told us about.

The room the owner showed us was constructed with a framework of tree branches covered with mud and roofed with sheets of corrugated iron. Inside stood a bed with a firm straw mattress, two sheets, a blanket and two large, thick, hard pillows stuffed with straw. It was clean and cozy, just what we needed.

But, what we really wanted was a shower. The owner pointed across the dusty compound to a small square structure with two-metre-high walls of vertical bamboo strips tied together with cord. It was a shower stall built on a concrete pad, open to the sky. We could hardly wait to use it.

We had just put down our backpacks in our hut when a young man knocked on the door and handed the first of two buckets of steaming hot water to Penny who marched straight to the shower with it. Mine came later but it wasn't in the bucket for long; I poured it over my aching, grimy body and scrubbed until I felt rejuvenated.

The next morning Odipio knocked on our door at seven-twenty and told us the truck to Bunia was leaving at eight. Then he left. We packed quickly and strode to the Kilo Moto office but the truck wasn't there, nor was Odipio. We assumed the worst – that it had already left. I saw a man in the office. "There is no truck going to Bunia today," he said.

Feeling dejected, we sat awhile to consider our options. But we seemed to be stuck here. By chance Penny saw a foreigner, a short, broad shouldered man with bushy, ginger hair pass by the office. We caught up to him, a Belgian who, in addition to French, spoke some English. When I explained our predicament he went into the office and asked about transport to Bunia. The man who had told me there wasn't a truck leaving had been called away from the office. His replacement said there would be a truck departing within a few minutes. So Penny and I stayed and the Belgian continued on his way.

We heard the roar of the truck as it approached. I ambled over to the driver, the man who had driven us here, and asked if he was going to Bunia. He said "No" in a surly tone.

I called to the Belgian who was about to disappear around the corner. He returned and spoke to the driver on our behalf.

The driver told him of an outbreak of cholera in Bunia and that he was afraid to go there. He added that 186 people were in hospital. While this conversation was taking place, Penny went to the office where the clerk repeated that the truck was going to Bunia.

Who were we to believe?

I doubted the words of the driver because of yesterday's behaviour. For some reason, he held a grudge against us. I hadn't experienced this attitude before.

Daniels, the Belgian, invited us to relax at his house which was nearby and he asked the office clerk to come and get us when the truck was about to leave.

The Daniels' house – a gold-mining company's house, he told us – was red brick with a rust-coloured corrugated iron roof. We met his wife, a woman in her early thirties with close-cropped blonde hair and a generous smile, and their 9-year-old daughter Valery who was home-schooled. She had a lonely look in her eyes.

Daniels told us he and his family had been in Bambu for six years and were the last of 200 Belgian families to leave after the closing of the gold mine. They had been waiting seven weeks for a truck to transfer them and their two-and-a-half tonnes of household effects to Kisangani – and still had to wait a while longer.

Kisangani used to be eight hours by road but it now took three weeks because of the potholes.

I looked at Penny. "This information could change our plan to go east from Bunia to Kisangani and travel down the Congo River to Kinshasa. I think our goal should be to get out of Zaire by going south from Bunia to Goma." Penny agreed with the change.

I mentioned to the Daniels our encounter with I'mande who had helped us with food, accommodation and transport.

"A smart man," said Daniels. "He was a politician when independence was given by Belgium in 1960. He and a few cronies took over coffee plantations from fleeing Belgian planters. I'mande got two plantations and employed the existing managers to continue running them for a percentage of the profits. He prospered. His cronies tried to run their plantations by themselves but they failed."

Penny relayed the account of the fourteen-hour truck trip and mentioned how quiet the babies were.

"They were doped with a porridge of manioc and bananas, as were the men and women. The mixture ferments in their stomachs, relaxing them almost into a stupor. You can often smell it on their breath. And it causes the whites of the eyes to redden. It is detrimental to their sight and mind. Of course, they don't try intentionally to harm themselves or their babies; they just don't know the consequences."

By now it was lunchtime and Madame Daniels rustled up a lunch of an omelette, boiled rice, spinach and canned sardines. "Getting a variety of European food is difficult because there are so few Europeans in Bambu," Madame Daniels said. Mention of other Europeans triggered a thought in Monsieur Daniels' head. "The French priest at the Catholic mission has good contacts and may know if vehicles are going to Bunia." Monsieur Daniels doubted whether the personnel at Kilo Moto really knew who or what was going where.

After a short walk Penny and I arrived at the high, solid brick church that loomed over the surrounding eucalyptus trees. We found the white-robed, mild-mannered priest in the church. He telephoned the Kilo Moto office and learned that the truck had left and that there wasn't a cholera scare. I glanced at Penny. She responded with a nod. We were completely convinced that the truck driver didn't like us.

The priest added that another company vehicle was about to leave, then dashed to his Citroën van. We rushed after him, jumped in and he drove like a maniac to the mining office but we arrived too late – the other company vehicle had already left. "It was full," the office clerk explained. "There is nothing else going today, nor tomorrow which is Martyr's Day, a holiday. But there may be a vehicle the next day, Friday."

I felt exasperated. Penny looked disappointed. We seemed doomed to spend a few days in a town that wasn't even on our map. But we liked the name. Bambu had an exotic ring to it. Maybe the misinformation would be to our overall benefit. We resigned ourselves to fate.

The priest went on his way and we headed towards the hotel – the one which had been full when we arrived the previous day.

It was a low building, and we headed to the entrance through an earthen compound where a pig nudged cobs of corn with his snout, much to the chagrin of some hens who tried to peck at them.

We found the clerk, a serious man picking at mosquito bites on his arms. He led us to the only vacant room. It was tiny with a bed that almost filled the space, and the air reeked of faulty plumbing. We booked in for two nights.

That evening we fired up our portable propane gas stove and boiled hard, unripened, plantain bananas and sprinkled them with sugar. Unappetizing but sustaining.

The next day, Thursday, we searched for Odipio to thank him for his help but no one knew where he had gone. He was another special person who unexpectedly entered our lives in time of need.

On Friday morning we arrived at the Kilo Moto office at seven. The office clerk announced a Land Rover would be leaving in a few minutes and it had space for two. We could hardly believe our good fortune. As we got in, we noticed Monsieur Daniels in front of the office. He came over, said good-bye and told us of an American missionary couple in Bunia who may know of onward transport. He then explained to the driver where to drop us in Bunia.

We picked up a mining official and a school teacher, both local Zaireans, and set off in the cool of the morning along a narrow road that wound around low hills. Thirty minutes later we arrived in Nizi, a few kilometres short of Bunia, where we dropped off the mining official. But there was another mining official who had to go to Bambu. So, we drove back to Bambu! Soon we headed south again. We stopped again in Nizi and picked up another mining official but this man, fortunately for us, was heading for Bunia. We arrived at eleven-thirty a.m. outside the home of Reverend Don Dix and his wife Alene.

The front door opened and a petite woman with greying hair

came forward to meet us; she had a quizzical look. We mentioned our meeting the Daniels and our plan to travel south to Goma.

"Come in," she said. "A lot of people, mainly missionaries, stay here when they pass through Bunia. You're welcome to stay. Unfortunately my husband Don can't be with us as he's visiting another mission station." As she led us into her home, she added: "There's a mission plane arriving tomorrow which is going to Goma. I think there may be a couple of empty seats but I won't know until tomorrow."

This was fantastic news!

Goma was 600 kilometres to the south. A flight would be a godsend rather than be jostled, pummelled and battered for many days in the back of trucks. From Goma we would have a choice of leaving by public transport towards Uganda, Rwanda or Tanzania.

"That's the good news," said Alene. "The bad news is that I'm obliged to charge a fare to non-missionary personnel."

We assured her that paying our way was not a problem.

The next morning we heard Alene on the two-way radio discussing the arrival of the airplane. She turned as we approached. "Good news. You'll be on the flight."

"We can't thank you enough," Penny exclaimed. I felt a flutter of excitement in my stomach.

A missionary couple in their twenties, David and Lilla, and their two preteen children stopped by the house. Alene mentioned they were living African-style.

David explained: "We're living in a bamboo hut in a nearby village to get closer to the people. And we're learning the local dialect to teach the bible."

Having seen the primitive conditions many of the locals lived in, I admired this couple.

A Land Rover pulled up outside. "It's Gordon." Alene said. "He'll be taking you to the airport after lunch."

Gordon was a tall, thin, sandy-haired man with a strong voice. He was a teacher at the Bunia Seminary. He and David had been born and raised in Africa, both of them sons of missionary parents.

Conversation over a lunch of rice, squash, cauliflower and a meat gravy focused on problems confronting the missionaries: delivery of medicines, mail, provisions and motor fuel, and how to convert more local people to Christianity.

Without warning Gordon leapt to his feet. "The plane's due to arrive." We scrambled into the Land Rover.

We stood by the tarmac and watched a little black speck in the blue sky grow larger as it approached. Very soon a Cessna 208 made a smooth landing. Two men disembarked. We took their places and stowed our backpacks behind the seats. Already on board were two missionary women who told us they "did a kinda bit of ev'rything" at the hospital complex of the Presbyterian American Mission at Nyankunde but had business to attend to in Goma. The flight took us over thick jungle, green grassy plains, village huts, cultivated fields, rivers and Lake Idi Amin.

I looked at Penny to share the wonderment below us but her face showed concern. "What's up?" I asked.

"I'll tell you later," she said nervously. "In the meantime, start praying."

I was baffled. Start praying? For what?

I looked out and saw we were flying past a volcano, Nyirangongo, which had recently spewed lava that reached the outskirts of Goma. A few minutes later, after a two-hour flight, we touched down.

I turned to Penny. "What's the problem?"

She pointed to a warning sign above the window that read: 'Propane tanks or cylinders and other explosive items not permitted on board.' I shuddered when I read it. In our backpacks we carried a half-dozen full propane cylinders for our stove, and a partly used one.

"They could have exploded," Penny said. "When I realized the danger I started praying."

I squeezed her hand. "You must have a direct line to the Big Man upstairs."

I felt as if we had just completed a survival course. It was hard to believe that in a couple of inches on the map so many difficulties could pop up to challenge us. But in that little area there was a variety of people who helped us on our journey to whom we are extremely thankful.

Three days later we found onward transport in a truck with comfortable seats, heading through Rwanda and Tanzania to Nairobi, Kenya.

China

Saving face

Adventures in dining in Xian, October 1982
See map, page 11

Inquisitive eyes followed us.

Penny, Pam and I wended our way between diners in the noisy, crowded worker's restaurant in Xian to the only empty table.

Because we were foreigners treading new ground in such a restaurant, we drew enquiring eyes from the diners as we sat down. Pam, our eighteen-year-old niece with long, blonde hair probably helped generate some of the attention.

More than three years had passed since our last long-haul journey in Africa and Asia. China had only recently opened its doors to independent travellers. The chance to journey through the 'Middle Kingdom' alone, not on a tour, intrigued us. We would have to buy tickets for trains, buses and boats and check into hotels without knowing a word of Chinese. We invited Pam to share the experience.

It was noon and there must have been a hundred men and women, chopsticks in hand, who looked up from their bowls of noodles and stared at us. It was almost impossible to differentiate between the sexes because everyone wore a Mao suit – a blue or green square cut, collarless jacket with loose trousers and a cloth cap. These formless suits were designed to equalize people in this communist state. In that, the designers were successful.

This type of eatery, often called a "restaurant of the masses," was in a large room at street level with about thirty round, wooden tables set on rough-hewn floorboards. The grey walls were devoid of paintings or decorations. Swinging doors led to the kitchen from where we heard the clatter of plates and the chatter of cooks. From the stoves, steamy aromas filled the air then floated up to the harsh fluorescent tubes that burned brightly overhead.

There were no menus on the table, not that we could have read them anyway. We glanced around to see what others had on their tables and decided to share a light lunch of one plate of dumplings, a bowl of noodles and a dish of meat and vegetables.

When a waiter approached we ordered by pointing to the bowls of nearby diners. Then we waited. Customers continued to stare curiously at us while they murmured to each other. Our guess was that few, if any, foreign visitors had eaten at this restaurant. We seemed to be causing a disturbance.

I observed the four men at a nearby table, all wearing identical dark blue Mao suits and blue caps. They deftly manipulated their wooden chopsticks, selected morsels of chicken, pork fat, bok choy, and bamboo shoots from large platters on their table and transferred them to a small bowl of rice each man had in front of him. They continually sipped green tea and, when the teapot was empty, one of them would turn the lid upside down on the pot to signal the waiter that more tea was needed.

The kitchen door swung open and three waiters headed our way, balancing plates on their arms and attracting comments from their worker clientele. With a flourish they put the plates on our small round table: three plates of dumplings, three bowls of noodles and three dishes of meat and vegetables. Our order had been tripled! We looked in amazement at all the food in front of us. The waiters' faces remained expressionless as they served us. But back in the kitchen they probably had a good chuckle.

Diners nearby smiled broadly at us, the crazy foreigners who didn't know how to order their meal. Or they probably thought foreigners ate far too much. There is a practice in China of saving face by not admitting defeat when confronted by adversity, challenges or embarrassment. As tourists we didn't have to follow the practice but because we were encircled by diners watching our every move, we remained very aware of the custom.

As it turned out, we were hungrier than we thought and ate more than we expected. We left small portions in the bowls to show we had been sufficiently fed, paid our bill and walked out, proud that we had saved face by not letting on we had made a mistake in ordering.

In the evening we returned to the same restaurant, believing familiarity would make it easier to order. As soon as I pushed open the door the man behind the cashier's counter recognized us, leapt off his chair and whisked us upstairs to a private room where our presence would not disturb the other diners. He obviously didn't want another lunch-hour distraction. He motioned us to sit in the high-backed wooden chairs at a long wooden table. The room appeared to be for small banquets and other special occasions.

This time we decided to order something simple. We agreed on one large dish of diced chicken, rice and mixed vegetables. Because of a language barrier in ordering the chicken I stood up, bent my arms, flapped like a chicken and clucked and squawked. The waiter caught on, laughed, nodded and left the room.

The minutes ticked by. What we thought was a simple dinner request was proving to be a long, drawn-out affair. Thirty minutes ticked by, then forty-five. Finally the door opened and two waiters carried in a large, golden, roasted chicken on a bed of boiled rice and mounds of mixed vegetables. The price was about seven times what we had expected to pay for dinner but we thanked them as if this was what we had ordered and enjoyed the sumptuous repast.

Again we saved face.

The next day we tried a new eating place: Xian's Renmin Hotel. Penny, Pam and I sat at a table near six fellow travellers. Waiters hovered around their table watching their sign language and listening to the fractured Mandarin the travellers struggled with to order their meal. The waiters nodded as if they understood, and disappeared into the kitchen.

"What have you ordered?" I asked Nick, an Englishman, who

was seated closest to me.

"We're going to share a tureen of soup," he said, "and dishes of noodles, vegetables, meat and a big bowl of rice."

After a few minutes the kitchen door swung open. Six white-jacketed waiters marched to the table in single file, each carrying a large tureen of soup, one for each person.

We could hardly believe our eyes and had trouble containing our smirks as we watched the waiters, one by one, plunk down a tureen, then hand each of them a large soup ladle. The travellers' eyes popped when they realized what they had ordered. The waiters smiled as they disappeared into the kitchen.

In China, soup is normally served during the meal, not at the beginning. The waiters, I felt sure, broke with custom so they could make a grand entrance together to play their joke on the foreigners.

During our travels in China we tried various ways to order a meal. Pointing to what other customers were eating was often success-ful. Going into the kitchen, surprising the cooks and choosing food from the various pots also worked. We even selected from menus written in Chinese characters, guessing that main dishes would be listed near the top of the menu and drinks farther down. This method didn't always work.

On one occasion Penny received a dish of diced pork and vegetables while I got a small plate of pineapple pieces. There's no guarantee that you'll get what you ordered no matter how you do it, especially if the waiters want to play a joke on you.

Despite receiving an excessive amount of soup, the six travel-lers picked up their ladles and attacked it with gusto, drawing stares from the other diners. The waiters looked amazed.

The travellers finished their soup and ate everything they'd ordered.

They had the last laugh.

By not admitting defeat, the travellers saved face.

Togo

The helpful witch-doctor

Dr Dako in Lomé, February 1987
See map, page 14

The morning sun, already hot and oppressive, beat down on Penny and me as we ambled through the open-air market located on the northeastern outskirts of Lomé in Togo.

About the size of three tennis courts, it specialized in fetishes used by witch-doctors. Market stalls – rickety tables roofed with palm fronds – were arranged in a rectangle around a cleared area of sandy ground. The stalls provided shade to the vendors who sat fanning themselves with horse tails to keep away the flies. Their brown skin glistened with perspiration in the humid heat. The entire scene was bathed in drab hues of brown, beige and off-white.

The tables, and the reed mats spread on the ground in front of them, were covered with fetishes. My mind boggled at the extensive array: skulls of monkeys, crocodiles, cats, baboons, horses, cows, pigs and birds. The large crocodile heads, lined up in neat rows on the mats, looked particularly ominous with their sabre-like teeth and their hollow eye sockets. As we walked away I had an eerie feeling that the eyes of the crocodiles were following us.

Cow and horse tails hung on a rope strung between two poles; they swished to and fro in the gentle breeze. There were also warthog teeth, porcupine skins, antelope horns, an assortment of loose bones as well as roots and bark for witch-doctors' potions and herbal medicines.

The local people worship spirits of dead ancestors and nature spirits. They believe that spirits, or souls, are everywhere – in trees, rocks, homes and the air. They contend that the spirits control various aspects of nature and that witch-doctors provide the link between this world and the spirit world.

This belief system, which we call animism (from the Latin anima, meaning soul), has developed over countless centuries.

Animists believe that illnesses, and medical problems such as infertility of a person or animal, are due to bewitchment. Bewitchment occurs when a sorcerer (one who communicates with evil spirits), casts a spell on a victim.

For a person to be healed, his family or a friend will consult with a witch-doctor who does good works. Witch-doctors are also known as medicine men, healers, fetish priests, and shamans.

An ill person may be told to buy herbs. A woman unable to become pregnant may be told to buy a spearhead – a phallic symbol – and to sleep with it by her side. A farmer who is concerned that he has ignored nature spirits may be told to buy a crocodile skull to appease the guardian spirit or deity in control of soil fertility. He would place it in a corner of his field to encourage a good harvest.

As Penny and I strolled through the market we watched farmers and city-dwellers shop for the fetishes suggested by their various witch-doctors.

"Crocodile head, very cheap," a friendly vendor called to us, crouching beside an array of animal skulls.

"Just looking, thank you," I said, "my crops are doing well."

While wandering around we passed a square hut with walls of reeds and a roof of corrugated iron supported by slim tree trunks. A man stood in the doorway, his charcoal complexion a direct contrast with the white trousers and white T-shirt he wore. Wearing white in this dusty place surprised me, but his clothes were spotless.

"I am Doctor Dako," he said in French. (France was the last colonial power in Togo.) He beckoned us into his hut. His black

skin was wrinkled and leathery and when he smiled he showed
bottom teeth that stood up like untended tombstones. We guessed
he was about fifty. Many people age quickly in West Africa because
of malnutrition and the harsh sun drying their skin. He pointed
to two short wooden stools and we sat down. He squatted on his
haunches on the earthen floor and showed us a finger-stained
business card that described him as *Docteur des cultes des forces
voudous africaines*. We decided that an approximate translation
was voodoo-doctor or witch-doctor.

The hut – the doctor's office and consultation room – was
gloomy and small, about eight feet by eight feet.

When our eyes adjusted to the dimness we saw in a dark corner
a strange structure. It was an altar made of an assortment of
wooden masks, feathers, bells, cowrie shells, snake skins, whitened bones, voodoo dolls, cow horns, long antelope horns, and a
fly whisk made from a cow's tail. It was erected on a clay base with
embedded clam shells. I wondered what ailments, physical or
mental, he could cure with these fetishes.

He stared at us. I guess he realized we had no ailments to cure,
nor crops to nurture.

"You are travellers," he said finally, "so you need protection for
your journey. I'll pray for you."

He suggested we buy a bottle of gin for his god.

I was taken aback. In India we had seen a mix of milk and
honey offered as a libation to the gods, but never alcohol. But this
was Africa, a different culture. Up to this point I had been willing
to go along with his rituals but when he wanted a five-dollar bottle
of gin "for his god" I became sceptical.

"Is it for you to drink?" I asked.

"No, no," he said emphatically, "we'll all share the gin but the
god gets most of it."

I relented and handed over some banknotes which he took
eagerly then got up off his haunches and called to a colleague in
the market. A man in a blue-striped T-shirt appeared. He wore a
permanent grin. His dark-brown eyes, big and round, bugged out
of his head. They gave him a wild look. He turned his back and

loped across the market square. Within two minutes he was back with a bottle of Gordon's Gin. I checked the cap. It was still sealed. The wild one sat on the earthen floor to join the party, grinning all the while.

As part of the ritual, Doctor Dako poured the gin into a battered tin bowl and passed it around so we could all have a drink. I figured that the gin, being raw alcohol, wouldn't harbour any bugs to play havoc in our gullets. Although I prefer my gin with tonic and a slice of lemon I raised the bowl to where hundreds of lips had touched before, and sipped. It burned my tongue. It was too early in the morning to enjoy it. Penny was next. She reeled. She doesn't like alcohol. I thought she was a good sport to have her share.

As he poured the remaining gin over the altar he chanted in his own language. We heard "Russell, Penny" over and over again. When he finished he told us, in French, we should have a safe journey but if we did have some problems we could get help from the spirit protector by contacting the spirit through amulets. With that said, he showed us two carved wooden figures about the length of an index finger. Must be the African equivalent of a lucky horseshoe or rabbit's foot, I thought.

"Ask for help by talking to the amulets," the doctor said. Then, with a smug grin, offered both of them to us for the exorbitant price of $190. After some friendly bargaining we settled on five dollars for the two.

I enjoyed the guy even though he tried to rip us off.

Because of their influence on everyday life, witch-doctors have a high status in the towns and villages of sub-Saharan Africa. The respect grows if, through their personality, they have a good doctor-client relationship. Doctor Dako had such a personality.

I felt good vibes in the hut. I'm not able to explain it. Penny felt them too. There are many subtle messages we pick up which bypass the threshold of the conscious mind and go straight to the subconscious. They are supposed to be the basis for our judging whether or not we think someone is believable.

I believed in him. Penny believed he was sincere.

We left Lomé with the amulets stashed safely in our backpacks and travelled for another seven months without mishap.

Did Doctor Dako's prayers and amulets protect us?

Can anyone say they didn't?

Togo

Cultural encounter

At home with the Tamberma, February 1987
See map, page 14

Pleased with her purchase, she devoured the rodent with gusto, stripping its flesh with her teeth and smacking her lips. Then she sucked loudly on one of its legs.

I could hardly believe my eyes. Penny looked away repulsed. I almost gagged.

Our truck had stopped at lunchtime in a village in central Togo to let off a passenger. Vendors gathered around the truck with trays of gum, matches and fruit, except for one man. He sold rodents which he had gutted, spread-eagled on wooden frames and roasted to a glistening brown.

It was one of these rodents that was bought by our fellow passenger – a lean, coffee-coloured woman. It was as big as a large rat. Its hollow eye sockets stared blankly.

Another man approached the truck selling pills for diarrhea. Good timing! But the woman waved him away.

Other passengers bought kebabs of skewered goat meat. Our oranges and cookies satisfied us.

Our destination was northern Togo where we hoped to visit the Tamberma people who lived in a region of mountains and fertile plains. They have largely retained their culture and traditions in the face of Western encroachment. The most visible example of this has been in the architecture of their homes. They built them like small fortified castles with circular towers and ramparts, all made from sticks, mud, clay and straw. They were designed long ago as places of refuge in time of attack by neighbouring tribes. Their housing style intrigued us.

In our travels we favoured the "old Africa" with its culture intact rather than the big towns and cities of modern Africa where different tribal groups are thrown together into a melting pot. We preferred to experience the way of life of a people: how they built their homes, what clothing and ornaments they wore, what tools they used, food they ate, their religious beliefs, their rituals and customs and their artwork and language.

Our journey to Tamberma country started that morning in Lomé, Togo's capital. Penny and I boarded a Nissan passenger truck at Lomé's bus and truck terminal. The back of the truck contained wooden benches to accommodate fourteen adults but we were crammed together with eighteen locals and four young children. At about eight in the morning, with the sun well-risen and the heat of the day already being felt, the truck pulled away and headed north.

The road was paved and the terrain fairly flat. The breeze blowing through the windows provided a welcome relief from the tropical heat. We passed homes, rectangular in shape, with mud-brick walls and roofs of thatch or sometimes corrugated iron.

Baobab trees grew intermittently along the roadside. Often called the upside down tree because its branches looked like roots, it is a popular shade tree. Its seed pods resembled big sausages – as long as one's forearm. When we stopped to stretch our legs we broke open a fuzzy skinned pod that had dropped to the ground. Inside, the edible pulp had dried out, turned white and chalky with age. I nibbled on it. Tasteless. And so dry it stuck in my mouth. Thankfully it wasn't part of my diet. The local people, however, eat it when it's young and pulpy and with a tangy taste. The traditional food is still popular fare.

Farther north we passed oil palm trees, sugarcane fields, banana trees and tracts of dry scrub. Traditionally, the local people have extracted oil for cooking from the pulp and kernel of the oil palm nut.

At lunchtime we reached the village where our fellow passenger ate the rodent. It was an *agouti* – a bush rat – widely considered as one of the most delicious types of bush meat. Snacking on agoutis was customary in this region.

As we continued north through other villages we drove by roadside vendors seated under shady baobab trees with their wares: sacks of charcoal, saplings for the building of huts, and grass thatch for roofs – the traditional building materials of tropical Africa.

Occasionally we spotted a herd of goats, a few guinea fowl and some skinny cows.

In the late afternoon we arrived in Kandé and checked into the Government Guest House. Definitely a no-star hotel. Our door lock was broken, the light bulb had burnt out, the fan didn't work and the tap water came out brown. There was no food available at the Guest House, nor in the area. Fortunately we carried food rations of canned fruit and stale buns. With no fan, and a bed as hard as an ironing board, we suffered a sleepless night.

The next day the sun had already risen when we got up at six-thirty. We wanted to get an early start to visit the Tamberma people who lived about twenty miles to the east.

In the lobby we saw a tall man in his mid-thirties who looked business-like in a well-worn black suit and white shirt which contrasted with his copper coloured skin. I asked him if he knew how to get to the Tamberma country and he replied in clear English, "I am a Tamberma. That's where I'm going." He introduced himself as Mr. N'Pohyetouho, a health inspector who came originally from Nadoba village in the Tamberma country, and who was returning to visit friends.

With his reasonably good command of English, his education and his wearing of a suit, how much of his Tamberma way of life remained in him? It would be interesting to visit the villagers he left behind to see if they had retained their traditions.

When he suggested we go together we readily agreed, and felt fortunate for the chance meeting.

The three of us sat by the roadside under a shady tree and waited two hours for a passenger truck that never came. We walked to the truck terminal and the man in charge told us that nothing was scheduled to leave today, nor tomorrow. In fact, there was no schedule. I thought our new acquaintance would have known this, but the hotel clerk had misinformed him.

A few trucks sat idly in the terminal parking lot. I realized that to get there today we would have to rent a truck and driver. After concerted bargaining with our friend's help, Penny and I arranged to pay twenty dollars for a driver and truck for the forty-mile round trip.

We set off with our new acquaintance and picked up a few villagers on the way, giving them a free ride. The rough dirt road cut through undulating terrain of scrub and baobab trees. Along the way castle-like homes dotted the flat, semi-arid landscape. We were in Tamberma country, approaching Nadoba village.

Po, as we called him, met a Tamberma friend – a short, stocky man with a dark round face, large lips, a flattened nose and dressed in bright red shorts. Po explained that the villagers wore few clothes.

He added that prior to 1960, the year of independence from France, many of his people didn't wear anything. It was the incoming African government that told them to modernize by wearing clothes – an example of an African custom being frowned upon by their own people.

Po's friend's face lit up with a smile of goodwill as he welcomed us to his home, or *tata*. The building, constructed with bricks of mud mixed with chopped straw, was about forty-five feet long with walls rising to fifteen feet. At the corners of the building, turrets or towers were capped with a conical roof of thatch. They loomed above the walls, giving the place a castle-like appearance. By not having windows, the homes were easier to defend from the parapets.

We were intrigued when, near the entrance, we saw a cow's skull, bleached white by the sun, hanging from a pole about six feet high.

"It is for protection of the house and the people inside," Po explained. "The skull is the home of a guardian spirit."

In the wall a small doorway had been cut – a circular opening about three feet in diameter. The owner invited us into his home. We had to bend down to enter. He and Po followed. Inside I found the coolness refreshing after enduring the 100°F temperature outside. Mud brick, a poor conductor of heat, kept the inside temperature up to 30°F cooler than outside, a fact often overlooked in the rush to modernize villages and towns with concrete buildings which are subject to the rise and fall of temperature.

We could stand up but we were in semi-darkness because of the lack of windows. The ground floor was reserved for animals; stakes for tethering goats and a cow had been driven into the ground. Chickens clucked and pecked at scraps on the earthen floor. In a corner stood a mound of mud covered with feathers and bones.

"That is the family shrine," Po explained, "where my friend will kill a chicken or another animal and sprinkle its blood on the shrine in the hope of having good harvests of millet and sorghum, or for divine protection."

He went on to say they believed the spirits of their ancestors controlled their lives and that they offered sacrifices to keep them happy.

I felt privileged to witness this lifestyle which had not been influenced by Western ways.

We climbed up a short wooden ladder to a room with a low ceiling where a large iron pot was perched on rocks over a fire. Except for the glow of the flames there was no natural light. Steam from the pot and smoke from the fire drifted up towards a small vent, a hole in the clay roof. In the smoky room our eyes watered but we spotted a woman sitting beside the pot, the colour of her skin blending with the darkness. Then there was a flash of white teeth when she grinned at us. We smiled back and apologized for barging in unannounced, not that she could understand.

On seeing the woman grinning through the smoke and steam, Po, who was right behind us, explained she was his friend's wife, making beer from millet. She will cook the millet several times and throw away the dregs. To the remaining liquid she will add yeast, taken from a previous batch of brew, then allow the new beverage to ferment. She was keeping alive the old custom of home-brewing.

In the confined room the fire had raised the temperature by a few degrees. The woman's large, bare upper torso glistened with perspiration. Po's friend continued to guide us through his home. He led us up an internal stairway constructed of mud bricks to the next level where we saw two bedrooms, both three feet high with a diameter of about ten feet. To enter the bedrooms one had to crawl on all fours. I felt claustrophobic in these cramped quarters.

We followed more mud-brick steps up to the parapet from where we looked towards distant mountains and fertile plains. In the foreground stood half-a-dozen castle-like homes surrounded by fields of millet, sorghum and grazing cows.

On the parapet lay piles of sorghum stalks, similar to corn stalks. These sweet tasting stalks were a favourite fodder among the cows. Heads of sorghum grain to be eaten by the family had been cut from the stalks and were lying in the sun to dry. We discovered that the towers which gave the homes a fairy-tale, castle-like appearance were actually granaries. Beneath the conical thatched roofs, the Tamberma stored their reserve supplies of sorghum, millet and corn.

The homeowner had work to do in the fields so he excused himself and we thanked him for the privilege of visiting his home.

From the parapet Po pointed to a storage shed not far away. "Cotton is brought from neighbouring areas and stored in the shed until it is trucked out," he said.

Penny looked down and pointed to a mud-walled rectangular building with a corrugated iron roof, unlike any of the other buildings in the village, and asked what it was.

"That's a bar," he said.

I hadn't expected to see a bar in a small village where they brewed their own hooch.

"You mean they sell beer? Real beer?"

Po nodded.

I offered to buy him a beer.

The bar was a plain room with a concrete floor and one long, roughly hewn wooden table flanked by two wooden benches. The barman, casually dressed in brown shorts and displaying his brown torso, served the bottles of commercially brewed Togo Lager at room temperature. No refrigeration here. But still the beer was thirst quenching.

We didn't want to overstay our welcome. Po told us he planned on visiting other friends and would stay overnight in one of the little bedrooms in his friend's tata.

As he walked us to our waiting passenger truck, I mulled over our good fortune in meeting Mr. Po who enabled us to have an insider's view of life in a tata.

Mr. Po interrupted my thoughts. "It was my good luck to meet you," he said. "I like to keep in touch with my roots. You solved my problem of getting here. Thank you for coming to my village."

"*We* should be thanking *you* for introducing us to your culture," I said.

We shook his hand, thanked him, boarded the truck and waved goodbye.

Once again a benevolent person had come into our lives just when we needed help.

Ghana

Painful journey

Bolgatanga to Kumasi, February 1987
See map, page 14

Encouraged by a light breeze, dust swirled around the bus station at Bolgatanga, the arid border town in northern Ghana. Penny and I had just arrived from Burkina Faso, the republic to the north, and hoped to find a bus going south to the coast.

At a ticket office we asked about southbound transport to Kumasi. We were pleased to be in a country where English was the official language. The man behind the counter, his dark face aglow with a toothy smile, told us the State Transport Corporation's first class bus had left earlier that morning.

"There are seats on that truck," he continued, pointing to an old British Bedford with a bus body built behind the cab. "But I wouldn't recommend it. It's uncomfortable."

We weren't daunted, having already experienced rough travel on the plains of West Africa. We didn't need soft seats and the protection of a bus's thick, tinted glass windows. We bought tickets on the truck to Kumasi, the former capital of the Ashanti kingdom, 350 miles south. The ticket seller told us the truck would be leaving soon and suggested we wait on a wooden bench that was propped against the trunk of a shady tree.

The shade provided some respite from the midday sun, a silver orb of searing heat. We were here in the dry season when the sky was hazy with dust and grit carried by harmattan winds from the Sahara.

From our vantage point we watched baggage handlers carry passengers' large bundles and sacks up ladders to the roof. For no apparent reason they were taken down and the owners had to claim them. Then they were loaded again. People shouted their frustrations. While some men and women pushed and shoved to get on the truck others battled to get off, then lined up to board again. Voices grew louder and angrier. Women laden with parcels and babies slung over their backs struggled onto the truck.

There must have been someone bossing these passengers around but we couldn't see him. "I bet someone wearing a badge is abusing his power," I said to Penny. "Those defenceless people are being tyrannized."

I could hardly believe what we were witnessing. It was chaotic. Nothing made any sense. There were more people waiting to board than there were seats. I doubted there would be space for us despite our tickets. Baggage handlers continued to add more bags and boxes to the pile on the roof. Without alternative transportation we had no choice but to sit and wait.

Finally, after five hours of this charade, the ticket seller beckoned us to head for the truck. A baggage handler tied our bags onto the roof, then told us we had to wait until everyone had boarded before we could get on. Finally, a dispatcher invited us to board.

The two seats saved for us were near the door on a wooden bench bolted to the rear of the cab. We and four local women, with our backs to the cab, faced the rest of the passengers, many of whom craned to glimpse the two foreigners in their midst.

The interior was crowded and oppressively hot. Perspiration beaded on my brow while we waited to leave. The air, heavy with humidity, stifled my breathing.

We left in the late afternoon. What happened to our "leaving soon" as the ticket seller said we would? The Ghanaian sense of time obviously differed from ours.

The advantage of the bench, we discovered when we got moving, was a refreshing breeze that blew through the door's open window.

The disadvantage was the need to face young male passengers who were so close that our knees pressed against theirs and there was little room for our feet.

A faded sign screwed to the back of the cab stated the truck was built to carry forty-two passengers but we counted about sixty and ten babies. I glanced at the solemn faces of the crowd who seemed upset that the truck company had sold too many tickets. More than half of the passengers were young men heading south for work. Freeloaders included a box of live chickens, a box of rabbits and a bleating goat.

We drove south through land that was cracked and brittle. Heat hazes shimmered along the horizon until the orange sun began its slow descent towards the western ridges. Thorn trees cast long thin shadows until the pitch black of the night swallowed our lonely truck as it rumbled along the potholed road.

Each time a wheel hit a pothole everyone in the truck suffered a jolt. We gritted our teeth as we winced in pain and our knees knocked against those of the fellows who faced us. The goat bleated frantically every time we hit a rough spot. Some of the potholes were small, the size of a wheel; others had grown as large as the truck itself.

Near Kedia the truck drove headlong into a hole as deep as the truck was high. We gripped the seats as the tires slid on the moist clay. The driver revved the engine and the Bedford started to grind its way to the other end of the crater-like pothole with a gnashing of gears. The heavily laden truck swayed dangerously to either side and pitched the passengers against each other before crawling up and out of the hole.

The young men opposite us stared impassively ahead while we all endured the torture. Because they appeared so relaxed it was obvious they had resigned themselves to these conditions.

The only relief experienced during this horrific journey was at the half-dozen police stops where the police checked passengers' identification documents. Each time the truck stopped we had the chance to file off to limber our legs.

At the police stop on the outskirts of Tamale we climbed down from the truck and milled around in the pitch dark, waiting to have our documents checked.

The police were ambiguous with their orders. One policeman ordered the passengers not to move from where they stood while another policeman, a bulky figure with the head of a pit-bull, barked an order. "Move! Get into line." If they were slow to move he pushed and shoved them.

He wouldn't earn my vote as the Policeman of the Month. We lined up with the others who had been verbally bullied into submission.

At the same check point a police officer materialized beside Penny and me and escorted us farther along the dark road, away from the other passengers. I felt the guy was up to no good otherwise why would he lead us away?

Penny stayed close beside me, nervous about the officer's intentions. I guessed extortion. I had experienced extortion attempts before and knew the way to foil the perpetrator: be uncooperative, play dumb and call his bluff if the need arose.

"Passport," he demanded.

I handed him my passport. With long, loosely fleshed fingers he flipped through the pages as a formality. He would rather be riffling through my little roll of American dollars. But I wouldn't allow him to get that far. He returned my passport, scanned Penny's and gave hers back.

Then he got down to business. "Money," he demanded. His mouth salivated, probably at the thought of a handful of greenbacks.

I pretended not to understand. He said it again. I stared at him blankly. Unable to get his message across he became irritated. Little beads of perspiration on his forehead told me he was uncomfortable. He appeared to lack experience in the sport of extortion.

"Money," he said again.

He was saved from further frustration when the driver called all passengers back to the truck. I was relieved.

As we headed back along the road Penny and I quickened our pace and stepped into the glare of the truck's headlight beam to thwart any further attempts. The officer gave up his demands, joined his cronies and stood aside while we reboarded the vehicle.

Police checks were common in West Africa, even many miles from a border. It seemed to us that these checks were an unnecessary inconvenience with no apparent benefit to anyone except some policemen. Our driver often gave bribes to the bullies in uniform to avoid extensive delays. I assumed the cost of bribery was reflected in the price of the ticket.

On the outskirts of Techiman we stopped at another police check point. A police sergeant looked at the driver's licence and vehicle documents, sauntered around the truck and kicked a couple of tires. This was his subtle way of giving the driver enough time to count the number of bank notes necessary to pay the bribe so we wouldn't be delayed longer by a detailed inspection of the truck.

The driver climbed out of the cab and muttered something to the policeman as he handed over the money. This definitely wasn't a payment for which an official receipt would be issued!

As we continued our journey the sun rose above the distant horizon and showered us with its golden rays. We tried to appreciate the hills and grassland around us but trying to overcome the pain in our bodies was uppermost in our minds.

After nineteen hours of punishment we rolled into Kumasi in the early afternoon. Our legs were stiff and our posteriors covered with welts from being storm-tossed on the wooden bench. Our only sustenance during the trip had been water and the bananas we had bought enroute.

We found a hotel and collapsed on the bed. About nine hours later we woke up, ate a banana and fell asleep again until five-thirty the next morning.

When we told the hotel proprietor we had arrived by truck from Bolgatanga he looked horrified. "That is how the poorest village people travel. You should have come on a government-run STC bus which leaves Bolga in the mornings. It is very comfortable; first class." We told him we had known about the STC bus but it had already left by the time we arrived at Bolgatanga.

Even though we were unable to sit down comfortably for a few days we felt humbled to have travelled with the tolerant, uncomplaining villagers who had to endure harsh conditions and be humiliated by bullies in uniform who pushed and shoved them around.

We set out to explore Kumasi. At the nearby Accra Road intersection we approached a policeman who appeared to be watching for vehicle infractions. I asked for directions to the Cultural Centre which housed the Ashanti Museum. He politely gave us his full attention and pointed down the road. He was on his way to win my vote for Policeman of the Month.

He then turned back to focus on the traffic. I watched him call to a taxi driver.

The policeman swaggered to the driver's window and flicked his fingers for the licence. Then he sauntered around the taxi.

And, as expected, kicked a couple of tires.

Ghana

Almost in the movies

Incident at Elmina, March 1987
See map, page 14

From beyond the wall ahead of us Penny and I heard rhythmic drumbeats accompanied by warlike chants. Above the din the French movie director yelled something to his film crew through a loud speaker. The drumbeats thundered louder and faster and the warlike chants grew to a series of whoops and yells as the Ghanaian film extras worked themselves into a frenzy. I turned to Penny. She looked hesitant. "I'm not sure we should go ahead," she said.

Earlier in the day when we boarded a bus in Accra, Ghana's capital, we never imagined we would be involved in a movie.

The bus travelled west along a blacktopped road which occasionally hugged the coastline.

After three hours we arrived at the coastal fishing village of Elmina, dwarfed by a gigantic lime-white castle, the earliest known European building in tropical Africa. The Portuguese built it in 1482 as a trading post, using rock from the headland on which the castle stood. This was just one of more than fifty castles and forts built by Europeans along Ghana's 560-kilometre coastline. They had been reasonably secure places from which to trade in gold, ivory and slaves.

Most of Europe's maritime nations were involved in trade with

West Africa, and this led to rivalry. In 1637, during the slave trading era, the Dutch captured the castle from the Portuguese, but sold it to the British in 1872 who named it Saint George's Castle. It was about this time that slavery was abolished.

We arrived to find cars and trucks marked "Ghana Films" parked outside the castle and a horde of people, mainly blacks, milling around the castle entrance. Probably hoping to be extras, I thought.

A skinny blonde French woman with bright red lips popped out of the crowd, told us a French company was making an historical film and that the castle was closed. We were dismayed. I told her we had come a long way to see the castle and we weren't able to come back another day. She conferred with her peers and, thankfully, permitted us to enter provided we kept a low profile.

For two hours we explored the battlements with their cannons, storage rooms and slave prisons, all the time staying out of sight. The storerooms and dungeons that housed slaves awaiting shipment to the New World were pitiful: windowless, little ventilation, a lack of toilet facilities and drainage. We were horrified that humans would treat other humans in this shameful way.

There had been no shortage of slaves to be traded as human cargo. Conflicts increased between tribes when they realized they could sell prisoners of war for profit at the castles or forts. We walked in silence and tried to imagine the degradation that had been suffered between these walls.

When we were ready to leave, a Ghanaian film crew member said he would show us out. He would take us behind the audio crew, down the stairs and off the set. It seemed like a good plan. He checked ahead and waved us forward. But we hesitated.

Rhythmic drumbeats pounded from beyond the wall ahead of us. Whoops and yells filled the afternoon air, and got louder as the drumming grew more frenetic. The French director's voice over the loud speaker sounded demanding as he yelled to his film crew.

Should we be going ahead?

Penny didn't think so, nor did I. But the Ghanaian crew member ahead of us seemed confident. He turned, whispered to us to follow him and waved his arm urgently. I hoped he knew what he was doing.

We crept towards the back of the sound stage, waiting for the right time to cross. He nodded and pointed forward.

We stepped onto the darkened stage. Just when we were half way across it, the flood lights came on, catching us in their glare, and the cameras rolled.

We stood fixed to the floor, horrified.

At that moment a hundred or more Ashanti warriors, a mass of bare torsos, loincloths and feathers, entered the castle compound. They waved spears and clubs as they war-danced their way onto the stage to re-enact a battle.

We were caught in the middle.

When the French woman spotted us she frantically waved us back. The director yelled "Stop" and waved us forward. We were confused. I wish I could have evaporated. My face burned with embarrassment. I repeated "Sorry" and *"Excusez-moi."* Penny was right behind me, also apologizing profusely.

We crossed the stage, scurried past the furious director, the camera crews, actors, extras, hangers-on and the French woman who was now wild eyed, tearing at her hair with long red fingernails. We darted towards the exit without looking back.

We didn't wait to be called for a second take!

Côte d'Ivoire (also known as Ivory Coast)

Try the bus!

The road from Accra to Abidjan, March 1987
See map, page 14

"Please write it all down and tell the world what is happening to us," Thomas said.

"Yes, Thomas," I said. "Penny is recording all the stops and the amount of the bribes."

We could hardly believe the treatment the bus passengers had to endure at the police and customs check points. We were now into the ninth hour of our ordeal from Accra, Ghana to Abidjan, Côte d'Ivoire, also known as Ivory Coast.

A few days earlier we had gone to the Canadian High Commission in Accra to read the current newspapers. We met Brian, a government official on business from the Canadian Embassy in Abidjan. A friendly, clean cut guy in his thirties, he looked cool in his blue cotton shirt and pressed casual trousers. These contrasted noticeably with our clean, comfortable but travel-worn clothes that had covered many miles of overland travel under West Africa's broiling sun.

Brian, who spent most of his time working in air-conditioned comfort, was taking a 45-minute flight to Abidjan the next day. He was intrigued by our travels. "Join me for a tall, cool one when you get to Abidjan," he said. "You'll find me at the Embassy."

Our day to leave Accra started before dawn when Penny and I

arrived at the State Transport Corporation's International bus station in Accra, Ghana. We were heading to Abidjan in Côte d'Ivoire – the republic next door – for what we expected would be a pleasant drive along the coast.

Baggage handlers arrived to load the luggage onto the top of the bus. Most of the passengers' belongings were wrapped in blankets tied with rope. There were a few bulging suitcases with snaps and ropes holding them closed and large red, white and blue striped shopping bags similarly tied with rope, and our two backpacks. Penny boarded the bus to choose our seats while I stayed to make sure our backpacks were positioned so they would not bounce off the top of the bus. Everything was well-organized – the workers pulled a tarpaulin over all the luggage and tied it down. The work took longer than expected; instead of leaving at six we left at seven-thirty.

We followed the road westwards, passing plantations of rubber trees, oil palms and coconut palms. The forty passengers on the bus comprised Ghanaians and Ivoireans and us. There was also a man in the co-driver's seat. It appeared to be a happy crowd, judging by the animated conversations in English, French and regional dialects. The women wore brightly coloured long skirts with matching blouses and headscarves. Most of the men were dressed in caftans but some wore slacks and cotton shirts.

In the seat ahead of us sat a jovial man, his complexion matching his black shirt. "I'm from Ghana," he told us, "but I live in Sweden, married to a Swede." I think he was trying to tell us he was different from the other passengers. "I carry a Swedish passport," he added, and told us his name was Thomas.

At one-fifteen in the afternoon we arrived at the Ghanaian border post where our passports were stamped. We changed Ghanaian cedis for CFAs with moneychangers who strolled around with wads of different currency notes stuffed in their pockets. The CFA (*Communauté Financière Africaine*) is the currency used in Côte d'Ivoire and most other former French colonies in West Africa. This business took about an hour; we left at two-twenty p.m. and arrived two minutes later at the Côte d'Ivoire border post.

Everyone got off. The driver and his helper (or courier) handed down the bags from the roof. We all lined up outside the customs office where two men were on duty. I expected a lengthy delay. A couple travelling together were the first to go into the office with their bags. A few moments later they emerged frowning, and muttered something to the other passengers.

Next to go in with his roped belongings was a man travelling alone. When he came out he ranted to the others. Thomas called to us. "The customs men are searching the bags then demanding 1,000 CFAs from each person." I felt sympathy for these people as 1,000 CFAs is about five dollars which is roughly three days' pay for many people in West Africa.

Our turn came to enter the office. The customs officials, dressed in khaki uniforms, greeted us, checked through our bags and discovered our unused Super-8 movie and slide films. They removed our belongings, spread them on counters around the room in the hope, I believed, we would lose track of them, but we kept our eyes on every item. One officer spoke rapidly in French to his colleague but I caught the word *douane* which means customs. I realized they may consider a customs duty charge on the film. This would not have been legal because films are regarded as non-dutiable personal effects. I protested loudly before he could speak to us and he backed down and indicated we could repack.

We quickly gathered our belongings from around the room and stuffed them into our backpacks. He waved us out without demanding a bribe. When we emerged everyone in the line-up looked concerned as we had been in the office for about fifteen minutes. Penny told them we weren't asked for a *cadeau* (gift) of 1,000 CFAs each.

I felt guilty that we were treated differently by not being asked for a bribe. It could have been because we were Western tourists who may have reported the incident.

The next office to visit was Immigration. We added our passports to a stack on the desk and waited outside while they were perused and stamped with the date of entry. When the passports were ready, the passengers were called into the office one by one and told that to get their passport back they would have to pay 500 CFAs each. For some unknown reason we were not charged the fee. We figured they did not want to start an international incident by extorting from foreigners. But they charged Thomas despite his Swedish passport. Perhaps, because he was African, he was fair game.

While the passengers paid the bribes the driver and his courier loaded the bags.

Finally at three-fifty-five p.m., with passengers and bags on board, we left the border. Everyone spoke in animated voices. I sensed the conversations were about the recent experience.

The road was paved and in good condition. The bus was comfortable and we sat back to enjoy the views. Oil palms grew on both sides of the road and occasionally we saw the ocean waves pounding the shore.

Presently the courier, who sat in the co-driver's seat, stood and announced in English, French and a local dialect that we would encounter a number of police and customs checkpoints enroute to Abidjan and that they would ask for bribes. If we refused to pay they would order everyone off the bus, search all the bags and demand a bribe from each person, individually. He suggested we pass around a hat and collect 1,000 CFAs from each passenger for a kitty from which to pay the bribes. We were shocked by this announcement but there was no use in our protesting; we were at their mercy.

There was an uproar in the bus. By the time the announcement had been made in three languages, everyone was talking at once. Thomas jumped up and said it was because of corruption that Africans wanted to migrate to Western countries. He added that he could drive all over Europe and cross borders without having to pay a bribe to anyone. Some men and women said they would refuse to pay.

The courier spoke again when the arguments had ceased and said we had no alternative but to pay if we wanted to reach Abidjan. Penny and I felt sorry for some passengers who looked destitute. We could have offered to pay for them, but in controversial situations like this it was better to keep a low profile.

A hat was passed among the forty passengers and filled with 36,000 CFAs.

At four-thirty p.m. we stopped at another customs checkpoint. The officer demanded 10,000 CFAs or he would order all the bags on the roof to be unloaded and individually inspected by his men. The courier handed over ten thousand.

Thomas saw Penny making notes. "Please write it all down and tell the world what is happening to us," he said. We could hardly believe these rip-offs and knew we had to record them to remember.

The bus left, but incredibly, six minutes later we arrived at a police post. The police wanted to see all passports and all yellow health cards. The officer in charge added that all Ghanaian women had AIDS and must be tested. A passenger called out, "How long will that take?"

The policeman answered: "The doctor is away. He will be here in three days." Then he said we could proceed immediately by paying 40,000 CFAs. This was becoming bizarre. I thought it outrageous these passengers had to endure these injustices.

"You are holding us hostage," a voice screamed from the rear.

A lot of heated discussion broke out among the passengers. The courier jumped off the bus to negotiate with the officer but was unable to reduce the demand so he got back on.

A male passenger strode to the front of the bus and yelled at the officer that his comment about all Ghanaian women having AIDS was a slur on the womanhood of Ghana and that it would not be tolerated. The other passengers roared their agreement.

The police officer ignored the outburst and stood his ground. The courier again got off the bus. Thomas stood at the door listening, then called out, "He'll accept 20,000 CFAs." Then Thomas said to Penny, "The officer's name-badge says Sanhouman. Please write it down."

The courier counted out 20,000 into the officer's hand.

This stop lasted an hour-and-a-half. At six-ten p.m. we left but Penny hardly had time to record the last stop in our note book when, at six-fifteen, we slowed down at another police post but a policeman waved us on. I was amazed at this leniency and didn't understand why. I expected more bribery farther down the road.

At six-twenty p.m. we arrived at another police post. After a brief five-minute negotiation our courier paid 4,000 CFAs and we drove away.

When the police stopped us again at six-thirty-four, passengers' voices grew louder and more agitated as they discussed the situation. A policeman boarded and asked to see all passports. As the courier started to collect the passports a skinny young man with a nut-brown face rose and said he had not been given back his passport from a previous police stop.

Why didn't he say something before? I wouldn't have let the bus leave a checkpoint if my passport was missing. And where is the guy from?

The courier asked his nationality.

"Philippines. And my name is Patrick."

The courier conferred with the driver then announced we would turn around and go back. We drove to a small town, Aboisso, where we all disembarked to wait while the driver, courier and Patrick kept going to the last checkpoint. I surmised that his passport was mislaid where Sanhouman collected the 20,000 CFAs.

Forty minutes later the bus returned. They had not found Patrick's passport. Penny and I spoke to him and he told us the driver and courier appeared to be on jovial terms with the police and that he would be very surprised if they were not in league with them, sharing some of the bribe money.

Patrick seemed more interested in the driver and courier than his passport, which he didn't even mention.

We considered sharing with Thomas and the other passengers Patrick's observations of the driver and courier but decided against it. The passengers were in a lynching mood, and we didn't want to make the situation worse.

At eight p.m. we reboarded the bus and set off again but five minutes later stopped at the police post where we had previously paid 4,000 CFAs. After a five-minute negotiation we proceeded without paying again.

At eight-forty-five, as if all the police stops weren't enough, the bus sagged and jerked to a stop in the middle of a town. We had a flat tire. We filed off the bus. I was frustrated; it was now the thirteenth hour of a trip supposed to take only eight hours. While the driver and courier changed the tire, four policemen, obviously recognizing a rare opportunity, descended on the bus like vultures and rummaged through people's bags. Whether any money changed hands we didn't know because we stayed out of sight.

At ten-fifteen p.m. we left but three minutes later, on the outskirts of the town, we stopped at another police post. They demanded 7,000 CFAs but we only had 2,000 left in the kitty. Negotiations handled by the courier could not reduce the demand so he announced the hat would be passed around again.

People protested. Some said they had no more money to give. However, the courier collected 9,000 CFAs, boosting the kitty to 11,000, then doled out 7,000 to the police officer.

At ten-forty-seven p.m. we left but twenty minutes later stopped at another police post. People were too tired to complain. Thomas marched to the front to listen to the negotiation between the courier and the police officer. Indignant, he returned and blurted out, "We have 4,000 CFAs in the kitty and he wants all of it. You'll write that down, won't you?"

"It's all written down," I confirmed to Thomas.

The courier parted with the money.

At twenty minutes past midnight we arrived in Abidjan. We had survived eleven checkpoints on the 530-kilometre journey which lasted seventeen hours. We were exhausted .

We shook Thomas' hand and said goodbye. He was in Abidjan to visit friends. We told him we would let as many people as possible know about the injustices we had just witnessed. We wished him well as he went on his way.

I felt sorry for Patrick who had lost his passport and had not changed any money into CFAs. I asked him to come to a hotel with us and offered to pay for his room. After we checked in and prepaid the rooms, he told us he hadn't really lost his passport. He had just wanted to frighten the driver and courier to make them aware that handling other people's passports was a serious business.

"Are you saying that the trip back to the police checkpoint

wasn't necessary?"

"That's right."

Annoyed, I said, "That little lesson for the courier added an extra two hours to our trip."

"That's right. I'm sorry."

"Well, where is your passport?"

"You've got it."

"Where have I got it?" My voice rose.

"It's in your shoulder bag. On the bus I put it there when you weren't looking."

I was irate as I rifled through the bag, found it and tossed it to him. I could hardly believe that he would plant his passport in my bag. I expected him to apologize and offer to reimburse us for his room, but he didn't do so. I didn't press the point. He was a skinny little guy; I hoped he would use the savings to buy a good meal.

The next day Penny and I visited the Canadian Embassy and looked up Brian in his air-conditioned office. When we told him about the seventeen-hour bus ordeal he shook his head in disbelief.

"I'm shocked. I do the trip quite often in the Embassy's Land Cruiser. I'm never bribed and it only takes six hours."

"Just for the experience," I said, "you should try the bus!"

Mali

Noisy nights

A busy hotel in Mopti, March 1987
See map, page 14

The afternoon's high-altitude sun shimmered as it breathed dry heat over the land. Penny and I had just arrived in Mopti, a desert town in Mali located at the confluence of the Niger and Bani Rivers. We had journeyed by train from Abidjan on the coast to Bobo Dioulasso in Burkina Faso then travelled by bush taxis to Mopti. Our plan was to visit the Dogon tribe. But first, we needed a hotel.

We plodded along narrow, sandy lanes lined with high mud walls, double our height, that gave privacy to the townspeople's homes. Tall wooden gates provided access and occasionally one was ajar. We saw a neat courtyard, where a woman pounded sorghum in a mortar and another hung laundry on a line. Children played in the lanes but stopped and stared when we walked by. We greeted them with a friendly wave.

Around the next corner we saw a two-storey building with a faded red sign which read Hotel Bar Mali. The yellow paint on its stuccoed walls had peeled with age, and green wooden window shutters hung crookedly. We were in luck. This place looked like our kind of hotel: it had character.

We squeezed through the narrow half-open doorway which kept out most of the daylight and entered a gloomy room. When our eyes adjusted to the darkened interior we saw a man standing at the check-in desk.

"How much is a room?" I asked.

"Nine dollars a night."

"Can we see it?" Penny asked.

We followed the thin, solemn-faced proprietor up a dim stairway and along a narrow corridor lined with doors. He pushed a door which opened into a small room with a huge bed. The heat inside the room was as oppressive as the hot, humid air outside. A large electric fan hung from the ceiling. "What a relief," I said as I switched it to ON. The fan didn't move. I flicked the switch again, not wanting to believe that it didn't work. Nothing happened.

"The electricity doesn't come on until six-thirty in the evening," the hotel proprietor said. I hoped he was right; we checked in. It was not unusual in Mali for power to be off for a few hours per day.

A door at the end of the corridor opened onto a balcony crammed with potted shrubs – a tiny Garden of Eden. With just enough room for two chairs it would be a great vantage point for soaking up the culture from the street below.

As we unpacked our bags we heard doors open and close, and laughter fill the corridor and the rooms. It appeared to be a popular hotel with a happy clientele. Armed with towel and soap I strolled along the corridor to the shower cubicles but both were occupied. I returned to our room to wait. Each time I went to a cubicle I found it was occupied or someone had just beaten me to the door. After several tries I gave up.

We relaxed on the balcony in the cool of the evening and watched the lights of Mopti come on night duty. The sun set behind a mound of cloud, trimming it with pink. Women set up food stalls in the street below. Orange flames licked at the bottoms of their woks as they cooked corn fritters for evening customers. We watched with interest as men and women came in and out of the hotel.

I pointed out to Penny a woman on the street who had beaten me into a shower cubicle. Her flowing yellow dress contrasted vibrantly with her blue-black skin. We watched a man approach her, discuss something, shake his head and walk away. The woman shrugged, ambled over to a street vendor and bought a corn fritter.

Just as she finished it, another man approached and spoke briefly. She nodded. I guessed he knew her because he followed her into the hotel.

We retired for the night but sleep was almost impossible. Footsteps padded along the corridor and noisy voices erupted from the rooms.

It finally dawned on us. "We were in a brothel!"

Mali

Villages beyond the horizon

By donkey cart to visit the Dogon, March 1987
See map, page 14

Mopti was the town from where Penny and I planned to visit one or two small villages of the Dogon tribe. The Dogon numbered about 250,000 and lived in about 700 villages scattered along a 200-kilometre escarpment in Mali. Their oral history tells of their retreat to the escarpment 600 years ago to escape the marauding Fulani and other ethnic groups who were threatening their granaries. Today they continue to build their granaries on the cliff-faces, cultivate their staple diet of millet, sorghum and beans on the plain below the cliffs and grow onions on the plateau above the cliffs.

The Dogon are animists, believing that natural objects such as rocks and trees are inhabited by spirits. Since the mists of time they have exalted the bright star Sirius – a relatively stationary star – and its satellite, Sirius B.

In the 1930s two distinguished French anthropologists lived with the Dogon and learned of their animist religion and their erudite knowledge of Sirius and Sirius B (as they are called by modern astronomers). Although long known to the Dogon, Sirius B was first seen by Western astronomers only in the mid-1800s.

Some historians believe the Dogon people gained knowledge of the satellite by extra-sensory perception – the ability to perceive scenes far beyond the horizon of immediate eyesight. They also exalt

Sirius C, but this has not been located by today's astronomers.

Conversely, some historians say the Dogon gained their knowledge about Sirius from cultural exchanges with Islamic and European scholars.

We were keen to visit one or more of their villages to help satisfy our curiosity about them. But they lived in the desert. Getting there could be a challenge.

While we were roaming through Mopti's riverside market a lanky man in his twenties approached and offered to be our guide if we wanted to visit the Dogon. He arrived at an opportune time because Penny and I had just been trying to figure out how to get to one of their villages. It was as if he had read our minds!

His name was Omar, he told us, and he spoke some of the Dogon language and French, but no English. We liked the young man immediately. He had an aura of calmness and quiet efficiency about him. We agreed to employ him despite our need to converse in fractured French.

We decided to leave the following day and asked Omar if there was anything we should take to the village. When he suggested rice we gave him money to buy it for us.

The next day, just after sunrise, Omar met us at our hotel and led us along some of Mopti's narrow dusty lanes lined with three-metre high mud walls. He wanted us to meet his family and to pick up the rice.

He pushed open a wooden gate in the mud wall and there, in a courtyard the size of a basketball court, people were going about their daily chores. Women tended their babies, young boys pulled water from the well and girls washed clothes in basins on the ground. We didn't see any men. We assumed they were involved in trade in the town.

The women wore the *bou bou* – a skirt of colourful fabric worn with a long blouse. The people were Omar's immediate family and cousins. Around the courtyard, doors opened into bedrooms, kitchens and storage rooms. Each family had its separate living quarters.

Omar had bought a paper sack containing five kilograms of rice which he poured into a more durable cloth bag for the trip.

We strode to the taxi-truck station from where passenger vehicles headed out of Mopti. Omar suggested we board a pickup truck going to Bankas, a desert town about three hours to the southeast.

The vehicles do not leave the station until they are full of passengers. Sometimes you wait five minutes before you leave or sometimes five hours. In our case we waited five hours while passengers were found and a bald tire was changed for a less-bald one. An iron bed frame and other household goods, and people's belongings, were loaded onto the roof rack.

The Peugeot 404 we were to travel in was fitted with wooden bench seats along both sides. Built to carry ten people, it was overloaded with sixteen passengers, including Penny and me. Where there should have been space by our feet for luggage, three men sat there instead. We balanced our backpacks on our laps. Boxes and bags that would normally be carried inside the truck were tied precariously to the roof rack, causing the vehicle to lean dangerously to one side.

Finally the wheels spun forward and our journey began.

Under West Africa's hot noonday sun, the pickup truck gained speed and thundered along the blacktopped highway. The road sliced across a broad, arid plain of grass and stunted trees. The driver drove at breakneck speed, swerving only to dodge potholes.

Without warning we all jolted off our seats. The truck rocked violently. A pothole! Then a loud bang! Chunks of rubber shot into the air. I gripped the seat in terror. Penny, her eyes shut tight, clung to my arm. The truck shook out of control. I feared it would flip and toss us onto the road. It veered crazily onto the gravel shoulder, skidded and gradually drifted to a stop.

We stepped down, shaking, thankful to be alive. Adrenalin pumped overtime. I realized we could have been snuffed out in seconds. Scattered along the road lay the chunks of rubber tire which had torn off the rim.

The driver caught a ride back to Mopti to get help while we

waited under a shady tree. The other passengers, probably all from Bankas, seemed to know each other; they chatted constantly while Penny and I passed the time solving crossword puzzles. Three hours later the driver returned with another pickup truck and we reached Bankas at dusk.

Bankas was a town of one- and two-storey homes that loomed above the desolate, flat terrain. The homes, and the three-metre high walls that surrounded them, were built with the reddish-brown earth that covered the landscape. The town appeared deserted except for the Bar-Ben Restaurant. Omar led us to one of the outdoor tables to meet the owner. A wiry man bounced off his chair and greeted us with "My name is Ben."

He was a jolly soul with a mobile mouth that smiled easily. He guessed why we were in Bankas.

"So," he said, "you want to go across the desert to visit the Dogon. Konikombole is the nearest village. The next is Tele." Then he added proudly, "I'm half-Dogon and half-Fulani."

He was copper-skinned, a legacy of his Fulani roots. The Fulani were cattle herders who came into contact with farming groups, such as the Dogon, to trade cattle for farm products and engage in the occasional liaison.

"How can you help us?" I asked.

"I can arrange a donkey cart and driver. You can leave at first light tomorrow if you wish."

He spoke understandable English which made negotiations easier.

After we settled on a price Ben showed us to a free-standing mud-walled room where we could stay the night.

"I don't think I can sleep in here," Penny said as she stepped into a curtain of hot, stale air. "Maybe we can sleep outside."

Ben agreed and handed us some reed mats which we spread on the ground.

Meanwhile, I checked out the toilet facility a short distance away. It consisted of a hole in the ground surrounded by a low, one-metre high wall of mud bricks. In an adjoining compound I spied a bucket of cold water to be used for a body wash. I felt refreshed after dowsing myself to get rid of the day's travel grime of red dust and sweat.

Nearby, the locals drank beer and played cards long into the evening; their loud voices, music and laughter kept us awake.

We had a restless night on the stony ground but were compensated by the spectacle of the large, yellow, full moon which hung like a shiny ball in the clear night sky.

In the morning, as the sun climbed out of its fiery haven in the east, Omar introduced us to our 15-year-old donkey cart driver, Braymar. He was a docile boy with a smooth, brown face and dark, deep set eyes and whose khaki shirt and shorts blended with the landscape.

The donkey, whose name was Toh-loh, was harnessed to a flat-decked cart with two wheels of bald rubber tires. But it didn't matter, we weren't going anywhere fast! We hoisted ourselves onto the deck of the cart with our day packs and provisions of rice and water and set out in the cool morning air. Omar joined us on the cart while Braymar walked beside the donkey.

Toh-loh pulled the cart along a sandy track through fields of harvested millet. The stalks lay strewn over the ground, waiting to be collected and placed in the branches of a tree for later use as fodder for the animals. Some acacia trees already had piles of millet stalks stowed safely in their branches, out of reach of the domestic animals: the cows, goats, sheep and donkeys.

A caravan of half a dozen donkeys trotted towards us loaded with cowhide sacks of millet on their backs, bound for the Tuesday market in Bankas. Behind them a farmer in dusty, beige coloured shorts and shirt, goaded the animals forward.

In the distance women headed towards us, dressed in bright red blouses and black skirts, a striking contrast to the short, dry, yellow grass of the plain. They each carried on their head two or three large baskets balanced on top of one another, all supported by an upstretched arm as they headed to the market. They walked with their backs straight and proud, their gait so fluid they seemed to glide along the trail. We waved to them; they waved back cheerfully with their free hand.

As the track became sandier and less distinct, the donkey refused to continue. Braymar pulled Toh-loh while Omar and I pushed the cart, but to no avail. Toh-loh was showing his stubborn streak.

I had a heart-to-heart talk with Toh-loh. We agreed if I walked in front, he would follow. He kept his part of the agreement. It turned out to be a long walk for me.

Meanwhile, Penny rode on the flat-deck to prevent our bags, the rice and canteens of precious water from bouncing off the cart. Fortunately Toh-loh didn't need our water. Donkeys only drink every two or three days.

On the way we passed four people camped in the middle of a harvested millet field in homes made of millet stalks. The two men wore blue robes and turbans; the women wore black robes. All looked gaunt. There were no children around. Omar looked concerned. "They are different," he said. "They don't belong here." He left us to speak to them and find out who they were.

Members of the Bella tribe, he told us, who had worked in the region between Timbuktu and Gao tending livestock owned by the Tuareg, the principal nomads in the Saharan region. Because of lack of pasture during the recent drought the Tuareg lost thousands of camels, sheep and goats and became impoverished. The Bella lost their jobs, forcing them to wander in search of work. People in this harsh environment had to be resilient. Through Omar we wished them well and marched onwards.

Farther along the track cotton bushes struggled to grow within fenced compounds. Beyond them the parched land looked like an artist's palette of browns, creams and rusts. This was the season when hot, dry, harmattan winds blew from the Sahara. We saw dry earth scooped up by the wind and sent spiralling upward to become a dust devil – a funnel of spinning sand, dust and leaves. Dust devils pirouetted over the land and, as they petered out, new ones developed.

I trudged ahead of Toh-loh along a narrow track faintly etched in the plain. I focused on the haze ahead where the brown flatness touched the nicotine sky, a colour caused by the dust laden harmattan.

After a short time Penny yelled excitedly from the cart: "There's a bump on the horizon. It's only a blur, but it must be an escarpment."

I felt invigorated and wanted to hurry forward but Toh-loh didn't share my enthusiasm. He just plodded along at his own pace. As we got closer, the escarpment seemed to grow until it loomed over us.

Three and a half hours after leaving Bankas we arrived at the Dogon village of Konikombole nestled below the escarpment.

The huts were built of rocks fallen from the overhanging cliffs, and the usual sun-dried mud. One hut with an earthen floor was a combination of home and restaurant. A low table was covered with a blue plastic cloth printed with large red flowers. Two metal chairs served as dining furniture on one side of the table while the owner's bed served as seating for the other side.

Outside the hut a few scrawny chickens scratched at the dirt. The restaurateur, a thin man with a smooth leathery face who smiled constantly, grabbed a chicken and offered it to us. It would go well with the rice, we decided, and we would share it with Omar and Braymar. We bought it for the evening meal.

We explored the village. In a small mud pool a man mixed water with clay and millet straw, making bricks. Completed bricks lay in neat lines to dry in the sun. Cattle milled about a well where men drew water. Village women carried calabash buckets and tin buckets on their heads to get water for their homes. The women wore long, dark blue skirts with pale blue horizontal stripes – the traditional Dogon cloth – and loose fitting floral blouses. Curious children gathered around us while others peeked from behind walls as we watched some young boys play a traditional African game with small stones.

Omar appeared and told us the donkey was hungry and that we should buy some millet stalks. I handed him a few francs so he could arrange it. Fodder for donkeys, goats and cattle was stored on platforms in trees out of reach of the animals. The village men began pulling down sheaves of stalks. More sheaves were pulled down. Then even more. It was party time for the animals.

The Dogon are known for their masks used in ritual dances at festivals and funerals, which are said to connect them with supernatural forces. Masks are worn to hide the identity of the wearer. About eighty different types are used, some of which can be viewed by the public. Other masks are religious and are kept hidden from view.

A village elder showed us into a hut where they kept a Kanaga mask which had a double cross, said to represent a mythical bird, and a white mask which was worn to stop floods. I could not imagine a flood in this parched land, but it must be possible.

As we emerged from the hut a woman held out to us her sick baby boy. He was hot with a fever. Penny, fortunately, carried aspirins in her day pack. She crushed a quarter of an aspirin, mixed it in a cup of water and let the mother give it to the child. The woman smiled her thanks. I wished we could have done more.

In mid-afternoon we left with Omar, Braymar and two villagers to walk to Tele, another Dogon village one hour away. We followed a sandy track that meandered below the escarpment and encountered a man who addressed us in English.

"Could you spare some change so I can buy some beer?" he asked. He was a small, lean man with a short grey beard and a wrinkled face that was as black as carbon paper. He wore a caftan with pink and white stripes – unusual colours in the desert. Sitting at a jaunty angle on his head was a matching pink and white striped cap. A trendsetter in desert fashion, I wondered?

He told us he had spent twenty-four years working in Ghana where he learned English, and was now on his way home to his village. It wasn't our usual practice to give money to anyone who simply asked for it, but the man had a twinkle in his eye and he looked genuinely thirsty. I dropped a dollar's worth of francs into his hand which he accepted gleefully. We bade him good luck, then continued towards Tele.

As we neared the village we spotted granaries grouped together like village huts on the sloping cliff-face. High above the granaries the sandstone cliffs were pockmarked with dark, cave-like recesses. Perched on ledges at the cave entrances stood clay urns of different sizes. Omar explained they were burial urns. The deceased would be placed in an urn in the fetal position. He told us the large urns held adults and the smaller ones, children and babies.

Penny gazed upwards. "Years ago I saw pictures of this place. I never thought I'd see it with my own eyes."

When we arrived at the village Omar suggested we find the headman to make a courtesy call and ask permission to visit the cliffside. To look for him we spread out among the forty or so thatch-roofed huts which were huddled together. Children scampered around; some amused themselves by blowing crudely carved wooden whistles. Women sat in front of their doors while they twisted and wound cotton onto spindles. A few elderly men pottered around but no young men were in sight. Maybe they were working in the fields.

Omar found the headman, a short, grey-haired man with a bony countenance and a welcoming smile. His leathery face was indented with deep wrinkles. His brown chest was bare and he wore a beige pair of well worn baggy knee-length shorts tied with a string at the waist. We made the customary donation of 1,000 francs, about three dollars, for village improvements and he gave us permission to climb up the escarpment to get closer to the granaries and burial chambers.

We struggled up the rocky path to the granaries. They were built of sun-dried mud bricks and stood about four metres tall, with a square base about two metres per side. Among the granaries we found some that had been converted into homes.

In one of them, a wispy little old man twisted strands of bark fibre to make twine. In another a gaunt, toothless man lay agitated, and pointed to a gash above his eye. But we had nothing to relieve his pain or cover the wound. He needed more than just an aspirin. I wished we had brought some medical supplies, but who would have thought we would be administering first aid to the Dogon?

We climbed higher to a vantage point from where we looked over the village huts below us, all with thatched, pointed roofs. Beyond the huts stretched a rocky, sandy plain of semi-desert which looked like a bleak lunar landscape. The distant edges of the pale brown flat land were blurred by a permanent heat haze. It was the plain we had crossed that morning. I hoped Toh-loh had the confidence to cross it without depending on me to lead the way when we returned to Bankas the next day. It can be lonely at the front!

We attempted to climb higher. We could see the burial chambers above us and tried to get closer but the rocky route was steep and slippery with small stones and gravel. It was not safe to go farther up the escarpment for fear of twisting or spraining an ankle. Failing to reach the burial chambers was a disappointment. I thought if we saw them at close range we'd have a better insight of their culture concerning burial rites.

Penny and I sat on a fallen boulder to rest and look down upon the plain. It had been an amazing journey to get here and we were pleased with what we had seen – the village women in their traditional blue striped skirts, homes, crops, masks, granaries and the funerary urns. Because of the difficulty we had communicating, I realized we would not be able to learn directly from them about their culture, including their understanding of Sirius. We were simply observers.

We surveyed the scene below us. A herd of goats appeared from behind some huts, kicking up a cloud of desert dust. A man followed, goading them into a mud-walled corral.

As late afternoon approached, the sun became gentler and the air contained a hint of the desert chill to follow. The scene below us, and the stark, dun-coloured desert beyond looked so peaceful and contained a beauty of its own. It was just a little piece of heaven reserved for Penny and me to cherish for the moment. As the sun lowered, the colours of the desert plain softened to grey. It was time to leave. We picked our way around the rocks on the pathway and called to Omar and Braymar that we were ready to return to Konikombole.

On the way we encountered the man to whom I had given beer money. He waved, hurried forward with a big grin on his face and told us he had become a beer seller with the money we had given him. He insisted on our having a free drink and pulled a glass from his cloth bag. From the gourd slung over his shoulder he poured a beer – a pleasantly palatable brew called *chakalow*, made from millet.

He spoke with enthusiasm when he told us he was able to buy a bulk supply of beer from a group of men who were distilling it in a nearby hut. I was amazed and pleased that our small contribution was enough for the entrepreneur to start a little moneymaking business.

As dusk approached, the sky displayed different shades of yellow and purple. By the time we reached Konikombole a pale yellow moon started to glow on the eastern horizon.

The cook had boiled the rice, the chicken was roasting on a spit and heavenly aromas swirled around my head, biting my nostrils. I was pleased Penny and I were sharing the mini-feast with Omar and Braymar. We both felt an attachment to our two fellow trekkers in just a short time.

Konikombole was rustic; there was no accommodation for visitors except under the stars. We borrowed reed mats, spread them on the rocky ground, and settled down for the night. Sleep was nearly impossible as we tried to find comfortable spots between the pebbles. The yellow moon shone through the baobab trees, casting eerie shadows. Donkeys brayed occasionally, breaking the silence, and little frogs jumped around us.

In the dark, early hours of the morning, sheep raised a cloud of dust and bleated as they scampered past. We covered our faces, our mouths already gritty from breathing in the dust-laden air. Women appeared through the haze on their way to the well to draw water to start their day's chores.

The sun rose, changing the mud huts from brown to gold.

We decided to leave before the full force of the sun beat down. We signalled Omar and Braymar that we were ready to return to Bankas. They hitched the donkey to the cart and we headed out, pleased we had made the effort to visit these people who live far off the beaten track. They appeared to have a semblance of security with their permanent homes and fields, unlike the Bella we had met in the millet field. When we passed the field on our return journey there was no evidence of their having been there.

Three hours later the low skyline of Bankas came into view.

Morocco

Hassan's story

With Berbers of the Atlas Mountains, April 1987

A chicken squawked and scurried past us.

Aunt Fatima, a human dynamo, wiry and grey-haired, chased it, running as fast as her little legs would carry her. With adept, practised hands she caught the frightened chicken.

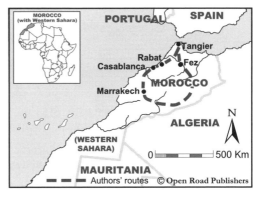

Feathers flew. The squawking stopped.

Moments later it ran around wildly without its head.

Aunt Fatima had boundless energy as she darted from one household chore to the next, chattering non-stop to whomever was in earshot. One minute she plucked the chicken and the next she repaired a hole in the courtyard wall using a pile of mud.

Penny and I were staying in a mud-brick, whitewashed home that stood by itself in a green wheatfield on a gently sloping hillside in Morocco's Atlas Mountains. In the courtyard we sat on clay steps sipping sweet, hot, mint tea as hens and a rooster argued over grain spilled on the ground. The deep lowing of a cow sounded from a stable across the yard. The cow was nursing her fifteen-day old calf.

We were experiencing life in this mountain home, thanks to Hassan.

We had met Hassan a few days earlier on a bus in northern Morocco, on our way to Fez. Penny and I chatted with him for six hours, enjoying his company. He was 27 years old, slightly built with a big friendly smile below his bushy black mustache. He had learned his halting English from students he'd met as a waiter in the restaurant at the University of Rabat. He was single, "but I would like to find a wife," he confided, and was on his annual holiday, heading to his Aunt Fatima's farm in the mountains.

He paused and leaned forward, his face beaming. "Would you," he asked, looking eagerly from Penny to me and back again, "like to come with me and spend a few days with my family?"

I glanced at Penny. It took all of two seconds for us to accept.

We stayed overnight in Fez in a hotel and the next morning, with Hassan's help, bought some gifts for the family: sugar, sweets, and mint leaves for the traditional mint tea.

We met Aziz, Hassan's 23-year-old cousin from the mountain farm who was visiting Fez for the day. He was a tall, sad-eyed man who lacked Hassan's natural cheerfulness. The four of us boarded a bus in Fez and headed for the mountains.

After two hours Hassan asked the driver to stop.

We leapt off the bus and stood in the middle of a lonely land, except for a farmhouse farther down the road.

"How far is it to your Aunt's home?" I asked.

"Only about twenty minutes."

Hassan pointed to a donkey trail that curved over the hill. "We follow that path."

To save us from carrying our backpacks up and down the mountain paths Aziz, who had a slow, easy-going manner, sauntered to the farmhouse and borrowed a donkey. He tied our bags to its back, and trotted ahead over the hills to advise the family of our impending arrival.

Squat, whitewashed mud homes nestled in the valleys, separated by acres of fields. Some of the hilltops were dominated by similar homes, none of which were connected by roads. All, however, were linked by donkey trails.

The clear blue sky provided a backdrop for the rolling mountains whose green slopes were clothed with wheat, barley and other crops. Bright red poppies poked up through the wheat. We climbed a hill carpeted with wild flowers of reds, yellows, pinks and blues. Another was studded with olive trees, their creamy blooms partly hidden by the foliage.

The only sounds were the chirps of birds and the occasional bray of a donkey on a distant hill. The air was pollution-free: no cars, no engines of any kind. We trudged up and down the hillsides for an hour, longer than Hassan's twenty minutes, stopping to take pictures and drink in the magnificent scenery. We were thankful the donkey was carrying our backpacks.

Finally Hassan pointed ahead. "My Aunt Fatima's home."

On a hillside stood a cluster of half a dozen flat-topped rooms built of sticks and mud and covered in whitewash. They were attached to each other by common walls.

Hassan led us into the courtyard and introduced us to the family. Aunt Fatima was gaunt with eyes that were bright and full of laughter. Her face was etched with deep valleys and a million wrinkles; she looked much older than her sixty years. Her husband, Mohammed, stood tall and rangy with the weathered look of a man who had spent years outdoors, planting and harvesting and raising livestock.

Their daughter-in-law Zoubedah smiled warmly. A mass of jet black hair swept back from her honey-coloured face. Her two young girls aged three and one clutched at her yellow skirt. The family was a mix of Arab and Berber, Berbers being the original inhabitants of Morocco.

We sat on clay steps in the courtyard and took in our new surroundings. The mud-brick walls of the enclosure stood about eight feet high. The ground had an uneven, natural slope, good for draining away rainwater. Various rooms with doors opening onto the courtyard served the needs of the family: bedrooms, a kitchen with a propane burner, a room with a clay oven for baking, a small barn for the cows. There was also ample space in the courtyard at night for the horse, donkey, three cows, one calf and the flock of chickens. Their few sheep were kept in a nearby field.

Fatima emerged from the kitchen with an engraved silver teapot and squat glasses for drinking mint tea. She poured the tea from a height of a foot or more above the glasses to enhance its flavour and create a froth. She then stuffed the teapot with extra sprigs of fresh mint leaves to maintain the taste. Mint tea is a symbol of welcome in Morocco.

A well established grape arbour clung to a trellis in a corner of the courtyard. Baby clothes and a traditional Moroccan gellabiah, pronounced jell-ar-ba, a long robe worn by men, hung from a clothesline. On the ground stood two half-metre-high black urns made of rubber tires. They were used for collecting water from the spring at the bottom of the hill.

Fatima and Zoubedah continued pouring tea and, to be polite, we kept drinking. In time I asked Hassan for the toilet. "There is no toilet," he said, "but you can use the wheatfield."

I left the courtyard for the wheatfield and enjoyed a million-dollar view of the mountains. When I returned I warned Penny: "If you use the wheatfield be careful because there are a few stinging nettles at squatting height."

She left the courtyard and came back a short time later looking amused.

"I didn't use the wheatfield," she confided. "Too public. I looked around and found a rough-looking mud hut, peeked in but it was pitch-dark. I stepped inside, chickens squawked and I ducked as they flew in a frenzy over my head and out the door. I got a shock. I didn't stay longer than necessary; the stench took my breath away."

"Where were you?" I said.

"In the donkey stable!"

I grimaced. "I'll stick with the wheatfield."

While Aziz returned the borrowed donkey, Hassan showed us the room we would share with him and Aziz. Compared with the hot daytime temperature outside, the interior was delightfully cool.

Because clay is not a good conductor of heat the interior temperature doesn't vary much between night and day. The room was oblong, furnished with a double bed and two single couches covered by paisley bedspreads. A paraffin lamp stood on a small table. There was no electricity.

The hardened floor consisted of clay mixed with straw and cow dung, a natural antiseptic. And it prevented bugs coming up from the ground. Woollen carpets and sheepskin rugs lay strewn on the floor. The interior clay walls, like the exterior, were coated in whitewash. A small mirror hung on a nail and a picture of Muslim pilgrims encircling the Kaaba in Mecca adorned one wall.

At dinnertime, Hassan carried into the room a communal bowl of potatoes in gravy to be shared between him, Aziz, Penny and me. We ate with our right hands and used bread to grip the bite-sized chunks of potato and to soak up the gravy. After this main course we enjoyed orange segments and mint tea.

In the morning we awoke at five-thirty when Fatima's high pitched voice cut through the air.

"Aziz! Aziz!" she screeched.

In the semi-darkness we saw Aziz pull the blanket over his head and roll over, obviously trying to shut out her voice.

Fatima continued to call his name until he dragged himself out of bed to attend his chores.

Then we heard milk squirt against the inside of a pail as Fatima milked the cows, all the while chattering to the animals.

Aziz took the horse, donkey and cows from the courtyard. He rode the donkey down to the spring to fill the rubber urns, a job he reluctantly did three times a day. Meanwhile, Fatima swept the courtyard clean of manure and hay to make it ready for the day's chores. Chickens scurried about, following Fatima until she scattered feed for them.

It was Zoubedah's responsibility to bake bread three times a day, every day. That was the custom. Zoubedah rose at sunrise to prepare the morning bread. It was thin and crêpe-like, served piping hot from the clay oven and spread with home-made butter. She served it with sweetened coffee. The lunch and dinner loaves were round but thicker, made with bean or wheat flour; preservatives weren't added.

During the third afternoon Penny helped Fatima shell peas for the evening meal. Seeing that each pea shell had a little weevil in it, Penny removed each one and squished it without Fatima noticing. However, Fatima was putting the peas with the weevils into the cooking pot. There were so many that Penny started doing the same. She figured we would just have a little extra protein that night.

The variety of meals, cooked by Aunt Fatima and Zoubedah on a propane burner, amazed us: lamb and onions, potatoes in gravy, and cous cous, a dish made with wheat semolina served with chicken, chick peas, tomatoes and onions. Before each meal a family member brought a kettle of warm water and a basin so we could wash our hands.

After a meal, Hassan would place the dishes in a basin on the ground in the courtyard so Zoubedah could wash them. But before she could clean the scraps off the plates, the chickens zeroed in for a pecking party.

We spent hours with Hassan, teaching him English and learning Arabic from him. The local people – farmers, cow herders, shepherds and donkey drivers – were always pleased when we tried to communicate with them using the few Arabic words we could remember.

One day as we sat enjoying the scenery and practising our Arabic, Hassan said, "Would you like to visit my Uncle Abdul?"

"That would be great," I said. "Where does he live?"

"Oh, on top of that mountain over there," he said, pointing to a distant peak.

To get there meant hiking down into a valley and up the other side, but we agreed.

We took an hour to walk through a beautiful patchwork of green fields which stretched to the tops of the surrounding hills.

We spotted Uncle Abdul waving to us from his house on the hilltop. In his white gellabiah, he stood out prominently against the blue sky.

He must have called to his family because they came out of the whitewashed house. He and his wife and six children – four girls and two boys – greeted Hassan with warm smiles. They hadn't seen him for many months. At first the four daughters, aged seven to fourteen, were hesitant and shy when they saw us. They hadn't met foreigners before, Hassan said. The two boys were nonchalant, engrossed in their own pursuits. One son was coaxing a tune out of a fiddle he had created from an old olive oil tin. His brother was memorizing verses of the Koran, the Muslim holy book, which were written in Arabic on flat boards.

The family had a mix of Arab and Berber blood. Although Muslims, they did not practise the Arab custom of veiling a woman's face.

Uncle Abdul's wife carried her wealth in her mouth. When she smiled, which was often, she displayed two gold-capped teeth. Her hair was swept under a black headscarf printed with pink roses. She wore a gold-coloured robe with a flowery blouse. Her daughters also wore headscarves, and bright dresses in reds and blues.

The girls warmed to Penny who encouraged them to look through her telephoto lens at a cow herder goading cows and a shepherdess leading her sheep along a distant donkey trail. They squealed with delight and chattered excitedly when they recognized people they knew, appearing so close. Hassan and I joined the happy group while the two boys went off to get the sheep.

The girls, wanting to show us the sunset, led us to the west side of the house where we caught the sky changing from yellow to orange, gilding the hillside crops below us. The sky became a splash of red then dimmed and saddened into a deep shade of lavender. As we wanted to return to Fatima's before dark, we bade goodbye to the warm, happy family.

On the hike down the hill Penny questioned Hassan about our being the first foreigners the girls had met.

"That's right," he said. "They are kept at home. They don't go to school. When they get married their lives won't change much. They'll stay home, become mothers, prepare food, plant a vegetable garden and gossip with other farming wives. That's the life of Uncle Abdul's wife."

Hassan spoke in a matter-of-fact tone, indicating this was the way of life in the mountains and nothing will change it. I looked around at the mountain landscape. It was part of a different world. I realized that although I could meet and interact with the people, I was only scratching the surface of understanding their lives.

Hassan's main concern was about finding the right girl to marry. "I don't want to marry a mountain girl," he said. "I live in a city. I want to marry a city girl who has seen more of life."

Just before dark we arrived at Aunt Fatima's. Mohammed had finished his field work and was resting. Fatima never rested. She was building a new clay oven for baking bread as the present one was doubling as an incubator for baby chicks. Hassan always referred to the farmstead as Aunt Fatima's because she appeared to run the place. That, I understood. It was common in all cultures.

Without electricity, bedtime usually came at sundown. However, Aziz brought gas lanterns into the room in case we needed them. Hassan and Aziz slept in the clothes they wore all day, as was the custom, and so did we.

We were awakened again by Fatima's call to Aziz. For us it was time to face another day of relaxation.

Hassan suggested the three of us go to a village market held a few miles away. To get there we retraced our steps over the hills to the main road. A truck stopped and the driver told Hassan he was heading for the market.

We climbed over the tailgate and half-fell into the back where there were wooden benches. The roof of the truck was a framework of iron bars, but without the canvas canopy. When the driver gunned the truck we grabbed the bars to keep our balance. Rather than be bounced around on a wooden bench, we stood. Or tried to stand. As we careened around mountain curves, gripping the overhead bars, our bodies twisted and shook like rag dolls. We held on as if our life depended on it. Which it did.

When we topped a hill we saw the market in the valley below. A sea of white canvas awnings protected the vendors from the sun. Corrals held donkeys, cows, sheep and goats. Our truck driver dropped us near the donkeys who, chasing each other, brayed loudly, kicked and nipped at each other. The donkey owners had difficulty separating the troublemakers.

Dust from the corral swirled in the air and blew into our faces.

We left the men with their challenges and headed for the canvas awnings where vendors sold a variety of products: baskets, nuts, dates, herbs, green beans, olive oil, AA batteries, blocks of salt and dresses. A cobbler hand-stitched the torn straps of my sandals for just a few cents.

Men pedalled Singer treadle sewing machines, making shirts and dresses. A grey-bearded man in a brown and white striped gellabiah held a green dress in front of him. Then he tried a blue one. He was having a problem figuring out his wife's size. Was it long enough? Were the sleeves the right length? Was it the best colour? In a culture where women usually stayed at home it was a common sight to see men shop for their wives.

"Look around you," Hassan said. "There are no women or girls at the market. Boys can't meet girls if girls are kept at home." It was the first time we had heard Hassan disgruntled.

Tantalizing aromas of spiced kebabs that sizzled on skewers over charcoal braziers permeated the air from the three open air restaurants that were set up for this weekly market. As we strolled around, men acknowledged Hassan with either *Salaam aleikoum* (Peace be with you), a few friendly words or a wave. He was obviously well-liked.

The market gave Penny and me the opportunity to buy provisions for our hosts: sacks of oranges, potatoes, onions and the freshly butchered leg from a lamb which, just hours before, had been gambolling in the field. We added two headscarves for Fatima and Zoubedah as thank-you gifts.

In the late afternoon we returned to the serenity of the mountains and rested under an olive tree near the house to enjoy the peaceful atmosphere.

There was a commotion at the house and Hassan went to investigate. We heard raised voices and saw a man gallop away on horseback. When Hassan returned we asked if there was a problem but he assured us everything was fine. We weren't convinced.

The next day we left before breakfast; we had a bus to catch. We had been their guests for five days and had grown fond of the family. We bade *B'slama* (Goodbye) and told the family we hoped to return one day. Fatima, Mohammed, Zoubedah and Aziz responded warmly with *Insh'allah* (God willing).

With our backpacks tied to either side of the donkey we followed the winding trail down the mountainside. Hassan led the way. Half-an-hour later at the main road he asked us to look after the donkey until he returned. Then he set off.

Fifteen minutes later Penny spotted him. "He's been to the farm-house down the road. He's carrying a tray of something."

"Breakfast," he announced.

He wore a smile as he produced a silver tray with a pot of mint tea, bread and cous cous.

But soon Hassan's mood changed. He grew pensive.

Our departure could not be causing this change of mood. It must be something else.

Penny looked at him. "What is worrying you?"

"Nothing."

Penny persisted. "Did the man on horseback bring you bad news?"

He looked down at the ground for a few seconds then raised his head.

"Yes," he said, then added in his fractured English: "Someone from the market reported to the police that you were staying with my family. I didn't know I was supposed to report to the police that you were there. I am now in trouble."

Penny looked sympathetically into his eyes. "Who would want to cause you trouble?"

"I'm not sure. Someone who doesn't like me; someone envious of me. Who knows? The law is an old one. I didn't know it still applied in Morocco. I don't think it does. Certainly not in the cities anyway. But the elders in the countryside don't know that. Or if they do know, they can ignore it because they make their own rules."

"What's going to happen?" I asked.

"He said I have to give one of Uncle Mohammed's sheep or pay a fine. I can't give them one of my uncle's sheep and I do not have money to pay a fine."

I felt that we were responsible for Hassan's predicament and gave him forty dollars which I thought would cover the fine. He was reluctant to accept until I insisted, pointing out it could be the difference between jail and freedom.

We heard the roar of the engine of the Fez-bound bus before it came around the mountain curve. We jumped up, thanked Hassan again for the wonderful time with him and his family, ran to the bus and called out that we would write.

Over the next five months Penny and I travelled in Europe and were not able to give an address to receive mail until we arrived in England to stay with friends. We wrote to Hassan and received a reply – a tale of woe.

The money we had given him for the fine had not been enough. The authorities insisted on a sheep or a month in jail. Hassan would lose face with his family if he gave away a sheep that wasn't his so he served thirty days.

He lost his job as a waiter at the University of Rabat because he didn't return to work. He said it was pointless to contact the university to say he'd be late in returning because he was in jail. He knew he wouldn't get his job back. Upon his release he went to Fez, his home town, and started a small business selling second hand shoes from a blanket on the sidewalk. The income was pitiful.

We corresponded with Hassan over the next few months. To write to us he had to dictate in Arabic to a scribe who would write it down and translate it into English for a fee.

What could we do to help?

Three years after first meeting him we escorted a tour group to Morocco. We wrote to Hassan to let him know we would visit him in Fez at the end of the trip. However, upon our arrival in Casablanca, our first stop, Hassan was there with his big, welcoming smile and twinkling eyes. He asked if he could join us on the trip.

After we made the request to the tour company and we agreed to be responsible for him, he was able to travel with us. He fitted right in with the group with his outgoing personality.

Two weeks later we rolled into Fez with our tour group and Hassan. The streets were alive with a random mass of motion: swarming pedestrians; vendors selling fruit, vegetables and cigarettes; water sellers hawking cups of water from goatskin bags; porters hefting tables, leather and fabrics on their backs; men dragging and pushing carts of merchandise to shops in cool, shadowy alleyways.

Hassan told us that he had a girlfriend in Fez whom he loved and hoped to marry. I noticed his eyes sparkle with enthusiasm.

"That's wonderful," Penny and I said in unison.

"How did you meet her?" I was curious.

"My family has known her family for a long time. My mother arranged the meeting. My girlfriend lives with her parents. I am going to visit the family now."

When Hassan returned he said that her family had invited us to dinner at their apartment the next day.

We met Hassan the following day and trailed him through the *souk*, a maze of twisting alleyways containing hundreds of little shops selling spices, mysterious grains, mint leaves, woollen blankets, woven caps, gellabiahs, brass tea pots, leather purses, belts and shoes, and plates engraved with geometric designs. It was a one-stop market.

We reached the edge of the souk and arrived at a dun-coloured, five-storey building. Entry was through a heavy wooden door, stained with natural oils from the hands of hundreds of users over the years.

When we emerged from a darkened stairwell on the third floor we stepped into a bright, spacious living and dining room with Moroccan carpets on the tiled floor. First to greet us was Hassan's girlfriend Majda. She blushed when she saw Hassan and shyly welcomed us. She was pleasantly plump with smooth, light-olive skin and sparkling brown eyes. Her father stood behind her, smiling broadly. There was a warmth between him and Hassan when they shook hands. Majda's mother and sister entered the room and welcomed us with *Salaam aleikoum*.

We took an instant liking to Majda. She was a translator who spoke fluent French and Arabic but unfortunately for us, no English.

Pleasantries were exchanged, principally through Hassan who did his best to translate. We sat down to a meal of cous cous with chicken which we spooned onto our plates and ate with our fingers and a piece of bread. Also served was tajine, a beef and almond stew, followed by apples and bananas.

After the meal Hassan, Majda, Penny and I adjourned to the roof-top for an evening view of the city. Electric light bulbs flickered to life and paraffin lamps illuminated the night stalls of food vendors. We watched the sun sink in the west while the peach and blue sky faded into the indigo night.

Hassan and Majda did not display their emotions in public but as they stood closely together I noticed their hands brush together fondly. This special evening was theirs as well as ours.

The next day we asked Hassan how he was doing financially. He was loathe to talk about it but we understood life was not easy because although he had worked, he had not found a steady job since his time in jail.

We hoped to get him established in a business, if that's what he wanted. Under our gentle prodding, he admitted he'd like to have a small shop from which he could sell clothing and shoes. To set up a shop would cost the equivalent of about US$400, he told us.

We decided to give him four hundred and felt relieved we were doing something to help him on his way.

Two months later when home in Vancouver we received a fat envelope from Hassan. It was full of photos of his and Majda's wedding which took place three weeks after we left Morocco. We were surprised and thrilled, but stunned.

The money we had given Hassan obviously wasn't used to start a business. He had followed his heart when deciding how to spend it. In Morocco, among the people of Berber blood, the groom or his family paid for the wedding.

The photos showed Majda in several elaborate dresses. In one photo she was radiant in a white, full-skirted gown with jewels sewn onto the skirt and a jewelled tiara in her hair. In another she wore a traditional white Berber dress with red and black tassels tied around her waist. Her headdress was decorated with beads and red tassels. Temporary Berber tribal markings of dots and dashes adorned her chin and forehead. Hassan looked happy in a black suit, white shirt and red bow tie. Other photos showed smiling guests.

Hassan had found the right girl. We knew from experience that paths crossed for a reason. Hassan and Majda had met, fallen in love and were now married. They stood on the threshold of a new life.

We dashed off a letter of congratulations.

Addendum A

Preparing to go and what to take

What to carry in my backpack on my first trip out of Australia was a problem for me, a greenhorn traveller. I wanted to have the right clothing to suit the occasion. I imagined myself in Egypt on an archaeological dig in search of lost tombs.

I had seen enough movies to know what to wear in desert terrain. Into my clean, green, shiny backpack I threw khaki shorts and a shirt. For protection from the hot, penetrating Egyptian sun, I planned on buying a pith helmet in Cairo. (However, I travelled in Egypt but didn't go on a dig.)

When leafing through travel brochures of Switzerland I envisaged myself hiking and climbing the Swiss Alps. So into my backpack I stashed a too-heavy pair of hobnailed boots. (As it turned out, I hiked but never climbed.)

Northern Europe's temperature can drop to zero. I added sweaters in a variety of colours.

The backpack took the shape of a green, bulbous bullfrog. Into its cavernous mouth I popped a propane stove, cooking pot, plate and cutlery. It swallowed the lot and craved more. To appease it I rammed down its throat a tent and stakes, sleeping bag, sleeping sheet, nylon ground sheet, air mattress, two novels, the Youth Hostel Handbook, a large radio (one must have music) and innumerable odds and ends, including a compass. Packing my backpack was exciting!

As I strained to tighten its straps I heard the thump of footsteps in the hallway of the house. I turned to see my two best friends enter the room. First in was the lanky one, known to his friends as Streak. Behind him came Shorty, the chubby one. I rose to greet them but they ignored me, stunned by the massive backpack in the middle of the room.

Shorty squeaked, "Are you going to carry all that?"

"I sure am," I said bravely. "I'd like to leave something behind but I need everything."

Streak circled the backpack like a bird of prey and made disparaging sounds through pursed lips. He stuck out his foot and toed it gently but it didn't budge. Then he shoved his foot hard and it toppled over.

I rushed forward to rescue it and pleaded, "Come on, guys, help me put it on my back."

For a moment I teetered to and fro like a tightrope walker as I steadied myself. But I lost my balance. The pressing weight of the backpack propelled me towards the closed door. I slammed into it, my knees buckled and I crumpled to the floor like a punch-drunk boxer. The backpack lay on top of me, pinning me down. I squirmed with embarrassment.

After disentangling myself from the straps I rose and stood over the backpack and sighed. "I think it's too heavy."

"You don't say!" Streak said. "It's pretty obvious."

I ignored him as I forlornly proceeded to unpack. But by nature I am a hoarder so eventually I repacked everything but my compass. Shorty assured me that if I became lost in Europe I could ask for directions.

Despite objections and suggestions from well-meaning friends I left for Europe with my heavy backpack which weighed thirty-two kilos, or seventy pounds. I staggered around under its weight for a week with everyone I met making comments like "That's a heavy backpack," or "Don't strain yourself," or "You're a fool to carry so much."

I finally saw the wisdom of travelling light. My new motto became "Count every ounce because every ounce counts." The baggage I suggest is listed on the following pages. I am still working on ways to decrease the load.

What to take

The less baggage you carry, the better.

In addition to putting a tag on your luggage, put your name and address inside. Never overpack. After packing, check again and remove 20% or more of the weight.

The following list is a rough guide only. What you take depends on your type of holiday.

Basic Items
• Suitcase with a strap to go around it to prevent it popping open, or a backpack • Camera • Shoulder bag (for camera, maps)
• Money belt or neck pouch.

Documents
• Passport • Travellers cheques/checks • Credit cards • Airline ticket
• International Driver's License (if required).
• International Certificates of Vaccinations (if required).
• Hostelling International membership card if you plan on using the worldwide network of "Youth" hostels which are open to all ages.

Clothes
• Sturdy walking shoes • Sandals (depends on where you go)
• Rubber thongs (wear in showers to prevent foot diseases)
• 2 pairs of trousers for men • 2 pairs of slacks for women plus a drip dry skirt • 1 sweater •1 jacket • 3 shirts for men • 3 blouses for women • T-shirts • 3 changes of underwear • 3 handkerchiefs
• 1 hat (crushable) • Bathing suit • Towel • Shorts (optional)
• Sleep wear.

Toilet Articles
Soap in plastic container, toothbrush and paste, shampoo, shave cream, razor blades, nail scissors, comb or brush, small packs of paper tissues, aspirin, cold remedies, women's sanitary requisites, moisture lotion, package of moistened tissues to wipe face and hands, mosquito repellent, adhesive plasters, ointment for bites,

needle and thread, lip salve, sunscreen, water purifying tablets, half-roll of toilet paper, tablets for stomach upsets and constipation, possibly sleeping pills and vitamin tablets, and electrolytes. Electrolytes replace minerals lost through diarrhea. Take packages of electrolytes containing glucose, sodium chloride, sodium bicarbonate, potassium and chloride.

Odds and ends
• Spare plastic bags for laundry, film, fruit, odds and ends.
• Sunglasses • Spare set of reading glasses (if applicable)
• Lightweight travelling alarm clock • Guidebook and map
• Clothes pins and clothesline (for use in your hotel room)
• Swiss Army knife with corkscrew, bottle opener
• Knife or vegetable peeler (to peel fruit before eating)
• Small flashlight • Wash basin plug (universal type)
• Water bottle (1 quart or litre capacity) • Immersion heater and cup (for tea or coffee in your hotel room) • Writing paper • pen • envelopes •journal or diary • Duct tape to mend your luggage
• Food rations: A can of food in case restaurants are closed.

Optional extras could include
• Sleeping bag liner (for use in budget hotels) • Empty soft-sided bag to carry home purchases • Fold-up umbrella • Gloves
• Lightweight binoculars (for game viewing or bird watching)
• Trading items or giveaways for Africa or South America: pens, T-shirts, postcards of your city, or lapel pins of your country's flag
• Camping equipment if applicable: tent, sleeping bag, sleeping mat and cooking and eating utensils.

Notes regarding prescriptions
1. Prescription glasses. Take an extra pair or take the prescription.
2. Prescription drugs. If you are taking prescription drugs ensure that you have an adequate supply.
Ask your doctor for the generic name of the drug and carry the name with you, plus directions for use.

Addendum B

Bargaining tips

Bargaining is a normal way of doing business in most developing countries. Do not accept the first price asked otherwise you undermine the system upon which the trading economy is based.

The process can be fun for both sides. Sometimes after we have completed a bargaining session and paid for our purchases the vendor has added a "sweetener," a handkerchief, fan or bottle of perfume as a token of his appreciation. Or was it because he felt guilty about the high prices we paid? Maybe we should have bargained lower? We'll never know!

You will encounter young girls and boys selling single cigarettes or cheap items they have made themselves, things you possibly do not really want. Consider buying them anyway to encourage them in their work. It is better to encourage trade than to have them beg.

In some countries, items such as T-shirts can be offered in addition to some money.

When you go to bargain, dress casually. It is better not to show your wealth.

Before you go, place known amounts of money in your various pockets. If you bargain down the merchant to a price of say $10, you do not want to have to pull out a twenty and ask for change. (To simplify our discussion we will talk in dollars.)

There are various techniques you can try:
Technique A:

When you see something you really want, do not point to it immediately. Point to something nearby and ask how much. When he tells you, shake your head and point to something else, then again shake your head. Your disinterest in his prices could cause him to lower them. When you point to what you really want, the bargaining will be starting at a lower figure.

The amount you first offer varies from country to country, but generally you offer one third of his asking price and the bargaining will creep up from there.

Technique B:

You could decide how much you want to pay and put the money on the counter saying, "To me it is worth this much."

If he won't accept your offer you could say you will think about it and start making your way to the door. He may then come down further.

If you agree on a price but you still think it should be lower there are two techniques available.

Technique C:

If you have bargained him down to the equivalent of say $22 you then go to a pocket and extract exactly $20 which you count out slowly. Because you are short, you mention that you must go back to the hotel to get more. Rather than lose a sale he should accept $20.

Technique D:

The second technique after settling on a price in local currency is to ask what he will sell it to you for if you pay in hard currency such as U.S. dollars. His favourable exchange rate could reduce the real cost even further.

More bargaining tips:

Before going shopping for expensive items such as carpets,

jewelry or intricate carvings, visit city stores to establish prices and quality.

Street sellers abound in many cities frequented by tourists and can be quite persistent. If you do not want what they have, do not say it is too small, too big, the wrong colour, or too expensive because they will produce an alternative. Simply say, "I have one." If you learn to say "No thank you" in their own language, use it. These two methods usually work.

If they persist, take the object they are offering and place it on the ground, then walk away. This method has never been known to fail in getting across the message that you are not buying.

Do remember, however, that these people must be respected. They are doing a difficult job for usually little reward. Do not be rude to them; you are a guest in their country.

The seller has techniques that work for him. He may invite you into his shop for a cup of tea and/or invite you into a back room to watch craftsmen making items for sale. You could accept these offers but remember you are not under any obligation to buy.

Maintain a poker face. If you appear enthusiastic about the item you want to buy it will be difficult to bargain him down. Disregard the seller's first offer. Show your lack of interest to get him to start lower.

Carry a pen and paper to write down your offer if language is a problem. If the seller meets your price you must buy from him.

Resources

Travel Planner's Weather Guide, second edition.
by Russell and Penny Jennings
This quick-reference weather guide suggests the best time to visit over 200 countries and island dependencies.

The guide contains:
- •Weather tables for hundreds of cities showing temperatures, rainfall, days with rain and hours of sunshine.
- •Weather descriptions for every country, region by region, and season by season when necessary.
- •More than 240 maps.
- •List of name changes of countries and cities.
- •When to cruise, ski, trek, go on safari, dive, climb mountains, and visit national parks.

The guide also warns of seasons of strong desert winds, cyclones, monsoons, snowy conditions, freezing temperatures and searing heat.

The weather tables were compiled from thousands of pieces of raw data gathered over past decades by the World Meteorological Organization in Geneva, Switzerland, and the National Oceanic and Atmospheric Administration in North Carolina, USA.

Explanations of the effect of global warning and the ozone layer are included.

This easy-to-read guide, which contains over 400 pages, is an essential source for vacationers, business travellers and travel agents.

To order, see ORDER FORM, over page, or check the website: www.worldweatherguide.com

Book prices

Travel Planner's Weather Guide
Second edition published in 2003. 432 pages.
Cdn $34.95 or US $24.95

Around the World in Sandals
Published in 2005. 288 pages.
Cdn $14.95 or US $10.95

Postage and handling charges

Canadian orders: Cdn $8 for the first book and Cdn $2 for each additional book. Canadian residents must add 7% GST to total of book price and postage.

U.S. orders: US $8 for the first book and US $2 for each additional book.

International orders by surface mail: US $8 for the first book and US $2 for each additional book.

International orders by airmail: US $16 for the first book and US $10 for each additional book.

ORDER FORM
(see opposite page for prices and postage)

- *Travel Planner's Weather Guide*
- *Around the World in Sandals*

How to order:
E-mail orders: jennings@worldweatherguide.com (We accept payment by VISA.)
Fax orders: 604 734 1586. Send this form.
Postal orders: Open Road Publishers, 3316 West 8th Ave., Vancouver, BC, V6R 1Y4, CANADA
Books are mailed within 24 hours of receiving payment.

In this space specify quantity, add postage and handling, and calculate the total payable. Book prices and postage and handling charges are shown on opposite page.

Book	Quantity	Total $
Travel Planner's Weather Guide	_____	_____
Around the World in Sandals	_____	_____
Postage and handling	_____	_____
7% GST (Canadian orders only)	_____	_____
Total	_____	_____

Please send books to:
Name _____
Address _____
City _____ Province/State _____
Country _____ Postal/Zip code _____
Phone _____ E-mail _____

How to pay:
Pay by money order or check to Open Road Publishers drawn on a Canadian or US bank, or pay by VISA card.
Canadian orders: Pay in Canadian dollars.
U.S. and International orders: Pay in U.S. dollars.

If you are paying by VISA* we need the following information:
Exact name on card _____
Card number _____
Expiry date _____ Signature _____

*We accept only VISA. If our policy changes it will be on our web site.

Books by Russell and Penny Jennings

China On Your Own – a Guide for the Budget Traveller.

First published, 1984. The third edition, published in 1986 with 240 pages, includes "The Hiking Guide to China's Nine Sacred Mountains" contributed by Michael Kelsey.
Cdn $13.95 US $9.95

Travel Planner's Weather Guide

Second edition, 2003, 432 pages.
Advises the best time to go.
Cdn $34.95 US $24.95 See page 285 for more information.

Around the World in Sandals

Published 2005, 288 pages.
Includes the authors' stories of personal encounters during their off-beat journeys which include four months in Mexico, Central and South America in 1975, fifteen months in Asia and Africa in 1978 and 1979, one month in China in 1983 and nine months in West Africa and Europe in 1987.
Cdn $14.95 US $10.95

Future titles

For future releases, check the web site:
www.worldweatherguide.com